PRAISE FOR *THE EXPERIENCE MINDSET*

"Practical and enlightening, this book gives you the daily tools you need to complete the missing piece of the growth puzzle: improving employee experience."

—Arianna Huffington, founder and CEO of Thrive Global

"If you run an organization or if you work for one (and isn't that pretty much all of us?) you need to read this book. Tiffani Bova's research answers some of the most pressing questions of our time, including why there is so much churn in our labor markets, why the customer isn't always right, and why technology hasn't necessarily improved things for regular workers."

—Rita McGrath, author of *Seeing Around Corners* and professor at Columbia Business School

"The scourge of modern business is reductionism, the belief that a business can only focus on and optimize one thing. In this ground-breaking book, Tiffani Bova blows a hole in that shallow logic by showing how the most successful companies focus simultaneously and equivalently on customer *and* employee experience. This terrific book is full of practical insights for tossing aside prevailing management dogma to achieve unique success."

—Roger Martin, #1 ranked management thinker by Thinkers50 and bestselling author

"Experience really is everything! Tiffani Bova has a knack for cutting through the reams of research, the jungle of verbiage, and our habitual faith in complexity to get to the very heart of what business and organizations are all about, or should be: their people."

—Stuart Crainer and Des Dearlove, founders of Thinkers50

"What do the best companies in the world have in common? An employee experience and customer experience that works in harmony.

This book shows you how to marry these seemingly disparate experiences and align your company around one growth-oriented philosophy: an Experience Mindset."

—Deanna Singh, author of *Actions Speak Louder* and chief change agent at Flying Elephant

"Employees are critical to the success of your business—but do you treat them like it? Covering topics like culture, process, people, and technology, this book is every leader's must-have guide to the growth opportunities lying right under your nose."

—Michele Romanow, "Dragon" on CBC's *Dragons' Den* and cofounder and executive chairman of Clearco

"Very few business thought leaders can match Tiffani Bova's combination of deeply researched insights, real-life experience, and compelling storytelling. Everyone who manages anyone—from middle managers up to CEOs—should read, study, and internalize *The Experience Mindset*."

—Laura Gassner Otting, *Washington Post* bestselling author of *Limitless*

THE
EXPERIENCE
MINDSET

OTHER WORKS

Growth IQ

THE
EXPERIENCE
MINDSET

Changing the Way You
Think About Growth

TIFFANI BOVA

PORTFOLIO • PENGUIN

PORTFOLIO / PENGUIN
An imprint of Penguin Random House LLC
penguinrandomhouse.com

Most Portfolio books are available at a discount when purchased in quantity for
sales promotions or corporate use. Special editions, which include personalized
covers, excerpts, and corporate imprints, can be created when purchased in
large quantities. For more information, please call (212) 572-2232 or e-mail
specialmarkets@penguinrandomhouse.com. Your local bookstore can also
assist with discounted bulk purchases using the Penguin Random House
corporate Business-to-Business program. For assistance in locating a
participating retailer, e-mail B2B@penguinrandomhouse.com.

Library of Congress Cataloging-in-Publication Data
Names: Bova, Tiffani, author.
Title: The experience mindset : changing the way you think
about growth / Tiffani Bova.
Description: [New York] : Portfolio/Penguin, [2023] |
Includes bibliographical references.
Identifiers: LCCN 2022054558 (print) | LCCN 2022054559 (ebook) |
ISBN 9780593542699 (hardcover) | ISBN 9780593542705 (ebook)
Subjects: LCSH: Business planning. | Strategic planning. |
Corporations—Growth. | Success in business.
Classification: LCC HD30.28 .B68448 2023 (print) | LCC HD30.28 (ebook) |
DDC 658.4/06—dc23/eng/20221121
LC record available at https://lccn.loc.gov/2022054558
LC ebook record available at https://lccn.loc.gov/2022054559

Printed in the United States of America
1st Printing

Book design by Tanya Maiboroda

*"I could tell you to remember the million things I told you,
but the most important is to be happy."*
MOM (1933–2022)

*This book is dedicated to my mom, Dolors (Dee),
who passed away the week I turned in the final manuscript
to my publisher. This was the last thing she said to me,
and a perfect message to remember.*

She will forever be missed.

Me Ke Aloha

Contents

Foreword

*The one piece of advice which I believe will contribute
more to making you a better leader and commander—
will provide you greater happiness and self-esteem
and at the same time advance your career more—than
any other advice . . . and it doesn't call for a special
personality [or] any certain chemistry, any one of
you can do it, and that advice is—you must care.*

GENERAL MELVIN ZAIS,
address to mid-grade officers,
U.S. Army War College

I HAVE BEEN CHASING EXCELLENCE FOR OVER FOUR DECADES AND
General Zais's message is one of the most essential lessons I've
learned. Take care of people! Train them and treat them with
respect and kindness and prepare them for the mad, mad world.
Insist that every employee commits to encouraging growth and
caring for their mates. *This* is how you achieve excellence.

Tiffani Bova recognizes this and makes it plain in *The Experience Mindset*. She sees the necessity of putting people first—a
message I've literally shouted about for decades—and how that
is a close-to-guaranteed profit generator. In *The Experience
Mindset*, Tiffani reminds us of the true importance of an out-
standing employee experience. Have you heard this from me,
from others? Yes. But in this book, Tiffani backs it up with first-
hand research, intriguing stories, and her own experience, providing lessons along the way.

As Tiffani states in her introduction, "By strategically pursuing an exceptional, balanced experience for ALL stakeholders, you achieve a sum greater than its parts . . ." I couldn't agree more. A leader *exists* to create and maintain organizations desperately committed to the growth of all its members and the well-being of the communities in which they operate. It is the meaning of excellence and the pinnacle of human achievement.

Tom Peters, author of twenty books, including the bestselling *In Search of Excellence* (1982) and his latest, *The Compact Guide to Excellence* (2022)

Introduction

Employees carry the torch every day for the values and mission of their company. They are the facilitators of every moment that matters—the positive connections and negative pain points encountered by a customer or a fellow employee interacting with a brand or employer. As my friend Hubert Joly, former CEO and chairman of Best Buy, told me on my podcast, "The heart of business is the idea of pursuing a noble purpose, putting people at the center, creating the environment where you can release that human magic, embrace all stakeholders, and treat profit as an outcome."

I'm not sure how many executives would comfortably describe their business this way, not least because it spotlights an often overlooked but critical piece of any company's success: the day-to-day experiences of the people who work there and serve its customers. While many companies are clear on the importance of seamless customer experience and its impact on growth, the role employee experience plays has yet to be fully quantified or understood. This is often because leaders feel they can only focus on one stakeholder or the other: customers or employees.

Instead, they must leverage both customer experience and employee experience in a more intentional and balanced way to accelerate growth. An increased focus on employee experience can increase revenue by more than 50 percent, and profits by nearly as much. Companies with high customer experience *and* employee experience exhibit a three-year compound annual growth rate (CAGR) almost double (8.50 percent) those with low customer and employee experience (4.35 percent).

Unfortunately, regardless of what leaders may say about the importance of employees, according to new, groundbreaking research, nine in ten C-suite executives encourage their employees to focus on customer needs above all else. As a result, the pervasive view is that, when push comes to shove, executives must throw their time and resources behind the customer and their experience if they want to grow the business.

That's not to say *all* executives are missing the point. Southwest's Herb Kelleher once said, "If you treat your employees right, guess what? Your customers come back, and that makes your shareholders happy. Start with employees and the rest follows from that." Sir Richard Branson, founder of Virgin Group, concurred: "If you take care of your employees, they will take care of the clients." Or, as Anne M. Mulcahy, former CEO and chairperson of Xerox, said, "Employees who believe that management is concerned about them as a whole person—not just an employee—are more productive, more satisfied, more fulfilled. Satisfied employees mean satisfied customers, which leads to profitability."

In short, all of these uber-successful business leaders are saying the same thing: *if you want happy customers, start with your*

employees. When put that way, it seems obvious, but this simple statement runs counter to the operating philosophy of most businesses today. That dominant philosophy is rooted in the management thinking of the previous century. American economist Milton Friedman shaped the shareholder-value-above-all-else management culture of the second half of the twentieth century with the extreme view that "the sole purpose of a business is to generate profits for its shareholders." Even management giant Peter Drucker's words were appropriated to promote a particular narrative. He famously said both that "the purpose of business is to create a customer" and that "in the knowledge economy everyone is a volunteer, but we have trained our managers to manage conscripts." Because the first phrase fit the emerging shareholders and customers first narrative and the second most definitely didn't, only the first is widely remembered and taken commonly as "Drucker's view."

Therein lies the rub. For years, positive customer satisfaction scores and good enough growth rates masked what had been brewing under the surface—the employee experience had been suffering at the hands of a maniacal focus on customer experience. Companies can have good customer experience and poor employee experience and still grow. They can even have good enough employee experience and good enough customer experience and still grow. *But to multiply growth, you need to do BOTH well.*

While many leaders intuitively understand that concept, most still struggle to integrate that understanding into the strategic decisions they make and the organizational structures they put in place. They can't—or are unwilling to—connect the dots. *You grow exponentially by improving both, balancing improvements in employee and customer experiences in tandem in order to leverage a mutually beneficial combination of the two.* This does *not* mean employee experience and customer experience will be "equal" all the time—that should never be the goal. You still need to recognize when one constituency needs more attention than the other does. That said, the needs and preferences of both customers and employees must be considered *with every decision made*, large and small, thus requiring an entirely new operating mindset: **The Experience Mindset.**

Ultimately, the Experience Mindset is about fully maximizing the leverage points between a strong employee experience and customer experience to create a virtuous cycle of momentum that leads to significantly better growth rates. It is a new operating model and an intentional, holistic approach that considers both employee experience and customer experience when making decisions for a company. *By strategically pursuing an exceptional, balanced experience for ALL stakeholders, you achieve a sum greater than its parts, magnifying growth many times over.*

Connecting the Dots for Resilient Growth

As a global customer growth and innovation evangelist at Salesforce, my job is to study market trends to uncover best practices on improving sales performance and driving growth at companies of all sizes. My thought leadership role at Salesforce is the culmination of fifteen years spent leading sales, marketing, and customer service for start-ups and Fortune 500 companies, followed by a decade researching and advising companies on their growth strategies as a research fellow at Gartner, a technological research and consulting firm based in Stamford, Connecticut.

That focus—or, truth be told, obsession—on helping companies grow has landed me on the Thinkers50 list not once but twice. I've delivered over 750 keynote presentations around the globe to more than half a million people and my ideas have been published in outlets from *Harvard Business Review* to *Fast Company*. I say this not to brag but simply to point out that, even with my years of experience, I, too, missed what was right in front of me all this time.

After publishing my first book, *Growth IQ*—a *Wall Street Journal* bestseller that outlines ten paths to sustainable and repeatable growth—I realized, to my dismay, that although I had an entire chapter devoted to customer experience (CX), I had not dug deep enough into the interconnectedness of employee experience (EX) and its impact on CX. Like so many others, I intuitively knew these two were linked, but it wasn't until 2018, while I was on stage in Vancouver in front of a few thousand people, that it hit me: "Globally, Salesforce is one of the best places to work," I said. "It is one of the most innovative companies, and it is the fastest-growing enterprise software company." After pausing to let that sink in, I added: "I don't think these three things are a coincidence." (As a Salesforce employee, my words might have been seen as self-serving, but these merits had been established by external sources including *Fast Company*, *Fortune*, *Forbes*, Glassdoor, and IDC, to name a few.)

I realized those last words were true as soon as they left my mouth. It followed that there were points of connection—a cause and effect—between employees, customers, and growth, whereby each factor buoyed the others. Standing on that stage was when it occurred to me: *pleasing customers is about more than simply "putting customers first"; it has to start with a healthy, engaged, and productive employee base to make the vision of an organization come to life.*

This stark realization began a transformative two-year journey. Sure, Kelleher, Branson, Mulcahy, and others had made big claims about the importance of employee experience to the experience of the customer. But where were the facts? Where was the research to back up their assertions? *Furthermore, if this idea was so obvious, why wasn't everyone building stronger employee experiences as a way to improve CX?* On behalf of Salesforce, I spearheaded two primary research projects to answer that very question.

Along the way, I immersed myself in the existing literature on these topics and held hundreds of in-depth conversations with executives from around the world. In the process, I developed a far better understanding of the current state of EX and CX corporate initiatives, the connection between the two, and how a more symbiotic relationship between them could produce a virtuous cycle, resulting in incredible results for any company.

The bulk of this work was performed during the height of a global pandemic and the Great Resignation it sparked. This context forced an even greater focus on employees and their productivity and engagement, much to the benefit of the findings and conclusions. For all its tragic effects, COVID-19 opened the door to rich, vital discussions about the unmet needs of employees across a number of key areas.

Top of mind for leaders is no longer growth at any cost, but *resiliency*. Growth must become robust and flexible enough to persist in a constantly disrupted, rapidly changing business environment. Today's environment. <u>Companies have learned the hard way that growth at the cost of unhappy employees or customers is brittle and all too fleeting.</u> Any gained revenue momentum collapses under the pressure of a company's negligence and disregard toward its employees. Without their effort, engagement, and commitment to a company's goals, growth becomes more elusive.

To be clear, adopting an Experience Mindset is not about establishing a new executive position or business unit. There's no quick and easy fix to any such deeply embedded, systemic problem (sorry!). As discussed in *Growth IQ*, *the one thing about growth is that it is never one thing*. The same can be said for the Experience Mindset. *This mindset shift is about embracing a new, company-wide philosophy of tight, cross-functional operation and communication between all efforts surrounding employees and customers, especially as it relates to* **PEOPLE, PROCESS, TECHNOLOGY, AND CULTURE**. Aligning company support around this effort will require strong leadership at the top and complete buy-in from employees.

C-level leaders need to pull down the walls of their fiefdoms and learn to work with their employees, in a new, collaborative way. Managers must open themselves up to their employees for guidance and candid feedback. And everyone in the organization needs to recognize that employees, teams, and customers can accomplish more together than they could alone. *Companies need to remove the self-imposed tension between EX and CX and approach them for the first time as part of a new operating philosophy and enterprise strategy:*

The fastest way to get customers to love your brand is to get employees to love their jobs.

Developing Your Experience Mindset

Change is never easy. Whether you're spearheading transformation in your organization or working to solve society's most complex challenges, you won't get far without a shift in your mindset and behavior. As you'll see throughout these pages, the Experience Mindset supports a whole new way of thinking about your approach to business: *working* **FOR** *all your stakeholders*. Today's companies must stop doing things *to* customers and *to* employees and do things *for* them instead. Business-*to*-customer (B2C), business-*to*-business (B2B), or even business-*to*-employee

(B2E) must become B4C, B4B, and B4E: business-*for*-customer, business-*for*-business, and business-*for*-employee.

While that may seem like a trivial distinction, it is about changing your mindset. You must reframe how you think about your relationships with your customers and employees. Instead of focusing on the sale, you should view the transaction as a way to help your customers be more successful in some way, using your product or service in order to serve *their* customers or *their* employees better. The same goes for your employees. Instead of trying to get every last ounce of productivity out of them, what can you do for them to make their jobs and lives easier? How can you start orienting your operating mindset to provide a place where you do things FOR the collective success?

Whether you're a manager, a start-up founder, or a C-suite leader, the Experience Mindset will help you recruit and retain world-class talent, keep those employees fully engaged with your mission, attract more customers than ever before, and supercharge growth through the most difficult and trying economic times. Once you accept the research that proves Kelleher, Branson, and Mulcahy were right—that only happy employees can delight customers—every takeaway in this book will follow with inexorable logic.

This book, and its research-backed findings, confirms what many of us have suspected about the connection between EX and CX but have not yet been able to prove in bottom-line terms. It offers leaders a clear road map for achieving growth goals by identifying areas with the greatest potential impact and designing a robust strategy to go after them. After reading the following chapters, you will no longer experience the dilemma of choosing between being an employee- or customer-first organization. With the Experience Mindset, you can reap the mutually amplifying benefits of CX and EX together to drive resilient growth.

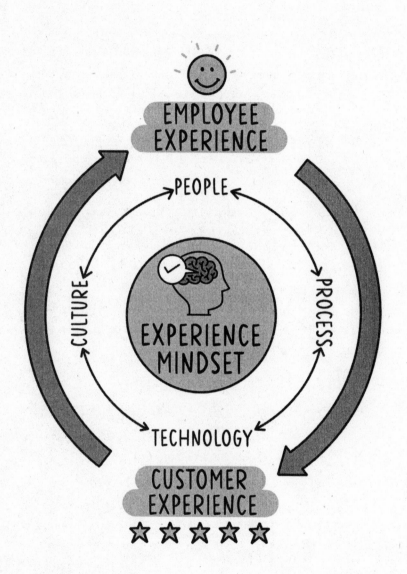

Chapter 1

Customer Experience

Innovation breeds a lot of focus and improvement—
whether it's in process, in people protocols,
infrastructure, architecture, it doesn't really matter—
toward the service of customers. And there's a loop,
which happens when happy team members drive a
better customer experience, which drives loyalty, which
closes the loop. That has to be the North Star.

SUMIT SINGH,
CEO of Chewy

LET'S BEGIN WITH A LITTLE BIT OF HISTORY. THOUGH MANY OF YOU
are likely familiar with these broad strokes, taking a step back
to understand how a maniacal focus on customer experience developed will shed some light on how we got to where we are today. The First and Second Industrial Revolutions were typified
by an increase in production capacity and output. Companies
were labeled as "product-centric" or "product-led," competing on
the basis of their advanced products, irrespective of whether people wanted these product improvements. The Third Industrial
Revolution, which began in the 1950s, welcomed advancements
in telecommunications, the rise of electronics, and the development of computers, forever changing how businesses operate.

With new capabilities to track and solve customers' problems,
meet their new demands, and provide increasingly better service,
the experiences customers had with brands improved. With a

growing global supply chain, there was also an increase in the diversity and availability of goods and services. Equally as important were new ways for customers to shop and buy products and services online. As a result, not only did their purchasing behaviors change, but their experience expectations continued to increase with the new capabilities technology provided, such as e-commerce.

In response, companies shifted away from a product-led model and focused instead on the *customer*. As compared to a one-size-fits-all model, specific customer data could be captured and used to create a better experience for a diverse set of customers and their needs. Embracing this attitude meant that new products, features, and functionality could be traced back to a real customer problem. Customer-centric companies also offered customers value at every interaction, based on their actual interests and desires.

This philosophy quickly caught on because it made logical sense: *Customers are the source of revenue. Without revenue, there is no company.* What's more, focusing on the customer, though myopic, works. Like hopping on one leg, it will move you forward, albeit slowly.

Becoming more customer-focused required an accompanying attention to customer experience. Providing positive CX then became the prime C-suite approach to strengthening competitive advantage. It wasn't that products no longer mattered; they did, and they still do. They just don't matter as much if great customer experience isn't there as well.

And today, with the Fourth Industrial Revolution upon us—pushing technological capabilities and uses to a whole new level with AI, IoT, Web 3.0, and the metaverse—customer experience is valued more heavily than ever, and for good reason. According to Salesforce, *88 percent of customers feel that the experience a company provides is as important as its product or* services (2022), up from 84 percent in 2019. Obviously, CX is vitally important.

Every company should strive to provide an incredible experience to the customers or businesses it serves. As discussed in the introduction, instead of doing something *to* customers, or *to* businesses, you must do something *for* them, reframing your thinking from B2C and B2B to *B4C and B4B*. To do so, you must first recognize what makes a memorable customer experience.

Raising the CX Bar

In 2004, Zappos's biggest challenge was customer service. Specifically, they were struggling to find the right employees to staff their call center. Though the online footwear retailer was an e-commerce company through and through, they realized that every new customer called them on the phone at least once on average. Handled well, that call could create an emotional connection and a lasting memory. Whiffed, it could lose that customer for good.

Tony Hsieh, Zappos's CEO at the time, had decided from the company's start to make service the company's main product. After all, customers could buy shoes anywhere. Hsieh believed they would only stick with Zappos if it "went the extra mile to WOW them," so he allocated the resources to staff the customer service line 24/7. Any similar company would have spent that money on advertising to drive awareness and demand. Rather than advertise, Hsieh wanted to make his customers so happy that they advertised for him via word of mouth, advocating on the company's behalf.

This was not the norm in 2004. Call centers were considered cost centers, not growth engines. But under Hsieh, Zappos looked at every interaction through a "branding lens instead of an expense-minimizing lens." This meant running and staffing its call center very differently.

For example, there are many stories of Zappos customer service agents staying on the phone for marathon sessions. The average call duration at most call centers is four minutes. The longest Zappos customer service call to date took place in 2016 and lasted ten hours and forty-three minutes. Now, not every call center agent should stay on the phone with a customer for ten-plus hours, but the mindset is what matters here. The rep knew he *could* stay on that call without worrying about an arbitrary metric or "getting in trouble" for spending so much time with one customer.

Stories like this one have become central to the Zappos culture. The company has never stopped raising the CX bar while also empowering its employees to go the extra mile for customers. Noting a drop in call volume at the start of the COVID-19 pandemic, the company decided against furloughs. Instead, it launched a special customer service line for people who just wanted to chat about anything: future travel plans, TV shows, whatever was on their minds. (The idea was the brainchild of a Zappos employee.) Customer service reps were known to sometimes help callers source items beyond shoes. As pointed out in a statement on its website, "Searching for flour to try that homemade bread recipe? We're happy to call around and find a grocery stocked with what you need."

The reps also proved willing to help with more urgent issues. When David Putrino, director of rehabilitation innovation for the Mount Sinai Health System, struggled to find pulse oximeters online due to pandemic demand, he reached out to Zappos. To his delight, the company located a stash of the critical devices, shipped five hundred to Mount Sinai within days, and went on to donate another fifty.

I had the pleasure of meeting Tony Hsieh a few times over the years before his tragic passing in 2020. Our conversations were always filled with laughter and joy, and the mark he left on so many people will keep his legacy of "delivering happiness" alive for many years to come. Hsieh recognized that investing in customer service could create "stronger brand loyalty and leave your customers coming back for more." He understood that customers recall brand experience and interactions far more than they do other differentiating factors like price.

You are much more likely to remember service reps that went far out of their way to help you than the amount you paid for a pair of sneakers. This emphasis on CX correlates to consumers who are "very likely to purchase more from a company" regardless of industry (Table 1.1). As you can see, the "very good" and "good" CX shows significantly better results than the others.

> A great CX experience is not defined by *what* you offer but *how* your customers feel when they engage with your products and services, your employees, and your brand, and how well you enable them to achieve the outcomes most important to them.

These interactions between a company's employees and their customers are truly significant as they are often *the moments that matter*. If the past decade is any indication, continuing to improve CX is unquestionably worthwhile. For example, mass-

U.S. Consumers Who Are Very Likely to Purchase More from a Company Based on Their Customer Experience (CX), by Select Industry, May 2020

% of respondents

	Very good CX	Good CX	Okay CX	Poor CX	Very poor CX
Banking	93%	79%	67%	46%	19%
Computer makers	93%	88%	75%	54%	23%
Electronics	92%	83%	71%	51%	22%
Fast food	96%	87%	72%	52%	22%
Grocery	96%	90%	79%	61%	25%
Retail	95%	90%	78%	58%	25%
Software firms	94%	84%	73%	49%	20%
Streaming media	92%	81%	70%	45%	21%
TV Internet service	90%	79%	64%	39%	14%
AVERAGE	94%	84%	72%	50%	20%

Figure 1.1: Providing Good CX Matters

market auto manufacturers that improve CX by 1 percent can generate more than $1 billion in additional revenue. Further, as shown in Figure 1.1, *CX leaders had three times higher returns to shareholders than CX laggards in the aftermath of the 2008 financial crisis.*

Customer Experience (CX) Leaders Are More Resilient During Recessionary Periods, Experiencing Shallower Troughs and Quicker Recovery

Financial performance (total shareholder returns) of CX leaders vs. laggards

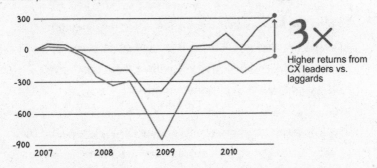

Figure 1.2: CX Leaders Are More Resilient in Tough Times

The Characteristics of Superior CX

So what is actually meant by a superior customer experience? Let's look at the specific characteristics businesses utilize to accomplish this feat:

- **Efficient:** Minimize the time and effort customers are required to spend to buy a product or service or to receive support for it. For example, many hotels no longer require customers to go to the front desk and talk to a clerk to check in and get a key. Instead, customers can use an app to not only check in and receive a digital room key but even order room service or make a housekeeping request. Done right, this "low-touch" approach—in which customers and employees have little contact—is highly effective at delivering a great experience.
- **Personalized:** Ensure employees know customers' names, purchase history, and any issues they've experienced in the past. Customers want to feel that their business is valued, not that they are dealing with a different company at every moment that matters.
- **Predictive:** Expect what customers may need next. For example, anticipate what products or services they may be interested in based on their prior buying data and compared against other customers like them. When done right, companies can uncover hidden buying signals and focus the efforts of a salesperson more effectively or use automation to streamline the sales process.
- **Proactive:** Anticipate reasons why customers may reach out and proactively reach out to customers. An example might be sending an e-mail alerting customers that their warranty or credit card expires in ninety days, which may disrupt ser-

vice. In a recurring revenue business, this type of proactive, value-based outreach is critical to minimize unnecessary churn.

- **Flexible:** Enable customers to buy, communicate, or engage through their preferred channels both online and offline. For example, provide multiple options for customer service and support via phone, e-mail, online FAQs, chatbots, and social media. By doing so, you can capture prospective customers where and how they prefer to buy.

- **Responsive:** Solve customers' problems in a timely manner. While it might not always be at first point of contact, being responsive is also about following up and following through on those issues that require more time and attention. With service expectations increasing, response time matters. If customers have to wait too long, it negatively impacts CX; if you are able to get back to them quickly and solve their issue, it positively impacts CX.

- **Value-based:** Focus on customers' needs so they can make a decision based on the potential value they'll get out of your product or service. For example, under a value-based health care model, health care providers (including hospitals and physicians) are compensated on the quality of services rendered based on patient health outcomes as opposed to the quantity of patients a physician might see. Being value-based is essential to the B4B and B4C approach. Ask yourself, what can you do *for* your customers to add value to their lives or their businesses? You want the customer to know you truly care about their needs and the outcome based on the tailored solution you've provided.

Each of these seven characteristics can be boiled down to *reducing customers' effort*, thereby bettering the experience they have with your brand and increasing their loyalty. As competitive advantage is increasingly defined by the experience you provide, rather than the products you sell, customer-centric solutions are paramount. However, those solutions alone will not remain competitive over the long term. _Long-term success will only come from creating frictionless and seamless interactions between employees and customers by decreasing the amount of effort both need to put into those interactions._

Interaction and Effort

There are two categories of effort to consider: the effort required of the customer to achieve their expected outcome and the effort required of the employee to meet the customer's expectations and do their job. Throughout recent history, customer effort and employee effort had decreased pretty much in sync, especially during the First and Second Industrial Revolutions when companies were, as mentioned, more product-centric. With an emphasis on productivity and output per person, machines and automation began taking over employees' redundant and tedious tasks, ultimately reducing their effort.

While there wasn't yet a full-court press focused on CX, there were new benefits to customers as it became easier for companies to procure products and services with greater consistency and quality. As new technology began to take hold in the Third Industrial Revolution, the effort needed to perform and complete tasks started decreasing, creating better results and experiences for both customers and employees. However, as the Third Industrial Revolution gave way to the Fourth, and digital technology investments further increased, the effort required for customers to engage with brands decreased. Subsequently, their

9

CX improved—but the same could not be said for employees. In fact, many employees saw the effort required to do their jobs increase. As a result, their satisfaction decreased, causing EX and CX to fall out of sync.

Take, for example, a hypothetical bank operating in today's economy. This institution, like many banks, has a mix of customers and small-business clients who have come to expect more and more digital banking capabilities. To increase customer loyalty and improve CX with its small-business customers, the bank conducted focus groups and surveys to determine what products and services they would be interested in.

It determined that video banking services would be a great addition to the in-branch services currently provided. This service would allow customers to converse "face-to-face" with their banker at their convenience, 24/7, without having to drive to a branch to do so. The goal was to reduce effort for the customer, increase the level of service, and establish a strong differentiator in the market.

It seemed like a foolproof plan, and the response from customers was overwhelming—too overwhelming. While customer satisfaction scores went up and overall CX improved, employee satisfaction in the newly created video team cratered. The video offering resulted in far more work for the employees than a traditional call center, taxing them with additional technology to navigate and processes to follow.

Furthermore, they weren't trained on the depth and breadth of questions they were now receiving, and they found themselves having to escalate a majority of the video calls to their managers to resolve. Unbeknownst to the customers, chaos reigned behind the scenes. Senior management was oblivious as well—until a third of the staff quit. While there was a lot of fanfare when the new service launched, the bank was forced to temporarily pause the video service after six weeks.

Though it proved to be a well-received service for customers, the bank didn't take into consideration what the downstream effect would be on its employees, their workload, or their inability to respond to such a diverse set of questions. Instead, the bank exclusively focused on improving customer experience and customer-based metrics, while employees paid the price in increased effort.

When companies leverage technology to reduce customer effort and improve CX, customer loyalty and revenue follow. CX then becomes an even greater priority for the C-suite. But so often, employees don't enjoy the same level of enhancement, and they find themselves bearing the brunt of the customer improvements.

It's worth noting that over time, brands' continuous pursuit of improving CX often results in diminishing returns, as "new" practices become widely adopted and customers are less easily wowed. While companies must keep up with rising CX expectations, or risk being replaced by others that do, to truly thrive as a company, businesses must stay ahead of trends and anticipate what customers may want or need in the future.

Incremental improvements have established norms and set expectations across segments and geographies. For example, retail businesses now know how to meet the expectations of new customers with digital onboarding routines. They have established best practices in e-commerce, like the rule of thumb that it should take no more than three clicks for a customer to find and purchase what they're looking for. Many of CX's fundamentals have become standard as more and more companies have realized the benefits of providing memorable experiences for their customers.

Since that's the case, simple, fast, clear, and intuitive experiences have become a de facto re-

> *The goal as a company is to have customer service that is not just the best, but legendary.*
>
> –SAM WALTON

quirement. At the same time, they're easier than ever to replicate, and therefore they don't differentiate a company enough to help it gain, or retain, customer mindshare. Investing in the improvement of CX has been a priority for companies for decades now, resulting in a "sea of sameness."

In short, *the seven characteristics of CX outlined above are becoming table stakes, expected from customers.* To that end, customers will always expect and want more from a company. But this increase in CX has given rise to a dilemma.

The CX Dilemma

Last week, I ordered an item on Amazon using the app on my phone. All told, the process took less than a minute: I found the item I was searching for after a short scroll through similar products and tapped the "Buy Now" button. At that point, related items were suggested, and one turned out to be something I actually needed: batteries to make what I was buying work. Later that day, an e-mail informed me that the items had been shipped and would arrive on my doorstep the next day before 10 p.m. Meanwhile, my credit card was automatically billed.

To our ancestors, Amazon's retail operation would appear to be a miracle: its seemingly infinite inventory, almost frictionless buying and return process, and nearly immediate front-door delivery. To our jaded eyes, the problem lies in those words "seemingly," "almost," and "nearly."

If the item promised by 10 p.m. arrived at 9 a.m. the next morning—still amazingly fast by last century's standards—I'm frustrated by Amazon's failure to meet my expectations. The added "effort" of waiting for the delivery impacts my feeling toward the company, and even toward the manufacturer of the product itself. While this one-off delay does not sway me to abandon the brand altogether, if another company came along that better met or exceeded my expectations, I wouldn't think twice about giving them a chance to win my business.

This is the CX dilemma every modern company faces. B2C retailers like Amazon, Walmart, Target, the UK's Tesco, Australia's MECCA, Brazil's Riachuelo, and Singapore's Uniqlo have done such an effective job of advancing CX over the past decade that customers not only expect an almost effortless experience but also anticipate a dizzying rate of improvement, companies doing all they can to push "almost" effortless ever closer to "completely." They vote with their wallets whenever any retailer fails to keep pace.

The problem is, in their attempts to keep up with these relentless demands, companies have pivoted too hard in favor of CX. Let's consider Amazon again. In his "2017 Letter to Shareholders," Jeff Bezos, Amazon's CEO and chairman at the time, highlighted these ever-increasing customer expectations: "One thing I love about customers is that they are divinely discontent. . . . People have a voracious appetite for a better way, and yesterday's 'wow' quickly becomes today's 'ordinary.'"

When Amazon launched its Prime offering in 2005, customers appreciated the value of two-day delivery with no minimum purchase required. As of 2019, Prime had expanded to free one-day delivery for members, with no minimum purchase required, on more than ten million products. In 2020, they topped themselves again: free one-day delivery on ten million items and same-day delivery on over three million items for qualifying orders of $35 or more. Then, in 2022 Amazon upped the CX ante even more. Amazon now allows customers to drop off returns at various locations without the original packaging and still get a refund, and even tells consumers to keep some returned items,

13

rather than dealing with the hassle and cost of shipping and processing a bulky, custom-made, or low-value item. This kind of maniacal focus—even for a company that has a mission to be "Earth's most customer-centric company"—has come with unforeseen consequences.

For example, shipping, returns, and restocking have always been enormously expensive to businesses, and returns tend to be even higher when consumers buy online. It's easy to toss items into a virtual basket but hard to visualize how they will look, fit, or work when they arrive. Online sales accounted for roughly 23 percent of the $4.583 trillion of total U.S. retail sales in 2021, according to the National Retail Federation (NRF), and the average rate of returns for online purchases was 20.8 percent. Considering that Amazon's total retail e-commerce sales in 2021 was $468.78 billion, this suggests that roughly $100 billion worth of merchandise was returned to the company in one year.

In Amazon's pursuit to be "Earth's most customer-centric company," by making returns easier than ever, the company now faces additional expenses and logistical supply chain challenges that could wipe out their increased profitability, along with the increased growth and customer loyalty they have realized by constantly striving to improve CX. What has helped keep Amazon sustainable is its sheer size—a small company would not be able to sustain itself under similar circumstances. With that in mind, when making long-term investments in CX, you must keep an eye on the downstream impact to profitability.

CX Is More Than "Good Tech"

Steve Jobs put it well when he said that "you've got to start with the customer experience and work back toward the technology, not the other way around." Superior CX doesn't come from simply throwing out an innovative new technological feature. This is where many companies stumble. They focus too heavily on the technology without paying attention to the most critical piece: how that tech is used, and by whom.

Just look at how much is spent on technology today. A 2020 McKinsey Global Survey of executives found that companies "have accelerated the digitization of their customer and supply-chain interactions and of their internal operations by *three to four years* since the start of the pandemic." Small and midsize businesses (SMBs) have been investing as well, with an eye on "catering to customer convenience" as a reason to digitize their organizations. Fifty-one percent of growing SMBs accelerated their investments in customer service technology between 2020 and 2021.

Further, 77 percent of information technology (IT) leaders are increasing investment in customer experience, with 93 percent stating that better customer-facing technology is crucial to remaining competitive in the marketplace. The overall customer experience software market is forecast to grow from $167.3 billion in 2021 to $295.7 billion in 2026 at a compound annual growth rate (CAGR) of 12.1 percent.

While the spend on CX technology is impressive, many consumers continue to be disappointed. In fact, when customers recall a brand experience, it's often "human-related": the prepared call center agent, the attentive waiter, the safe driver, the fair salesperson. Call it the experience disconnect: companies tout new technology or snappy design but have not invested in one of the most meaningful aspects of what customers view as an important part of a memorable experience—*people. Companies must find ways to create experiences that delight customers through the fusion of humanity and tech.*

Every day customers have a choice when they want to buy something. Do they shop and buy online, having the product delivered to their home? Do they buy online and pick up in a store (BOPIS)? Do they "showroom," in which they shop in a store and then buy online, typically at a cheaper price? Each customer will make a decision based on a few variables, including time and effort, personalized service, seamless experience, and price. It doesn't matter how much money or improvement a company puts into the online purchasing experience; customers will default to which engagement type they want (whether human or digital) based on their expectations and needs, so you must make sure your human-centered services are up to par.

The Employees on the Other End

In the name of efficiency and cost reduction, many organizations attempt to achieve a high-touch human feel during online transactions. They use digital tools to give the illusion of human intervention while maximizing scale and productivity. Simple transactions have become quicker and easier by orders of magnitude—and they improve by the day. While this CX-related technology has cultivated greater customer loyalty by reducing their effort—making customer transactions seamless and difficult transactions easier—it has had the opposite effect on employees, like we saw with the bank video service earlier in the chapter. Some of the improvements hyped by companies are not actually happening via tech alone; rather, they are happening thanks to some human intervention.

For example, in some companies, when customers place an order online, an employee must manually e-mail the receipt as well as add the order to the internal ordering system to be fulfilled. This process is *far* from automated and seamless for the employee, although it is much more so for the customer. An employee makes that process happen. Yet customers have no idea, nor do they really care. Once they hit "Order Now," it doesn't matter if a human fulfills it—it had better show up when expected. Though the employees are integral to the transaction, they are given little consideration by their employers and the customers they serve. In fact, businesses around the world have spent hundreds of billions of dollars and millions of people-hours aligning customer expectations with digital capabilities. But what they seem to often forget is EX, the one element that can help offset the diminishing returns of current CX investments, which has been neglected by employers for years.

This neglect has been thrown into sharp focus by the Great Resignation of millions of unhappy employees. Most companies, especially in the United States, believe the only way out of this growing morass is to sink even more money into improving the experience for customers without shoring up employee experience and reducing their effort. These companies lack a clear understanding that improving EX has a meaningful effect on a company's ability to provide better CX.

CX and EX, long treated as separate worlds, are, in fact, tightly bound—and share a common destiny. **Superior CX depends on superior EX.** The former can never keep pace with elevating customer expectations without the latter rising in synchrony. What is needed to solve the customer experience dilemma? How can you get beyond the experience disconnect and invest in what contributes the human aspect of a customer's experience? How do companies truly become B4C or B4B? For most companies, the answer seems to be hiding in plain sight: empowered, engaged employees who view enriching customers' lives, or businesses, as the core purpose of the company. In the next chapter, we take a look at how that's possible.

- The customer experience is better than ever . . . except when it isn't. And given the inflation of customer expectations for ever less effort and ever better support, those negative encounters are likely to only grow more common—no matter how great the fortunes companies spend on CX.
- As competitive advantage is increasingly defined by the experience you provide rather than the products or solutions you sell, solving customers' needs through innovative solutions is paramount.
- Long-term success will only come from creating frictionless and seamless interactions between employees and customers by decreasing the amount of effort both need to put into those interactions.

Conversation Starter Questions

- ▶ When you make strategic decisions to improve CX, do you consider the implications to employees?
- ▶ What value do you bring to your customers' businesses or lives?
- ▶ How do you define a compelling customer experience?
- ▶ Is customer-centricity integrated into your culture?

Chapter 2

Employee Experience

Your top employees aren't simply doing a job for you. They create outcomes that wouldn't be possible if they disappeared.

ROGER MARTIN

BY APRIL 2020, 2.6 BILLION PEOPLE HAD GONE INTO LOCKDOWN. Eighty-one percent of the global workforce's places of employment were fully or partially closed. From new rules for safety and well-being, to work-from-anywhere policies, to digital-first hiring and onboarding, the pandemic forced leaders to reimagine every part of the employer–employee relationship almost overnight.

If that first year taught us anything, it's that employees craved changes to the employer–employee relationship. In the wake of COVID-19, people around the world realized that work is not where you sit, but rather what you do. And many didn't want to go back to the *how* and *where* of the past, including even the employers they worked for. The resulting Great Resignation, or as I like to call it, the Great Reflection, was the beginning of a reckoning: today's employees demand more from employers, and they have proven willing to change jobs—and change them often—if *they don't get what they're looking for.* This reckoning will only continue if companies don't recognize and embrace the power shift taking place from employer to employee.

According to research by the global communications firm Edelman, employers have now woken up to the fact that *employees, not customers, are considered the most important group to a company's long-term success.* Edelman's research explained further, "This shift in power shouldn't come as a surprise. It's actually the culmination of a trend line that started a few years ago." *The pandemic reminded every company that they are in the people business.* And the commitment of a company to its employees directly affects their productivity, satisfaction, engagement, and ultimately, the revenue the employees generate for the business. The Edelman research further revealed that 74 percent of institutional investors agreed that a "company's ability to win the best talent is more important in gaining investors' trust than the ability of that company to attract new customers or increase a valuation multiple."

Fundamentally, companies previously saw employees as an "asset line item, human capital" that could be easily replaced if they left. Since March of 2020, business leaders are waking up to the central importance of employees—and the totality of their employment experience—but they still don't fully understand what elements drive a superior EX, let alone how to measure or improve it. And there is still reluctance, despite the greater recognition of the importance of employees, to implement policies and tools that would improve EX. People are the keepers of a company's brand promises. They design and develop products. And they are the ones who drive the differentiated, superior CX that impacts the bottom line.

That is why organizations must make the necessary investments to better an employee's experience, which ensures they are equipped to easily do their jobs and they are supported in their roles. From now on, employees must be viewed as "internal customers" who are a valuable, and sometimes irreplaceable, part of the business, working every day to serve "external customers."

Instead of enacting top-down mandates directed at employees without regard for what they want or need, businesses must see themselves as in service *for* them, B4E. *Employee experience is no more or less than the sum of every employer–employee, employee–employee, and employee–customer interaction. To win at EX, you should aim for positive, seamless interactions with and for your employees at every turn.* If you don't give EX the focus it deserves, you'll find yourself facing not only a talent shortage but also an absence of growth.

Raising the EX Bar

In August 1983, William B. Johnson—a major Waffle House franchisee who was once the franchise's largest owner—purchased the Ritz-Carlton Boston and its U.S. trademark for $75.5 million. He assembled a four-person development team, headed by hotelier Horst Schulze, to create a new luxury hotel brand, establishing the Ritz-Carlton Hotel Company as it is known today.

At Ritz-Carlton, Schulze created operating and service standards that have become famous not only in hospitality but throughout the broader service industry. Under Schulze's leadership, as cofounder and president, the Ritz-Carlton Hotel Company became the first service-based company, and the only hotel, to be awarded the prestigious Malcolm Baldrige National Quality Award—an honor it received not once but twice.

The company also held one of the highest J.D. Power rankings for guest satisfaction and has received all the significant awards the hospitality industry can offer. Ritz-Carlton has also ranked first in Employee Net Promoter Score (eNPS) versus its competitors. These awards would not have been possible without a relentless focus on maintaining a high experience culture, starting with its people.

Ritz-Carlton has a brand promise, coined by Schulze himself—"Ladies and Gentlemen serving Ladies and Gentlemen"—that has guided the organization for more than four decades. Schulze understood that creating a place where customers felt welcome and taken care of required its employees to feel the same way. He believed in hiring the right people and then setting them up for success.

"We hired people not to work for us," Schulze told me during a conversation on my podcast, "but to join us on the dream to create the finest hotel company in the world." That's why while Schulze was there, he went to the opening of every new hotel, personally heading up all orientation and training efforts himself. He knew he had to get three things right if he wanted people to be successful:

- Select the right employees.
- Align them with the organization and with the customer.
- Teach them their function.

He didn't just paint a picture for employees of a great customer experience; he directly influenced it, ensuring that, every day, every employee strove to make that CX a reality. The result was hotels that are legendary for their luxury and employees who are legendary for their service. But employees are only willing to go above and beyond because in addition to CX, the Ritz-Carlton focuses on EX, empowering their employees to make decisions and helping them to succeed in their roles.

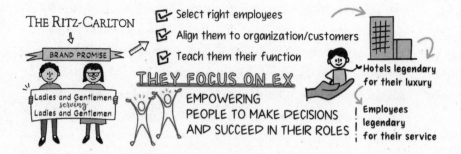

THE RITZ-CARLTON

BRAND PROMISE

Ladies and Gentlemen
serving
Ladies and Gentlemen

- ☑ Select right employees
- ☑ Align them to organization/customers
- ☑ Teach them their function

THEY FOCUS ON EX

EMPOWERING
PEOPLE TO MAKE DECISIONS
AND SUCCEED IN THEIR ROLES

Hotels legendary
for their luxury

Employees
legendary
for their service

For example, each Ritz-Carlton employee can spend up to $2,000 to fix a customer's problem before having to alert a manager. The company also enforces a "fifteen-minute rule," in which employees have fifteen minutes to solve a customer's room issue before others from the team come to the rescue. While that might seem like it would put undue pressure on employees, the culture encourages and rewards its people to go above and beyond and immediately resolve guest problems. With this kind of service-level expectation, Ritz-Carlton takes the new-hire selection process and training very seriously.

As part of that training, the Ritz-Carlton has a rigorous certification process for new hires, covering the employee's first twenty-one days, that prepares them for their specific job and aligns them with the hotel's "Gold Standards." Each day, they learn one of the "20 basics of service," a set of twenty principles and expected behaviors that help the employee better understand the brand's promise and their personal role in delivering on that promise. In Schulze's view, coaching employees on these points over and over puts Ritz-Carlton on its strong CX and EX footing.

These twenty principles are reinforced so that they become second nature to everyone regardless of their role in the company. This constant emphasis on the basics keeps employees engaged and helps coach those who need additional support. This

23

training was so legendary that the Ritz-Carlton soon became an inspiration to people in other industries. When the first Apple Stores were conceived in the early 2000s, Steve Jobs asked employees to share their best customer experiences and almost all pointed to a stay at a Ritz-Carlton. Jobs decided to send all future Apple Store managers through Ritz-Carlton's hospitality training.

As discussed later in the book, career development and appreciation are two top drivers of employee satisfaction, and by investing in their people with ongoing training and development, Ritz-Carlton helps make employees' jobs personally rewarding, increasing that satisfaction.

The Ritz-Carlton ensures that its people have what they need to do their job well. While Schulze was still with the company, if a hotel was experiencing a drop in Net Promoter Score (NPS)—which measures customer experience of your brand and provides the best metric to anchor your customer experience management program—or employee engagement scores, he would move into the hotel to work with management until that "Gold Standard" was back in place. Nobody got a pass from these high expectations of Ritz-Carlton employees, including the managers.

If you allow yourself to get too far away from individual contributors who touch and serve your customers every day, you risk running your business from a spreadsheet with no first-hand understanding of their day-to-day challenges. To improve EX, you need to be willing to connect with your employees on a direct level so you can better meet their needs. If you do, the result will be happier employees, and ultimately, happier customers.

> *Managers manage processes. Leaders create an environment in which people want to do the job excellently.*
>
> **–HORST SCHULZE**, cofounder and former COO/president of the Ritz-Carlton Hotel Company, and founder of Capella Hotel Group

The Characteristics of Superior EX

As we did in Chapter 1, let's ground the discussion in the specific ways businesses accomplish superior EX. With a few minor changes, and for very good reason, these characteristics mirror those that drive superior CX.

- **Efficient:** Minimize the time and effort employees need to expend to do their jobs, whether placing an order, providing customer service and support, collecting payments, or shipping out products. Examples include minimizing the systems employees need to log in to every day to perform basic tasks, providing an easy way for employees to find answers to general FAQs, and putting processes in place that reduce time spent on repetitive tasks.

- **Personalized:** Deliver a new kind of experience for employees that feels personal, relevant, and responsive to their individual wants and needs. Examples include tailoring communication specific to their role in the company, alerting them to changes in the systems and tools they must use, and informing them of required training they have to complete.

- **Predictive:** Surround employees with a platform able to anticipate their needs. Parental leave is a great example: once employees apply for parental leave, a series of activities should be put in motion that eliminates confusion of what needs to be done, alerts necessary personnel of the employees' time off, and backfills resources, all in a seamless way requiring little effort from the employees themselves.

- **Proactive:** Communicate both good and bad news in a timely fashion to help build trust and transparency with employees. If you purchase another company, close down a division or plant, or eliminate a product, do you want your employees to hear this news from someone else first? Of course not. Telling them yourself is a better approach.

- **Flexible:** Listen to employee feedback and develop a strong feedback loop to help improve employees' day-to-day experience. This will allow you to become more responsive, increase employee trust, and engender a safe space where people's voices are heard and respected. A common example today is a flexible working environment, including flex hours and remote work. Some companies are also testing in-office and at-home hybrid approaches and four-day workweeks.

- **Responsive:** Empower appropriate employees—such as those in HR, finance, recruiting, and benefits—to solve their fellow employees' issues in a timely fashion, and as close to the point of contact as possible.

- **Value-based:** Help instill employees with more personal value and purpose at work. With 70 percent of employees reporting their sense of purpose is defined by their work, companies that build connections with employees and facilitate success in that purpose will see greater productivity. Having a mission statement and the vision and values of the organization plastered on the wall is good, but actions speak louder than words.

Just as with superior CX, each of these characteristics helps reduce employees' effort, thereby bettering their experience. Also similar to superior CX, competitive advantage in EX is grounded in people. If employees are not enabled, supported, or empowered to do their jobs, they can't possibly have a superior work experience.

As discussed previously, companies have spent decades reducing effort for customers by shunting the lion's share of the mundane work onto their employees. In fact, many companies have flat-out ignored the needs of employees when designing CX enhancements, creating a major disconnect between employee effort and customer effort that ultimately hinders growth.

Increasing Employee Effort

Throughout the first three Industrial Revolutions, the primary use of technology was to increase productivity and efficiency within businesses. Technology helps this happen at scale through the automation of repetitive tasks and the elimination of legacy processes and systems, such as data entry, assembly line work, and automated time sheets and scheduling. In theory, technological improvements should help employees do their jobs with less effort.

Often, however, the improvements happen on the back end—the supply chain, manufacturing, and operations—not in the places where frontline employees work and serve customers. If a company reduces customers' efforts by removing steps they need to take to buy a product or receive customer service, but those steps are then pushed over to a sales or customer service representative, there is a negative impact on employees. CX and EX initiatives have to work in tandem; reducing effort for both sides should be the goal. But this won't happen until every leader throughout the organization understands how good EX drives good CX and vice versa.

When companies forego back-office technology investments that help streamline the business and expand toward more customer- and employee-facing technology, it is usually driven by an interest in improving employee productivity and CX. Notice I'm referring to "employee productivity," *not EX*.

But just like with CX, more technology for frontline employees isn't always the answer. Tech for tech's sake never helps employees. In fact, the proliferation of technology has actually overwhelmed many employees, the result of a lack of training and skills, a shortage of integration between the various systems, and inadequate processes. Even more basic than that, some new tech may not even be necessary for employees to do their jobs, and as an unintended result, it simply increases effort. (This is such an important topic, there are two entire chapters on technology and processes later in the book.)

Employees Expect More

Employees know exactly what's working—and what's not—through their day-to-day experiences. They're the ones dealing with the systems and processes that don't work quite right, the customer expectations that challenge the status quo, the onboarding and training that are far from ideal, and everything else in between. Furthermore, every employee is a customer of other brands. Outside of work, they have their own good CX experiences that demonstrate how seamless certain processes can be—if the company values their stakeholders' experiences and invests money into improving them. They know a better employee experience is possible. In fact, 56 percent of employees expect their work experiences to align with their own expectations as customers.

For example, in the B2C space, digital apps have removed long-standing frustrations and bottlenecks in legacy markets. You can purchase the latest fashions at the tap of a button. You never have to hail a cab again, nor step inside a grocery store or bank. Employees know what's out there, and they expect enterprise offerings (such as a company's internal software) to function as seamlessly as the products and services they use at home or in their cars. Many employees end up thinking enterprise offerings don't function seamlessly because their leaders don't care about their frustration and wasted effort. And in some ways, they're right.

More often than we'd like to admit, companies are *not* setting their employees up for success. After decades of ignoring EX, employers are finding themselves in a difficult situation. As mentioned in Chapter 1, the general business shift from product-centric to customer-centric led to an overcorrection. There is now a stark imbalance between customer- and employee-expended effort and subsequent experiences. Focusing on improving CX delivered results, but those results hid increasing damage to employee satisfaction, engagement, and loyalty. The extent of that damage is now undeniable.

Reasons Why Executives Prioritize CX over EX

Though the pandemic shone a light on the reality that companies have ignored the wants and needs of their employees for decades—while customers enjoyed steady investment into their overall experience—there has been little interest in improving EX from the C-suite. Even though nearly six in ten C-suite members say that providing a good employee experience is a top priority to the overall company, the leadership team, and them personally, most HR leaders (66 percent) report designing their post-pandemic workforce policies with little to no direct input from employees. There's obviously a disconnect here.

Employees, especially in customer-facing jobs, such as customer service, sales, and field service, want to work with customers and deliver great CX. Working with customers is often part of why they chose their profession in the first place. But studies have found that employees feel thwarted at every turn by management that is out of touch with the realities of the workforce. According to Gartner, "Eighty-seven percent of surveyed customer-facing employees agreed that they want to provide their customers with a superior experience. However, more than half of customer-facing employees do *not* believe their company or management is setting them up to be successful in customer interactions. In fact, a majority of respondents say that unnecessary effort in their day-to-day work prevents them from delivering a higher quality experience for customers."

In reality, companies have known about the pain points of employees for decades. Even though many companies have survey and employment data they have collected over time, a full 73 percent of the C-suite report they *don't know how to use their employee data to drive change* (as further explored in Chapter 3). And they don't want to dedicate time and/or money toward figuring it out. Let's dig into these two factors more deeply:

1. **Time:** Learning about pain points through surveys is one thing, but to truly understand pain points and devise solutions, executives must spend time learning about the employee experience firsthand. But how many executives sit down and listen to customer service calls on a regular basis? How often do they reach out to individual employees to ask what the company might do to make their jobs easier? How many get involved in training and orientation, like Horst Schulze?

2. **Money:** Leaders don't want to spend the money required to improve an inferior employee experience after inefficiencies are uncovered. Typically, this is because there is no inexpensive "quick fix." Decisions made in the C-suite are determined by long-standing but out-of-date return-on-investment (ROI) assumptions. When choices are made on where to invest, preference is given to solutions that

show immediate results. Solutions with a longer or even unknown time horizon are put off for "another day"—a day that rarely comes. All in all, CX has been prioritized over EX to the detriment of companies' resilience.

Instead of working on these problems, executives let working harder—not smarter—become the default solution. For example, many employees have to log in to multiple systems just to complete a simple task. Developing an integrated system would offer "a single source of truth," in which data is aggregated from multiple systems to a single location for ease of access. This would reduce errors, increase efficiency, and spare employee effort for more productive endeavors. Yet companies allow issues like this to persist.

The Results of Employee Dissatisfaction and Disengagement

A majority of employees have been disengaged from, or indifferent toward, their work for decades. They're frustrated by inadequate pay, limited career advancement opportunities, unrealistic productivity expectations, and long commutes that have become increasingly unnecessary. As shown in Figure 2.1, employee productivity and compensation were in alignment until the Digital Revolution, and they have diverged wildly since then. Between 1948 and 1979, productivity (measured as how much total income is generated in an average hour of work) and compensation (employees' average pay) rose in fairly close tandem. That was a result of specific policies with the "intentional goal of spreading the benefits of growth broadly across income classes."

Between 1979 and 2020, productivity went up 61 percent while compensation only went up by 17.5 percent. With productivity increasing, it is only natural to assume that income

The Gap Between Productivity and a Typical Worker's Compensation Has Increased Dramatically Since 1979

Productivity growth and hourly compensation growth, 1948–2021

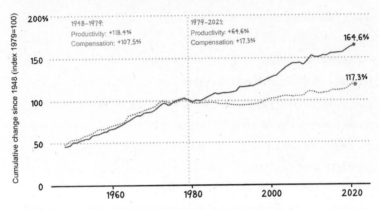

FIGURE 2.1: Productivity and Hourly Compensation Growth, 1948–2020

increased for businesses as well, and you'd be right. But that money wasn't making it into the pockets of the majority of employees. Instead, it went to the C-suite, other corporate and professional employees, and higher shareholder profits. A telling statistic to convey how much employers valued a majority of their employees.

Beyond compensation and productivity, companies need to pay attention to employee engagement when considering how to better EX. Engagement is currently at a miserable 32 percent—and hasn't budged in the United States since 2007, as shown in Figure 2.2. (In the rest of the world, the situation is even worse: just 20 percent engagement.) The engagement elements that declined the most from early 2021 to 2022 were employees' level of agreement that they have "clear expectations, the right materials and equipment, the opportunity to do what they do best every day, and a connection to the mission or purpose of their organization."

The percentage of actively *disengaged* employees—that is, workers who are disgruntled and disloyal because most of their workplace needs are going unmet—is slowly climbing, at 17 percent in the United States in 2022. Even more telling is the fact that from early 2021 to 2022, there was an eight-point decline in the percentage of employees who are *"extremely satisfied" with their organization as a place to work.*

This lack of engagement is estimated to cost the global economy $7.8 trillion in lost productivity each year. Human productivity is correlated with engagement of course, but unhappy or disengaged employees can still "do their jobs," checking the appropriate metric boxes and getting paid. They may, however, also be miserable. This disengagement shows up in places like a disinterest in collaboration and an unwillingness to go above and beyond or take on extra work. That ends up negatively impacting those employees who *are* actively engaged.

Digital productivity can also mask engagement issues. The fact that so much of the inner workings of any business—the tedious, mundane tasks—is now handled by technology and automation, and not humans, can result in higher productivity numbers. That doesn't mean, however, that your employees are engaged. As discussed, tech can help employees, but it's not a

U.S. Employee Engagement Trend, Annual Averages

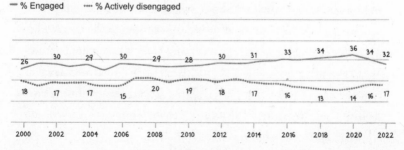

Figure 2.2

EMPLOYEE EXPERIENCE

cure-all. The impact of engagement on productivity has everything to do with the industry, the work being done, and the level of automation or human intervention involved.

Take the food service industry, for example. If you have unhappy, disengaged employees working in the kitchen and cooking in a busy restaurant (i.e., high productivity), but the quality of the food is low and the presentation is substandard, will that produce the best results? Well, if the metric is how many meals you can serve in a day, then things are going great—productivity is high. If the metric is quality, repeat customers, and good reviews online, then things might appear a bit different.

More directly, lack of engagement means employees are less likely to invest discretionary effort in organizational goals or outcomes. They are also more likely to quit or be fired due to poor performance, further exacerbating the talent crunch. Lost employees are expensive to replace: the average cost is approximately 90 percent to 200 percent of the previous employee's base salary, not including the impact of lost expertise as well as the new employee's training and learning curve.

Considering all this, it should come as no surprise that organizations that are the best in engaging their employees achieve earnings-per-share growth that is more than four times that of their competitors. If you don't have employee engagement, how could you possibly expect to see high productivity, innovation, and organizational agility? How can your company expect to provide superior EX when employee engagement is so dismal?

Business leaders are beginning to wake up to the central importance of employee engagement and the ways engagement affects revenue growth, but not quickly enough. The time has come to focus on EX: employees are begging for it, your customers are feeling the consequence of its neglect via poor service, and it's showing up in your bottom line.

Lead with Purpose

Fortunately, there are a number of companies that already understand the connection and, more importantly, operate according to that understanding. As mentioned earlier in the chapter, employee experience is foundational to the Ritz-Carlton philosophy and has been since its inception. Other companies have had the foresight to tend to EX when they've recognized a problem and understood the direct impact on CX. And not all of these companies are young, dynamic, tech-driven enterprises known for an agile approach. Take the nearly century-old giant manufacturing firm Unilever.

Founded in 1929 in the United Kingdom, Unilever has grown to become a multinational conglomerate with more than 145,000 employees, 400 brands, and 52.44 billion EUR (2021) in annual revenues. Considering its size, Unilever faces a huge task in responding to the changing nature of work, such as that brought about through technology advancements, like automation and AI, and the pandemic. In response, the company has launched numerous "Future of Work" programs to remain competitive and transform its workforce. In the process, they have stayed true to their stated mission of "making sustainable living commonplace"—including for employees.

While other companies cut costs to "improve profitability and find growth," Unilever believes "that such transactional approaches overlook opportunities and are ultimately counterproductive." It's not that Unilever doesn't cut costs; they had been cutting $1.5 billion per year in overhead through sustainable sourcing since 2008. Then, however, they reinvested three-quarters of that money into growth initiatives.

Paul Polman, Unilever CEO from 2009 to 2019, introduced the notion that *purpose* can "help reduce tensions in the workforce and create optimum conditions for growth." For that reason, he focused on giving the company, its products, and its people "a purpose beyond reducing costs and producing immediate profits." Their mission? Better the planet. The company created a long-term business model, the "Unilever Sustainable Living Plan," that focused on reducing its waste and greenhouse gas emissions and achieving 100 percent renewable grid electricity across its sites.

Polman didn't just inspire a purpose-led business inside of Unilever; he was one of the first CEOs to challenge others to do the same. Along with 181 other CEOs, he signed the Business Roundtable Pledge in 2019, stating that they would "lead their companies for the benefit of all stakeholders: customers, employees, suppliers, communities, and, of course, investors."

While Polman is no longer the CEO of Unilever, the idea of purpose and investing in employees has not slowed down—it has actually accelerated. As early as 2009, Unilever sought to ensure its employees were on board with the company's purpose-led approach, recognizing the approach would likely increase EX. To gain buy-in from employees, the company launched the Unilever Leadership Development program. What started out as a program exclusively for senior leaders soon expanded to all levels of the organization. Employees created their own individualized "future fit plans," including an eighteen-month skill development plan, focusing on a purpose important to them but in line with Unilever's goals.

These plans are paying off. In 2020, according to *Harvard Business Review*, "92% of those who had attended a 'discover your purpose' workshop reported having jobs that inspire them to go the extra mile, compared with only 33% of those who had not attended one."

Too often, companies view employee training as a double-edged sword. One side is the ROI in terms of employee productivity and capabilities. The other is the wasted investment when

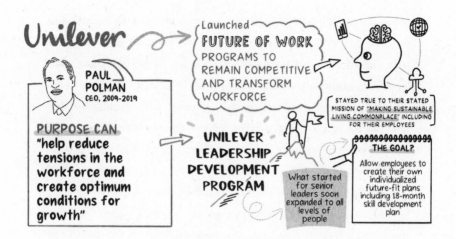

Unilever

PAUL POLMAN
CEO, 2009-2019

PURPOSE CAN "help reduce tensions in the workforce and create optimum conditions for growth"

Launched FUTURE OF WORK PROGRAMS TO REMAIN COMPETITIVE AND TRANSFORM WORKFORCE

STAYED TRUE TO THEIR STATED MISSION OF "MAKING SUSTAINABLE LIVING COMMONPLACE" INCLUDING FOR THEIR EMPLOYEES

UNILEVER LEADERSHIP DEVELOPMENT PROGRAM

What started for senior leaders soon expanded to all levels of people

THE GOAL?
Allow employees to create their own individualized future-fit plans including 18-month skill development plan

employees leave after training on the company dime. However, if you do not provide training or investment in your employees' careers, why would your best people stay? With so much uncertainty today, investing in employee development has long-term benefits far greater than the limited impact of a small percentage of employees departing the organization.

"We can't promise anyone a job for life," reads Unilever's website. "But we can do everything possible to equip our people with the skills and awareness to pursue meaningful work, whether at Unilever or elsewhere." That's the type of experience employees seek today. When they find it, the results for employers are very real. During Polman's tenure, Unilever delivered a total shareholder return of 290 percent, and annual sales rose from $38 billion to more than $60 billion.

Prioritize EX for Great Results

To solve the problem of declining EX, there's a simple though often overlooked approach: ask your employees what to improve. My friend Tom Peters, coauthor of *In Search of Excellence*, among other incredible books, believes in "management by wandering around (MBWA)." In other words, if you want to know what is going on in your business, get "close to where the work is done." This isn't aimlessly meandering around the office. It's a deliberate and genuine way to not only connect with employees but observe what it's like to work at your company. Don't put a wall around yourself as a manager; your people won't learn from your expertise and you won't from theirs.

What you'll discover can't be found on any company report or spreadsheet. Do they like what they are doing? Do they feel supported and heard? Are they able to do their job effectively? Are they wasting time and effort on outdated tech and processes? You may uncover sources of job dissatisfaction that could be avoided.

If companies were to stop and take the time to truly deconstruct the greatest areas of employee dissatisfaction, they could begin to fix these issues and show progress and good faith to the employees. They could start improving EX. And in return, CX will improve as well. The benefits are real:

- Sixty-nine percent of employees say they'd work harder if they were better appreciated.
- Companies that excel at customer experience have 1.5 times more engaged employees than companies with a record of poor customer experience.
- Sixty-one percent of employees agree that their primary employer needs to do a better job of listening to their feedback.
- On average, 62 percent of employees agree that they would work harder if their primary employer treated them better.
- Employees most committed to their organizations put in 57 percent more effort on the job—and are 87 percent less likely to resign—than employees who consider themselves disengaged.

- Eighty-one percent of employees and 58 percent of HR managers say, "creating and sustaining a positive culture" to enable a superior employee experience is important.

This process of improving EX starts at the top, with the C-suite, and works its way down through management to the employees. Everyone owns part of the employee experience and should see themselves as a stakeholder in its evolution. Organizations in which employees are primarily motivated by shared values and have a commitment to a shared purpose are far more likely to have high customer satisfaction than those that don't.

This revolution is already underway at top companies, where leaders are finally taking steps to treat their employees like "internal customers," increasing EX and CX in tandem. "We are treating our employees as customers," Allstate CEO Tom Wilson says. "They don't pay you in dollars, but in hard work." It's a win-win.

The onus is on companies to deal with poor EX. That's what the companies that will win the intense competition over the next decade will do. Creating a culture of engaged, invested, and happy employees will keep their organizations vibrant and successful. While increasing either EX or CX has the ability to increase revenue, improving both in concert generates a multiplier effect. We will explore the research that proves this connection is real throughout the next chapter.

CHAPTER TAKEAWAYS

- In reality, companies have known about the pain points of employees for decades. They recognize that the lack of investment in systems and tools increases the effort it takes for employees to do their jobs. Instead of working on these

39

problems, they let working harder–not smarter–become the default solution.

■ If a company reduces customers' efforts by removing steps they need to take to buy a product or receive customer service, but those steps are then pushed over to a sales or customer service representative, there is no net benefit. CX and EX initiatives have to work in tandem, reducing effort for both sides.

■ Instead of enacting top-down mandates directed at employees without regard for what they want or need, businesses must see themselves as in service *for* them. *It's no longer enough to win at CX alone.* You must also win at EX, which is no more or less than the sum of every employer-employee interaction.

Conversation Starter Questions

▶ Are the metrics used to manage your employees focused on task productivity, the value they provide to customers, or the overall business?

▶ Are you investing in training on a broad set of skills to help your people prepare for the future?

▶ Are technology improvements for customers being balanced with those for employees?

Chapter 3

The Big Research Findings

*Your people come first. And if you treat them right,
they'll treat the customers right, and the customers
will come back, and that'll make the shareholders
happy.*

HERB KELLEHER,
*cofounder, later CEO, and chairman emeritus of
Southwest Airlines until his death in 2019*

IN 2019, WHEN I SET OUT TO STUDY THE REAL LINK BETWEEN CX AND EX, my working hypothesis was as follows: *Happy employees are more engaged. That higher engagement translates into better customer experience. When EX and CX are improved in concert, the impact on growth will substantially exceed the effect of improving either one at the expense of the other.* Granted, as I outlined in the introduction, the "happy employees make happy customers" hypothesis seems obvious, and I am not the first to propose it. But if it's so obvious, why don't more companies develop an operating mindset along these lines? Why isn't this incredible opportunity to drive growth being leveraged more often?

As discussed earlier, for years, business leaders had acknowledged that a better employee experience will lead to a better customer experience, resulting in increased profits and growth, but little hard research had proven such direct linkage. When

Salesforce partnered with Forbes Insights, then Edelman, and then Talenteck, we set out to change that.

Over a two-year period, we dug up data to determine whether or not the facts could support these long-held claims. Those research findings provided strong evidence that *improving employee experience does indeed lead directly to better customer experience and, as a consequence, increased growth rates.* It is no coincidence that companies that perform well on employee experience metrics also tend to perform well on customer experience metrics, and, when they do both well, increase revenue results. All three components are deeply connected. And our research shows that when companies take a more holistic approach to delivering meaningful experiences for everyone, a number of benefits—in addition to growth—appear. Among them are:

- Stronger employee and customer brand loyalty and affinity
- A workforce more open to change, including technological
- A better organizational capacity for transformation and innovation
- Closer employee alignment with business goals
- Greater employee satisfaction with leadership
- Personal connection to the vision, values, and culture for both employee and customer

While it would be impossible to explain all the detailed findings from our research in one chapter, they have been sprinkled throughout the book to provide the greatest insights for companies looking to improve revenue performance and employee engagement. Meanwhile, this chapter highlights the major takeaways from all of the studies.

By sharing this information together in one place, my hope is that you fully understand the virtuous cycle created when you get both EX and CX more tightly aligned, and why that is so integral to company performance and resilience, today and in the future. But first, let's take a look at another company that already understands and embraces that virtuous cycle: Southwest Airlines.

World-Class EX Drives Industry-Leading CX

Over the course of half a century, business writer Tom Peters has taken thousands of flights all over the world. The one he remembers most, as he shared with me on my podcast, was with Southwest Airlines. Like most frequent fliers, Peters knew Southwest's reputation for superior customer service, a particularly unlikely one for a low-cost carrier. On that flight, however, he saw that famous customer service in action, and he never forgot it.

While exiting the plane, Peters noticed a man in a wheelchair waiting to be pushed up the ramp. Suddenly, one of the pilots exited the plane and walked over.

"Would you mind if I pushed you up the jet bridge?"

"Sure," the stunned passenger replied, and the pilot pushed the man's wheelchair up the ramp. For Peters, this was a fantastic "in the wild" example of delivering excellence at work.

Southwest, known for its quirky crew members and witty flight announcements, credits its top-rated customer service to an "employees first" mantra, one endlessly reinforced in everything the airline does. Southwest believes in treating its employees right, not least because it believes its employees will treat customers right in return. Ultimately, the company recognizes how this virtuous cycle begins with employees and increases business and profits.

This may explain why *Forbes* named Southwest a Best Employer for Women in 2019, *Military Times* named Southwest to the 2019 Best for Vets, and Indeed ranked Southwest Airlines number three on the list of Top-Rated Workplaces in 2019. It may also explain why, in 2020, the company had the lowest customer complaint levels, according to the Airline Quality Rating report, which ranked Southwest as number one.

When I had the opportunity to speak with Ginger Hardage, Southwest's former senior vice president of culture and communications, about the company's legendary employee and customer experiences, I jumped at the chance. Hardage spent twenty-five years at the company, serving on the executive leadership team before taking on the role of SVP of culture and communications. She attributes the company's dedication to customer service and employee experience to its founder, Herb Kelleher, and its president emerita, Colleen Barrett. "They put the foundation of service in place from day one," Hardage told me. "Especially the philosophy of *servant leadership*—that is, putting your people first and the rest will take care of itself."

When I told her about Peters's experience, she wasn't surprised. "We have so many of those stories," she said. "In fact, it's one of the things we did: encouraged the organization to collect and retell those stories to help reinforce great customer service behavior among employees—especially new ones."

Hardage visualizes the connection of happy employees and happy customers as a flywheel gathering momentum as EX and CX are successfully improved and propel growth for years to come. "The mistake too many companies make is that they try to start that flywheel by taking care of their shareholders first," she said. "It's really hard to get employees behind the process after the fact."

She once again credits Kelleher with taking a different approach to EX and CX. "Herb understood the magic of starting with happy employees so much so that, to this day, the company's promise states: '*Employees will be provided the same concern, respect, and caring attitude within the organization that they are expected to share externally with every Southwest Customer.*'" The flywheel spins fastest when *every* business decision is aligned with the experience of both the employee and the customer.

When I asked how Southwest first integrated this operating philosophy into its business model, she pointed to a process that started on day one: "All cultures start with hiring," Hardage told me. "Hire tough so you can manage easier." Organizations that truly care about their cultures are willing to spend time on hiring—and if they're a company with a reputation for great employee experience, like Southwest is, they get to be selective.

"Southwest historically receives about 370,000 applications in an average year," Hardage told me, "and they hire 6,000, which means only 2 percent of applicants get through. Hiring tough not only makes managing easier, but it also helps with retention. Southwest has about a 97 percent retention rate, which means only about 2 to 3 percent of the people leave voluntarily in a given year." Getting a lot of résumés in the door is one thing. Finding quality candidates who align with your corporate values

Southwest BELIEVES IN TREATING ITS EMPLOYEES RIGHT, WHO WILL TREAT CUSTOMERS RIGHT IN RETURN

CX

The connection of **happy employees** and **happy customers** is a flywheel, gathering momentum as improved EX and CX propel growth

EX

CX

THE FLYWHEEL SPINS FASTEST WHEN EVERY BUSINESS DECISION IS ALIGNED WITH BOTH **EMPLOYEE** AND **CUSTOMER EXPERIENCE**

SERVICE

"HIRE TOUGH SO YOU CAN MANAGE EASIER"

All cultures start with hiring

and want to keep working for your company over the long term is another.

"If you take care of every aspect of your employee journey," Hardage said, "that employee is going to take care of your customers, just like that helpful pilot. It's as simple as that."

The Hard Numbers

I love that story about Southwest, as it shows the true power of a combined, balanced EX-CX approach ingrained into the operating mindset of a business. But I also recognize it's an anecdote, and what you're likely looking for is the "wood behind the arrow," some facts to back up the platitudes. So here it goes.

Let's start with the *direct link*. Salesforce research found that those in the C-suite who feel their companies "place a high priority on EX" say they saw **1.3 times** more growth in their client satisfaction key performance indicators (KPIs) than those who do not. Companies that "place a high priority on CX" saw **1.4 times** more growth in employee satisfaction KPIs than those who do not (see Figure 3.1). *When both CX and EX increase in concert, the results are even greater.*

Without fail, whenever I make that statement, the question that comes up most often in response is "That sounds good, but how much of an increase are we talking about, and what is the revenue impact?" While this particular Salesforce study was conducted in the U.S. only, it provides a strong indicator that there is undoubtedly additional revenue to be realized. Companies with both high EX and high CX exhibited a three-year compound annual growth rate (CAGR) of 8.5 percent, almost double (1.8 times) that of firms with low EX and low CX (4.35 percent CAGR). *In other words, for a $1 billion company, such a growth rate would translate to $40 million in additional revenue per year.*

C-Suite Who Had...

...EX as a top priority

saw **1.3X** growth in their client satisfaction KPIs over those who do not

...CX as a top priority

saw **1.4X** growth in their employee satisfaction KPIs over those who do not

FIGURE 3.1: Corresponding Improvements with EX and CX Investments

Among the top U.S. performers were such iconic brands as FedEx, PepsiCo, Amazon, Apple, Netflix, Costco, Hilton, and Southwest Airlines. Even if you don't run a billion-dollar brand, this multiplier should be compelling enough to get your attention. *Optimizing and improving the efforts currently underway for employees and customers can and will increase revenue—it just requires doubling down on changing the way you think about growth.*

Because our study was based on organization-level data, it could not be definitively proven that the EX-CX connection was the actual driver behind improved revenue outcomes and not, for example, a good press cycle or a great new product launch. So Salesforce decided to go a step further and see whether we could get closer to identifying—and quantifying—this causal impact, including what elements of EX have the greatest effect on CX and growth. Proving that connection and result would not only represent compelling new evidence about how much employee investments matter but also show executives the power of those investments in their own organizations.

To sleuth this direct link, we determined a large, single U.S. retail store would provide the best conditions for creating a control environment of "on-the-ground" employees. We focused on the retail environment so we could directly study a business that relied heavily on customer-facing employees to zero in on the impact of employees on customer decisions. Our question was: *Does the composition of customer-facing employees in these locations— all else being equal—affect revenue and profits?*

The retail case study (three years of data) first identified employee experience as a combination of four elements:

1. Employee longevity
2. Full-time/part-time status
3. Prior internal rotations
4. Proxy for skill level

By combining financial data with people-related data—two sources of information that tend to be siloed in different departments and rarely integrated—we were set up to answer another central question: *Does the employee composition at the start of each month impact the sales generated in that store over the course of that month?* The results were striking. Not only were we able to establish a clear link between employees and revenue, but the impact was substantial. Put simply, stores whose customer-facing employee base: (1) was more tenured, (2) had more cross-departmental experience, (3) was more skilled, and (4) skewed toward full-time employment generated far more hourly sales.

How much more hourly sales? If an average store could move from the bottom quartile of performance to the top quartile in each of the aforementioned four elements of retail employee experience, it consequently would jump from generating $57 per

Employee Experience Drives Revenue and Profit

Improvements to employee experience metrics such as employee longevity, full-time status, internal rotation, and skill level impact store-level financial metrics.

Predicting hourly revenue and hourly profits by employee experience quartile

Figures shown are per person-hour worked

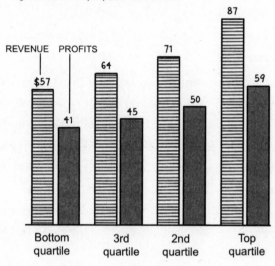

FIGURE 3.2

person-hour worked to $87 per person-hour. That's more than a 50 percent increase in revenue (shown above in Figure 3.2).

Also noteworthy, these revenue increases would not be accompanied by skyrocketing expenses. In fact, a parallel analysis of operating profits showed that improving employee experience through these four factors would result in a 45 percent increase in profits per person-hour, from $41 to $59.

The numbers presented here are of course specific to the company and industry studied (retail). But the effects should be large enough to convince executives that they are missing out

THE BIG RESEARCH FINDINGS

on a tremendous opportunity to improve performance. Customer-facing employees—or any employees, for that matter—are not simply a cost to be minimized (as retail, call center, and service employees are far too often thought of by executives) but potentially high-impact investment opportunities that can pay back significant returns if managed properly.

The Tension: A Crisis of Prioritization

So, the proof of a direct link is now starting to take shape: *EX is often the forgotten or overlooked contributor to improved CX and revenue growth*. While executives have caught on to the link, they still need help in overcoming a number of internal challenges, starting with what strategic choices they make when planning for growth. The C-suite and executive leaders talk a big game about prioritizing EX, but the reality is nowhere close. Note the apparent global contradiction (highlighted in Figure 3.4) to that statement.

While it is encouraging to see that the C-suite intuitively understands this direct link, with more than half (61 percent) saying that good EX equals good CX, and nearly six in ten C-suite leaders saying providing a good EX is a top priority, that

The C-Suite Recognizes the Link Between EX, CX, and Revenue, but Still Prioritizes CX

Good EX equals good CX

Providing good EX is a personal and company priority

Employees are encouraged to prioritize CX

FIGURE 3.3: The Aspiration and the Reality

Percentage of C-Suite Who Feel EX or CX Is Important to the Success of a Company

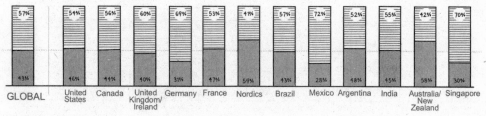

Employee Experience
Customer Experience

FIGURE 3.4: CX Still Prioritized by C-Suite
Globally Despite EX Importance

is where the backing of EX seems to end. Nearly nine in ten (88 percent) say that *all employees are encouraged to focus on the customer's needs above all else.*

This is not just a U.S. phenomenon. It was found that there are only two regions—the Nordic countries and Australia and New Zealand (ANZ)—in which the C-suite considers EX more important than CX to the success of a company. As shown in Figure 3.4, like in the United States, the rest of the world's business leaders feel CX is more important than EX, and Mexico, Singapore, and Germany feel it is *significantly* more so. No matter how much lip service company executives around the world give to improving EX, it remains stuck in between intention and action.

What is even more discouraging than the C-suite feeling CX is more important than EX to a company's success is that *employees agree* (Figure 3.5).

Overwhelmingly, on a global basis 63 percent of employees feel CX is more important than EX. This stat shows leadership continues to struggle with establishing a culture where employees feel they contribute to the success of an organization.

51

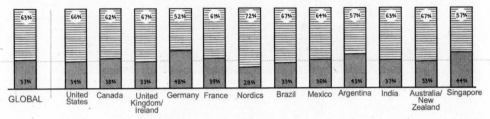

CX Still Prioritized Globally and Across Regions Despite EX Importance

Percentage of Employees Who Feel EX or CX Is Important to the Success of a Company

63%	66%	62%	67%	52%	61%	72%	67%	64%	57%	63%	67%	57%
37%	34%	38%	33%	48%	39%	28%	33%	36%	43%	37%	33%	44%
GLOBAL	United States	Canada	United Kingdom/ Ireland	Germany	France	Nordics	Brazil	Mexico	Argentina	India	Australia/ New Zealand	Singapore

≡ Customer Experience
▓ Employee Experience

*FIGURE 3.5: Employees Feel Less Important
to Company's Success Than Customers*

A Tale of Two Companies

Globally, there is a huge disconnect between C-suite perception
and the realities of the day-to-day experiences of employees.
This disconnect is undermining the ability for companies to improve EX, CX, and ultimately, growth. Further, a lack of C-suite
accountability and ownership of EX is deepening this disconnect. Only 51 percent of the C-suite and 33 percent of employees
agree that HR has a seat at the table for discussions on the
overarching company vision. It is no wonder there is such a significant divide—EX has no representation in the decisions that
matter.

In one of the most blatant misses by companies today, 74 percent of the C-suite say that no one actually "owns" EX. This problem persists across all sectors and markets examined, but it is
especially significant in Canada, where 91 percent of executives
agree that EX does not have a proper owner within the company. (That percentage was the highest out of any market in the
study.) The United States and Germany were the least likely to

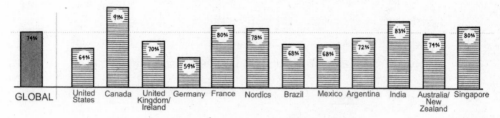

Who Owns the Employee Experience: Key Market Differences
Percent of C-suite who feel no one owns the employee experience

GLOBAL 74% | United States 64% | Canada 91% | United Kingdom/Ireland 70% | Germany 59% | France 80% | Nordics 78% | Brazil 68% | Mexico 68% | Argentina 72% | India 83% | Australia/New Zealand 74% | Singapore 80%

Figure 3.6: Globally, Ownership of EX Isn't Common

agree, at 64 percent and 59 percent, respectively (Figure 3.6), which could point to the fact that there is a greater level of effort directed at improving employee experience in those two markets.

When conducting dozens of executive roundtables around the globe, this lack of EX ownership was one of the most significant conversation starters, especially if there were chief human resources officers (CHROs) or chief people officers (CPOs) in attendance. Why was that the case? Most people believe—and research backs them up—that great customer experience drives revenue growth. But who claims credit for these successes? Marketing departments will point to advertising campaigns and brand awareness efforts that coincide with above-normal sales growth. Product teams can quantify the impact of specific features on customer satisfaction or increased revenue. Sales teams, of course, view themselves as the go-to group for bringing revenue in the door. But what about human resources departments?

CX has many champions in the org chart—including the chief marketing officer (CMO) or the chief customer officer (CCO)—but who stands up for the employees' experiences in the same way? When I asked those same CHROs if they believe they own EX, their responses were fairly consistent: "Parts of it, yes, and then various other executives own the rest." These responses validate the findings in Figure 3.6 even further.

Now, before any strategic adjustments happen based on the findings thus far, *executives and business leaders need to start with some context. They must truly recognize the state of EX today,* including the specific aspects of an employee's experience that drive an increase in reported client satisfaction and revenue.

Market Leadership
Does Not Mean High EX

This may come as a surprise—or it may be all too believable—but going into the pandemic, executives shared a long-held belief that if a company was successful, there should be no reason for employees to complain. While it is alluring to think that revenue growth will make employees happier, a company can only press their employees so hard before their nerves fray and they burn out.

Winning against the competition and dominating the marketplace are all well and good in theory, but the spoils must be divided among the company, including and beyond compensation. If you are a market leader with huge revenues and your CEO is compensated more than your frontline employees, they're going to notice. In 2021, S&P 500 CEOs averaged $18.3 million in compensation—324 times more than a typical worker—and the AFL-CIO report showed that workers' real wages increased 4.7 percent while CEOs' rose 18.2 percent in 2021. If the warehouses and employee spaces are getting run-down but the C-suite offices just received an opulent upgrade, there's a problem.

Success can't be achieved on the backs of employees without recognition and rewards for their hard work. Not if you expect to keep them, at least. So, forget the antiquated notion that growth and revenue translate to employee happiness—you must make the proper investments, guided by your employees and proper C-suite representation, if you expect to get the best out of them.

As discussed in Chapter 2, there is also a clear misunderstanding as to the realities of what the world of work *really* looks like in the trenches, as opposed to the view from the C-suite (Figure 3.7). Further, a significant number of executives don't know how to use their employee data to drive change. This is where the fact that nobody owns EX shows itself most. If there isn't a champion responsible for analyzing survey data, then putting insights into action, why do the survey in the first place?

This leadership–employee divide on engagement, happiness, and growth opportunities is resulting in millions of people leaving jobs for the promise of something better. To avoid this fate, you must determine where the disconnect between executive assumptions and employee experience exist, especially when it comes to those elements that create a sense of employee empowerment and drive CX. (More on this in Chapter 8.)

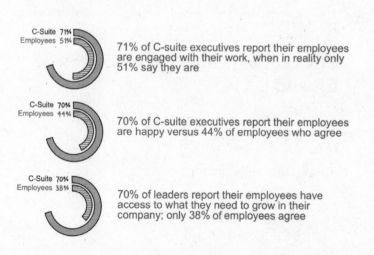

C-Suite 71%
Employees 51%

71% of C-suite executives report their employees are engaged with their work, when in reality only 51% say they are

C-Suite 70%
Employees 44%

70% of C-suite executives report their employees are happy versus 44% of employees who agree

C-Suite 70%
Employees 38%

70% of leaders report their employees have access to what they need to grow in their company; only 38% of employees agree

FIGURE 3.7: The C-Suite Is Out of Touch

Diverging Views and Priorities
of Executives

Diverging views and priorities exist not only between executives and employees but also within the C-suite itself. As I mentioned earlier, there are executives who already buy into the importance of prioritizing EX to improve CX and growth. And unlike some of their peers, they actually want to bring a greater focus toward improving EX. Let's call them EX executives. On the other side of the equation are CX executives, those who believe the most important way to sustain growth is to focus on customer experience. That said, they still see value in improving EX.

But even though both groups want to improve CX and EX, there appears to be some disagreement on the obstacles to getting there, as shown in Figure 3.8. While differing opinions among executives are neither unusual nor unexpected, those varying opinions can get in the way of getting anything done, leading to inaction and, in return, impacting future growth.

For 43 percent of EX executives, employees' *resistance to cultural transformation* is considered the biggest obstacle to im-

The Biggest Obstacle to Improving EX and CX is...

For **EX** executives
employee resistance to cultural transformation

For **CX** executives
lack of senior management vision

FIGURE 3.8

proving both employee and customer experience, whereas 31 percent of CX execs said the same. For 41 percent of CX executives, a _lack of senior management vision_ is the biggest obstacle to improving EX and CX, whereas 32 percent of EX execs said the same.

In addition to disagreeing on the obstacles, EX execs and CX execs also have divergent views about how best to _improve_ CX and EX. Significantly, more than 39 percent of EX execs say _instilling a vision for change is the best way to do so_, whereas only 32 percent of CX execs agree. By contrast, 47 percent of CX execs say the best way to improve CX and EX is to _redesign the organization to focus on **BOTH** high CX and high EX_, compared with 40 percent of EX execs (Figure 3.9). There should be no question that close coordination within the C-suite itself is crucial if the operational mindset is going to align around enhancing EX and CX in a more intentional and connected way.

Without agreement in the C-suite on the biggest obstacles and the best way to improve CX and EX, how can you even begin to create an action plan?

You can't.

There are also marked differences between EX and CX exec-

Best Way to Improve CX and EX is...

39% of EX executives say that senior management must instill a vision for change

47% of CX executives say that organizations must be redesigned to focus on high CX, high EX

FIGURE 3.9

utives' objectives over the next three years, and not in the way you would expect:

- EX executives say that **CX** will be the most important objective *or* among their top five objectives, by a wide margin over CX executives (81 percent vs. 64 percent).
- For CX executives, the priorities were reversed: 68 percent say **EX** will be the most important objective or among their top five objectives, compared with 52 percent of EX executives.

Yes, you read that right. Executives focused on EX say CX will be the most important objective or among their top five objectives, while CX executives state EX will be the most important objective or among their top five objectives. That means CX and EX executives are in agreement that both experiences are important, but they have come to an impasse in which they cannot agree on how to overcome the obstacles to, or improve, either experience.

It's therefore no wonder companies are still asking whether the employee or the customer is more essential to the business and are struggling to make progress. Understanding what the business priorities are is a prerequisite to decision making. Otherwise, you have different parts of the company heading in very different directions. In the next chapter, we explore the mindset that must exist at the center of any organization that wishes to bring EX and CX into alignment—and wishes to set that organization up for even greater success.

CHAPTER TAKEAWAYS

- The tension between CX and EX is real. There is an urgent need to prioritize EX and shore up the lag in dedicated EX resources, systems, and processes. Furthermore, metrics and accountability for EX must be created (more on this in Chapter 9), and cross-functional ownership of EX must take place at the highest levels of company leadership. Otherwise, employees will continue to feel they aren't an important part of a company's success.

- The leadership-employee divide on engagement, happiness, and growth opportunities is resulting in millions of people leaving jobs for the promise of something better. To avoid this fate, you must determine where the disconnect between executive assumptions and employee experience exists, especially when it comes to those elements that create a sense of employee empowerment and drive CX.
- Success can't be achieved on the backs of employees without recognition and rewards for their hard work. Not if you expect to keep them, at least. So, forget the antiquated notion that growth and revenue translate to employee happiness—you must make the proper investments, guided by your employees and proper C-suite representation, if you expect to get the best out of them.

Conversation Starter Questions

Whenever I get the chance to sit with an executive team and discuss the advantages of tightly linking CX and EX to drive growth, I begin the conversation with a series of questions:

▶ Are you aligned on what priorities will have the greatest impact on growth over the next three to five years?
▶ Do your employees feel like the company provides them with the best technology, processes, and culture to do their jobs effectively?

59

- Has your employee-focused technology kept pace with digital transformation investments for your customers?
- What are the tension points and gaps between your EX and CX initiatives? Is there a plan to resolve those differences?
- Do you know what the leverage points are between CX and EX? How are you harnessing them?
- Does your company know how to use employee data to drive change?
- Is there a clearly articulated definition of what good CX and EX look like?
- What metrics are you using to measure both CX and EX? Is there an executive or cross-functional team responsible for setting goals and metrics to measure against a stated goal?

If you have not asked yourself these questions—much less answered them—you are headed for rough times. Not only are your employees going to become even more unhappy than they already are, but your customers are going to become unhappier consequently. If it's any comfort, at least you're not alone. Far too many companies are in the same position.

Chapter 4

The Experience Mindset

When a company's founding generation hits upon a powerful formula for delighting customers, that new venture starts to rock and roll, energized by heady growth. But at the same time, it's not always common at that state for the company's leadership to focus on taking good care of their employees.

FRED REICHHELD,
Bain Fellow, creator of Net Promoter System

TO GET THE STORY OF EMPLOYEE EXPERIENCE AT ONE OF THE world's most celebrated companies, Airbnb, there is no one better to talk to than Employee Experience Advisor Mark Levy. When Levy joined the company in 2013, he was considered by many to be the first head of employee experience at a major U.S. corporation. As he shared with me, the position emerged from a conversation with the company's CEO, Brian Chesky. A few days after Chesky posted a Medium article entitled "Don't F*^k Up the Culture," Chesky brought Levy in to interview for global head of HR—a role that had been sitting vacant for over six months. "I don't really know what HR is," Chesky told him, "but everything I've heard about it, I don't necessarily like."

This was an interesting way to start a conversation with a potential HR leader. Chesky wanted to know whether Levy would be open to a completely new approach. "Are there ways that we could reinvent HR by putting everyone focused on the people activities in one group?" Chesky asked. "Could we flip the HR model on its head and figure out a different way to work with employees to ensure that, as we grow, we don't f*^k up the culture?" Well, now that's interesting, Levy thought. Levy recognized Chesky was a huge proponent of culture, so he decided to stop talking about HR narrowly and instead focus on the overall people at Airbnb.

"Who's working in areas of the company related to employees," Levy asked, "and are they all reporting into different parts of the company?" As it turned out, they were, as is the case at most companies. The twenty-five employees at Airbnb whose work touched on talent and recruiting were scattered across the organization. Technology recruiting reported to engineering, and all the regular HR functions and nontech recruiting reported to legal.

To Levy's surprise, he learned there was one unique internal group that could be a great resource for improving culture and experience: *Ground Control*. This self-organized employee group brought the company culture, mission, and values to life through employee events, employee recognition, employee celebration, and internal communications. Ground Control's goal was simple: *This is a special place to work, and we want to keep it that way.*

When Chesky described Ground Control to Levy, a lightbulb went on. "You have a Customer Experience team," Levy said. "Could we have an Employee Experience team as well?" Chesky agreed, so they set out to create one together. This was the start of a transformation in Airbnb's employee experience journey that would be led by Levy as its head of employee experience. Levy said, "A crucial step we took to drive the transformation of the company was to really change the remit for employee experience. It still included the traditional HR functions, but now it also included the ideas generated by Ground Control."

Then came another turning point. "Thanks to this new emphasis on EX," Levy told me, "there was a major shift in how we worked. Instead of doing things *to* our employees, we began working *with* them and *for* them to both define the priorities that would help set them up for success and do their jobs. That in turn led us to design the programs, processes, systems, and tools that enable them to be more engaged, more productive, and more connected to the hosts, our guests, and the community."

"While we began by cobbling together disparate parts," Levy told me, "we grew from four people doing everything into teams focused on areas like recruiting, total rewards, diversity, and so forth. We learned you need to be thoughtful about how these functions and teams interact to create that end-to-end journey for the employee. They all need to be connected or the experience will suffer.

"The goal was creating the container to empower employees to democratize the company culture." As Levy continued to explain, Airbnb did that through "very clearly defined values and then further defined behaviors, which included a 'core values interview process' where every prospective employee, every candidate went through a core values interview." These were done by people outside of the hiring function so there would be no bias on whether they would be a good engineer or marketer. To make that initiative even more powerful, Airbnb trained interviewers to look for "signals to ensure the person was joining for the right reason and would further drive the values."

Levy and his team also created a Core Values Council, which consisted of veteran employees from throughout the organization. As Levy described it, "They served as sage advisors to the CEO and the leadership team when it came to important decisions—everything from a marketing campaign to choosing a partnership to an organizational redesign to acquisition. Again, we were working to empower the workforce."

Chesky and Levy knew that improving the technology, processes, and tools used by employees would have a tremendous impact on their job satisfaction, and thus they reimagined the role IT would play in EX. In 2013, Airbnb hired a new director of IT, and Levy told him he needed to do as much to make things frictionless for employees as he would normally do for hosts and guests.

Together, Levy and the new IT director took a field trip to an Apple Store to inspect the Genius Bar. Just as Apple learned from Ritz-Carlton (discussed in Chapter 2), Airbnb would learn from Apple. Much like how at the Ritz-Carlton, employees are able to spend up to $2,000 to solve a customer's issue before having to alert a manager, at an Apple Store, employees don't need to request special approvals while helping customers. This type of employee autonomy leads to empowerment, and that empowerment creates better EX. CX also improves, as customers receive prompt, frictionless service from one attentive, caring employee.

To create a seamless experience similar to that of customers at the Apple Store, Levy wanted each of Airbnb's office locations to feature their own "Genius Bar," where employees could go to get fast, convenient service from the IT department. They would arrive at a help desk or service window with their laptop, smartphone, or other digital device in need of repair and be greeted by a member of IT. Just as the Genius Bar is seen as a place that provides friendly, useful, and welcoming interactions, Levy wanted to develop the same vibe. Often, office employees dread reaching out for IT help—calling or emailing, putting in a "ticket," dealing with multiple interactions. In this case, they would have more autonomy and access to IT, and IT employees could help them in real time, providing a more seamless experience. The environment was also meant to be inviting, somewhere employees felt comfortable sitting down and having a cup of coffee as they waited for assistance.

Having raised the status of EX to match that of CX, the final challenge was to tie the two universes together: "We decided to connect our employees with our guests and our hosts by giving them $2,000 a year for travel," Levy explained. "We even created special thank-you gifts for employees to give to hosts during their stay. We asked them to sit down with their hosts, talk about what it's like to work with Airbnb, and bring any thoughts and ideas back to the office when they returned."

Levy worked closely with his colleague Chip Conley, who led hospitality at Airbnb. After Levy's team successfully brought together all Airbnb employees to an event called One Airbnb, Conley decided it made sense to invite hosts from across the world to an event called the Airbnb Open. The two collaborated on the design of the event, and one important component was to involve as many employees as possible to be able to "host the hosts." The two also collaborated on other ways to integrate the employees, hosts/guests, and community through meetings, experiences, and volunteering.

"I think the moment when I realized we'd accomplished what we'd set out to do came when the company had its IPO in December 2020," Levy recalled with a smile. The event took place right in the middle of the COVID pandemic, so the traditional bell-ringing ceremony happened virtually. Airbnb marked the occasion by creating an ad featuring some of its over four million hosts simultaneously ringing their doorbells from Bhutan to Samoa to Iceland, the international community of hosts coming together as one giant Airbnb family to celebrate the company's success.

"That's when I knew that we hadn't just improved the experience of Airbnb employees and its customers," Levy told me, "but that the experience was now shared." Sparking all of this in Levy's view were Chesky's words in their first meeting, the idea of turning HR on its head.

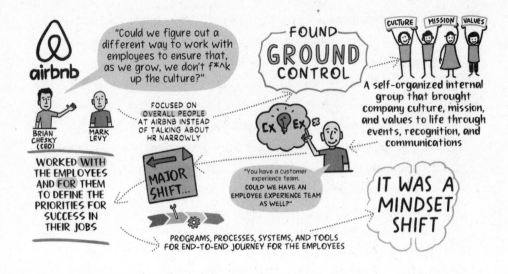

"It was a mindset shift," Levy said, "to see the solution as not simply an HR matter but something spread across the entire organization. We had to get anyone touching the employee experience process to understand that we were going to work with employees the same way our employees work with hosts and guests. That is, they needed to be in service to the employees." If every organization's smallest action and largest purpose were oriented in this way—to serve both the customer and employees at the same time—every source of friction between the two could begin to be eliminated.

An Intentional and Strategic Approach

The pandemic and Great Resignation have made it clear that conversations regarding employees' expectations and their experiences can no longer be limited to the HR department. Employee expectations are changing, and what they might have put up with in the past will no longer be tolerated. The entire organization must be aligned around a new operating mindset, an Experience Mindset.

> A quick reminder: an Experience Mindset is about fully maximizing the leverage points between a strong employee experience and customer experience to create a virtuous cycle of momentum that leads to significantly better growth rates.

It's no coincidence that companies that demonstrate an Experience Mindset—such as Airbnb, Qatar Airways, Costco, Lamborghini, Hilton, Zurich Insurance Group, and Chipotle—dramatically outperform similar companies within their respective sectors that focus on CX alone. These companies realize that any improvement to CX that diminishes EX, or vice versa, is counterproductive because of how closely they are intertwined. A cohesive, exponential revenue growth strategy is only possible through a decision-making approach dedicated to improving experience across the board for all stakeholders, internal and external.

Adopting an Experience Mindset will require nothing less than a true cultural shift. Furthermore, the Experience Mindset must become the standard operating philosophy, *intentional and strategic*. A company that applies an experience lens to strategic decision making will create a high-value, integrated employee and customer framework that will cascade throughout the organization.

The Experience Mindset approach aims to make sure both CX and EX are represented in the boardroom and beyond, taking them out of their separate silos and integrating them into one whole. The goal of this new corporate mindset is to serve customers better, beginning with the group described as "internal customers" in Chapter 2—that's right, your employees.

The Experience Mindset in Practice

Consider a situation where a company's customers demanded a new service that employees dread performing. Should the company offer that service anyway in the name of "customer-centricity"? What about firing the employees who are most disgruntled about this customer demand and replacing them with new hires who are less likely to share their real opinions? Applying the Experience Mindset to that question, the answer should be obvious: neither is the right response.

> *Everything starts with employee experience. Maximizing that employee experience in a hybrid working environment and focusing on physical, mental, financial, and social well-being is a real priority.*
>
> **–DAVID HENDERSON,**
> chief human resources officer
> of Zurich Insurance

In a scenario like this, a far better option would be for leaders to use employee pushback as a conversation starter, asking those who are most resistant to the new service for direct feedback. That feedback might end up uncovering a solution that would increase satisfaction for both the customer and the employee at the same time. Don't let the old saying "The customer is always right" lead you astray—a company shouldn't automatically do whatever the customer wants, or thinks they want, especially at the expense of employees.

Employees must be given the opportunity to provide feedback on new offerings (products or services), not just from a feature and functionality standpoint but also in terms of how these new offerings impact their day-to-day working lives. That way, when the challenge arises, employees, feeling heard, will be more likely to understand and accept why they have to do something a certain way, and know how to get it done.

Imagine if an IT department were to deploy a new sales technology called Chat that allowed the company's sales reps to engage with customers virtually. The company's executives are excited because they've been hearing that Chat is something their customers have been asking for. But there's an issue they had not foreseen. Chat was rolled out quickly so it isn't integrated into the existing customer relationship management (CRM) system, nor was there any true explanation on why it was being deployed or input from the sellers themselves about how they could use it.

In fact, if they had been asked, the sales reps would have explained that Chat was not something they wanted, unless it was easily accessible via their CRM system; otherwise, it only added more complexity to their jobs. In such a situation, do you think those reps would immediately embrace that tech or would they dread using it? Wouldn't the more ideal scenario be to ask sales what processes—if any—need to be changed, how they might use the new tech, and whether or not it should be integrated into the CRM system?

The short answer is, well of course. Yet, in reality, when sales doesn't use new tech they're provided with (and I can tell you from experience, this happens all the time), executives start to ask IT why no one is using the new tools that have been deployed. The standard response is to place blame on the sales team members and not on the fact that it was a less-than-optimal deployment (more on this in Chapter 7).

By comparison, if IT had shared the fact that customers

wanted the ability to chat with sales, then gotten the employees involved in how best to deploy such a feature—including integrating Chat with the CRM system, updating current processes, and enabling salespeople with the proper training—adoption would have been much less of an issue. Unfortunately, the option of asking employees what they need to do their jobs, and how they use the systems and tools given to them, is rarely part of the technology planning process. Instead, it happens *after* the fact, forcing unnecessary burdens and expectations on all involved.

The example can work in the other direction as well: you may have employees who love doing some aspect of their job, but customers no longer value it. Should you continue to offer that service to appease employees? Or should you simply eliminate it altogether? What if your employees don't feel a connection with, or commitment to, the customers because of this change in their responsibilities? Would you just hire new employees at that point?

Again, in this situation, it would be better to ensure employees' voices are empowered and protected. By asking your employees what they think, you show them you value their opinions and are willing to truly listen to their suggestions or complaints. This approach builds trust, which is sorely missing—no more than 46 percent of employees agree that their companies provide this type of two-way dialogue.

The ultimate goal should be to ensure alignment between the efforts and expectations of employees and those of the customers before settling on a solution to any problem. You must take into account the implications, good and bad, to each constituency everywhere and always. Though you may not be able to benefit both equally all the time, you can strike a fair balance.

This approach may make some leaders a bit uncomfortable since the default is usually to put customers first, as the research indicates. But it will enable companies to right the wrongs of the imbalance created by decades of putting the customer above all else. Employees will recognize and appreciate this change, with great results for the company and its growth.

The result of this kind of equity can be spectacular: research shows that employees who report having a positive employee experience have sixteen times the engagement versus their counterparts with a negative experience—and are eight times more likely to want to stay at a company.

Third Time's the Charm: Howard Schultz and Starbucks

For years, Starbucks had been synonymous with strong CX *and* EX. That combination has been one of its greatest competitive assets. The company originally developed its cafes with its customers in mind. It wanted to create places for customers to lounge and connect over espressos and lattes. Beginning in the 1990s, the company positioned itself as "the third place," a spot between home and work where customers could find "comfort, community, and good coffee." Meanwhile, since its inception, Starbucks has implemented groundbreaking people-first policies, including health care benefits for part-time employees, a purposefully inclusive workplace celebrating diversity, free college tuition, and paid parental leave . . . all starting on the first day of employment.

These employee policies were not developed out of altruism but hard-nosed business pragmatism. Starbucks founder Howard Schultz explained: "I believe [free education] will lower attrition, it'll increase performance, it'll attract and retain better people." Because of these perks, the company had been highly successful, ranked as a great place to work and the envy of those inside and outside the industry who aspired to grow and add value to both employees and customers.

Schultz retired in 2017, but in April 2022, he returned to Starbucks as interim CEO until April 2023, when his successor, Laxman Narasimhan, took the reins. The move came as the multinational coffee chain was struggling with staffing some of its locations, and as U.S. baristas ("partners," as they are called) had mounted the most serious unionization push in the company's history. Part of Schultz's focus, he told employees at the first all-hands employee forum upon his return, was "establishing a new tone with the roughly 230,000 workers staffing its U.S. cafes." It was an admission that Starbucks, long known for its employee experience, had begun to lose its way.

This would be Schultz's third stint as CEO. He had previously held the position from 1986 to 2000, taking the company public in 1992 at a valuation of $271 million. He next returned as CEO eight years later, in 2008, to help the company reconnect its brand with its CX roots after years of waning results. At that time, he said, "The most serious challenge we face is of our own doing. We became less passionate about customer rela-

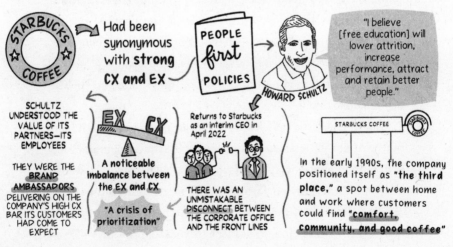

THE EXPERIENCE MINDSET

tionships and the coffee experience. _We spent time on efficiency rather than experience._" He stayed until 2017 after steering the company to 551 percent stock growth.

In March 2022, just five years after Schultz successfully refocused the company on CX, he was back at Starbucks, this time realizing that the company was no longer set up to fully "satisfy the evolving behaviors, needs and expectations of our partners or customers." They needed to refocus on the experiences of _both_ employees and customers.

Over the previous few years, changes in Starbucks's relationship with its employees had been brought about by forces both in and out of the company's control. Employees were regularly subjected to customer satisfaction surveys where they were at risk of being written up if they received bad reviews. When the pandemic hit, they were under pressure to meet drive-through time quotas, as drive-through sales and an emphasis on drive-through customers from Starbucks corporate increased during the COVID-19 pandemic.

No question March 2020 had wreaked havoc on the retail sector. Many frontline employees around the world found themselves struggling to stay safe and still collect a paycheck. This working environment was particularly difficult for Starbucks's employees and baristas. Facing staff shortages, many employees were overwhelmed. Meanwhile, in addition to managing orders coming in through drive-through windows and over the counter, mobile orders had become "out of control."

Worse yet, this new reality was forced upon them, with little training in the systems and health and safety processes they were now contending with. This challenge was exacerbated by the fact that employees had historically been measured on "their ability to connect with customers and the experiences of those customers inside the store."

According to a reporter for _Fast Company_ who interviewed a number of Starbucks employees, "A long-standing policy at the company is that one barista should be able to finish 10 customer orders—take payment, prepare the drinks, cook any food, and hand everything off—in 30 minutes. Some baristas argue that the expectation is outdated. They say the push toward mobile ordering has actually made some things more difficult. Consumers no longer face the barista's glare when ordering a 14-ingredient TikTok-famous drink; the Starbucks app judges them not."

In the United States, Starbucks's employees had already become frustrated with the demands brought about by mobile ordering before the pandemic, which then exacerbated the situation. They felt unheard by management, and there was an unmistakable disconnect between the corporate office and the front lines. Starbucks has said that after the pandemic set in, "the lack of contact between corporate and regional leaders and baristas hurt worker relations and the company's ability to address store problems promptly, fueling the current union drive." There was also a noticeable imbalance developing between EX and CX. As a result, the rumblings of unionization grew louder. There also appeared to be a crisis of prioritization in the Starbucks C-suite that may have played a part in Schultz's return, as executives struggled to balance stock prices, shareholder expectations, customer expectations, and employee needs.

During that first employee forum after he returned, Schultz announced he had suspended billions of dollars in share repurchases and stated that the company's "immediate focus would be on cafes, customers and employees, rather than the stock market." He added, "I am not in business, as a shareholder of Starbucks, to make every single decision based on the stock price for the quarter. Those days, ladies and gentlemen, are over." Regardless of the external pressures Starbucks was experiencing, it was clear that Schultz understood the value of its "partners"—its employees. They were the brand ambassadors delivering on the company's high CX bar its customers had come to expect.

At the time this book was being written (summer 2022), Schultz had announced a reinvention plan beginning with five bold moves. Two of the moves are particularly important to this story: *Renew the well-being of retail partners (employees) by radically improving their experience. Reconnect with our customers by delivering memorable and personalized moments.* This plan appears to be headed in the right direction, though it's too soon to tell if employees would get on board.

Starbucks also announced a plan to invest $200 million in wages, equipment, and training, among other benefits, and spend about $1 billion in fiscal year 2022 on employees *and* improving the in-store customer experience. In June 2022, they planned to double the amount of training time for new baristas, and then do the same for shift supervisors in August. They were also launching an employee app to keep workers connected.

Maybe most important, though, is that they announced they would raise wages. That sounded great, but there was a caveat that not all employees were likely to be happy about: wages for tenured workers and expanded training for new employees would be taking place, but those perks wouldn't apply to the approximately fifty company-owned locations that had voted to unionize, which precluded them from some of these benefits due to government regulations.

Whatever the result, Schultz's goal is to restore the culture that once had understood the connection, and value, between employee and customer experience. He fully realizes this is a journey that will take time. "The work of our Reinvention is ongoing—and all Starbucks partners who believe in our purpose

75

and potential as a company can make a significant contribution in building our path forward."

Only time will tell if Starbucks will succeed with its reinvention plan.

The Tipping Point

When our research first came back from the field, I began to share the results with executives at a few roundtable discussions. While speaking with a chief people officer (CPO) from a global multibillion-dollar software as a service (SaaS) company, I was intrigued to hear that even though the company was one of Glassdoor's 100 "Best Places to Work"—and extremely focused on employee experience—they had no formal connection between their EX and CX efforts.

I wanted to know more, so I asked, "Who owns EX at this company?" The answer was telling: "As far as employee and resource management, it would be me," said the executive, "but we don't have a formal structure between the various groups to look at the employee experience holistically."

A chief revenue officer (CRO) from an AI cloud provider said, "I think EX sits with HR—and employee engagement scores have been left off our executive-level KPIs—and that has impacted our ability to grow. To combat that, *we've been trying to break down that mindset, and elevate EX as a top priority*" (emphasis added).

As so many people have shared with me, this entire concept of superior EX leading to superior CX seems so obvious when said aloud. Executives from around the world understand the idea the moment they hear it—and more often than not, they acknowledge it as a blind spot in their own companies. But many successful execs also point out that they are already growing without making this kind of "disruptive shift" to their businesses.

They will not be able to make that rationalization much longer. We are at a tipping point—brought on by the pandemic and the Great Resignation—and companies cannot continue ignoring this connection between EX and CX, regardless of what past decisions resulted in revenue growth. **THE BIGGEST EMERGING**

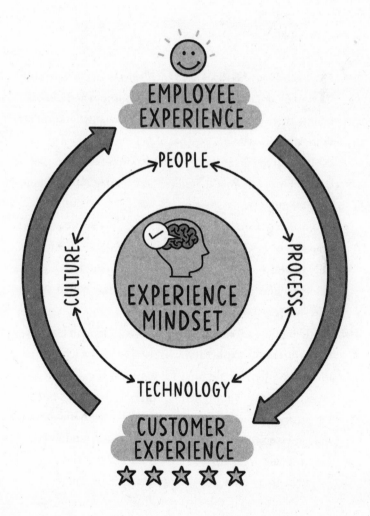

ORGANIZATIONAL OBSTACLE TO THE IMPROVEMENT OF CX AND EX WILL OCCUR WHEN A COMPANY CONTINUES TO EMPHASIZE ONE OR THE OTHER.

To ensure that obstacle is avoided, there are four variables that must be considered and balanced: people, process, technology, and culture. Prioritizing these four elements together, in a unified approach, in any business will not level EX and CX, but improve both. Next up, we'll explore each one of these priorities in detail.

CHAPTER TAKEAWAYS

- The Experience Mindset approach aims to make sure both CX and EX are represented in the boardroom and beyond, taking them out of their separate silos and integrating them into one whole. The goal of this new corporate mindset is to serve customers better, beginning with the group described as "internal customers" in Chapter 2—that's right, your employees.

- One-sided improvement is one step forward, one step back. A cohesive, exponential revenue growth strategy is only possible through a decision-making approach dedicated to improving experience across the board for all stakeholders, internal and external.

- The ultimate goal should be to ensure alignment between the efforts and expectations of employees and the customers before settling on a solution to any problem. You must take into account the implications, good and bad, to each constituency everywhere and always. Though you may not be able to benefit both equally all the time, you can strike a fair balance.

Conversation Starter Questions

- ▶ Does your company put equal time and investment into both CX and EX?
- ▶ Are you a product-led organization or a customer-led organization?
- ▶ Is your organization open to change?

Chapter 5

People: The Heartbeat of Business

Instead of focusing on productivity, focus on purpose, cultivate compassion, and give employees the agency to make decisions.

DR. AMIT SOOD,
expert on psychological resilience

IN THE EARLY 1960S, BUSINESS MANAGEMENT EXPERT HAROLD LEAVITT formulated a new model on the components of every business called Leavitt's Diamond Model. That model consisted of four variables: people, structure, tasks, and technology. Leavitt's theory was that one or more of these variables must be used for creating change in an organization. "Sometimes we may aim to change one of these as an end in itself," he said, "sometimes as a mechanism for effecting some changes in one or more of the others." Since the paper was published, Leavitt's model has morphed, combining structure and tasks to create "processes." PPT was born:

- **People** *are the employees of an organization and do the work.*
- **Process** *is the repeatable steps or actions that, when taken, culminate in a similar result or goal in a more efficient manner.*

- **Technology** *increases efficiency further by helping people perform their tasks.*

I'd like to suggest adding a fourth variable to this multidimensional framework, one that Leavitt likely took as part of the people discussion but which grows more imperative by the day: *culture*. Instead of PPT, companies looking to compete today and in the future need to consider PPTC: **People. Process. Technology. Culture.**

- **Culture** *refers to the beliefs and behaviors that determine how employees and management interact both internally and externally with other stakeholders.*

Remember, building an Experience Mindset is all about *balance* and *intention* between various CX and EX initiatives. The same applies here. The way to maximize organizational efficiency is not just to balance your PPTC efforts but also to intentionally

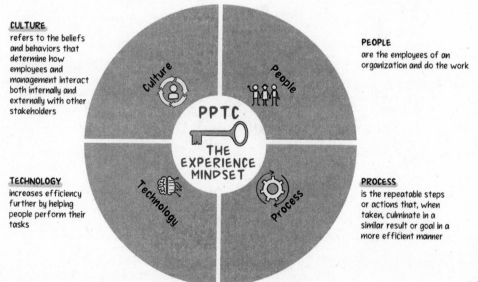

CULTURE
refers to the beliefs and behaviors that determine how employees and management interact both internally and externally with other stakeholders

PEOPLE
are the employees of an organization and do the work

TECHNOLOGY
increases efficiency further by helping people perform their tasks

PROCESS
is the repeatable steps or actions that, when taken, culminate in a similar result or goal in a more efficient manner

optimize the relationships between them on a continuous basis and track their progress.

For example, if your company's technology changes, you need to modify people and processes to adapt to that change. If people aren't efficient, start by looking at the technology and processes, then move on to employee development—don't assume the individual is the problem. If people don't know how to use the new technology properly and thus struggle to do their job, the company will take a hit on both employee and customer satisfaction.

Similarly, if an organization creates too many processes and rules, the bureaucracy in that organization will make people highly unproductive. All of which means the organization's culture and brand reputation will suffer. The point is, *PPTC variables are interconnected: focusing on one without considering the others is a recipe for suboptimal performance.* In this chapter and the following three, I dig deeply into PPTC as a way to integrate an Experience Mindset into your business in a more intentional and balanced way, starting with the first of the original PPT variables: *people*.

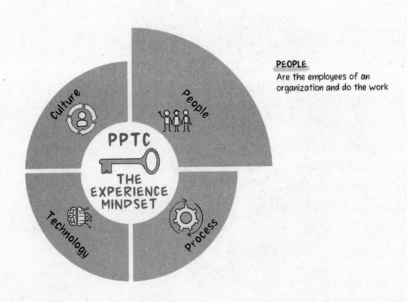

PEOPLE
Are the employees of an organization and do the work

As you've seen, customers and other external stakeholders often get the lion's share of attention while employees are overlooked. Too many businesses fall into the trap of concentrating heavily on technology and processes—streamlining both in an effort to reduce costs and increase human productivity—without any thought to improving overall employee experience. Needless to say, being overlooked or underappreciated is a consistent source of employee frustration and dissatisfaction. That damages EX, which negatively impacts CX, and together these factors weaken overall company growth.

You must understand the lived experiences of your people, similar to how most companies understand their customers. Only once you understand their experiences can you work purposefully toward improving them—before things get bad and they decide to leave.

CEOs say that customer experience (39 percent) and talent (20 percent) are the top two most effective methods for creating a competitive advantage.

A People-Centered Turnaround

In 2012, Best Buy found itself in severe financial straits. Sales and profits were declining, the company's stock price was plummeting, employees were disengaged, and pundits were predicting the brand's demise. Best Buy brought in a new CEO, Hubert Joly, new to the retail space, to turn the company around. During a conversation I had with him on my podcast, Joly explained that "there were zero buy recommendations on the stock. Everybody was saying, 'You better cut, cut, cut, close stores, fire a lot of people.'"

Instead, as part of his effort to bring accountability back to

83

Best Buy, Joly aimed to get "all hands on deck" and encouraged in-person collaboration to find ways to improve the business. Joly wasn't interested in inventing a totally new business model or "cut, cut, cutting" people. He wanted better financial results by managing the assets, including the people, that Best Buy already had.

Joly learned how to improve the business and cut unnecessary costs by listening to what he calls "the front liners." Turns out—surprise, surprise—they had the answers: "I spent a week in a store in St. Cloud with my blue shirt and my khaki pants—my badge said 'CEO in Training'—to just listen to the employees. They provided all of the solutions and it made our job easy.

"One thing I learned from that experience," Joly told me, "was that, as it relates to people, head count reduction should be the last resort. As leaders, we need to first focus on growing the top line. And with cost, our first focus should be what I call the 'non-salary expenses,' which are all of the elements of the cost structure that have nothing to do with people." At most companies, these "non-salary expenses" constitute the majority of the cost structure. "Of about $2 billion we took out in terms of cost," Joly explained, "about 70 percent was in these non-salary expenses." This is not to suggest there were no layoffs—some were made—but within the course of reducing head count, Joly wanted to do it in a "thoughtful, purposeful way."

"[There] are a few lessons that can be learned from that experience," Joly said. "The first thing is: we conducted a very people-centric turnaround. After all, a company is a human organization composed of individuals working together in pursuit of a common goal, isn't it? As leaders, sometimes we focus too much on the 'what' to do. But the 'how' is very important in finding ways to create that energy by co-creating the plan, getting going, and celebrating wins," Joly said.

From 2012 to 2019, Joly led the company through a successful "Renew Blue" transformation that resulted in five consecutive years of sales growth, improved customer satisfaction, market share gains, improved margins, and a 263 percent increase in shareholder return. This transformation placed a new emphasis on employee experience, attracting and growing "transformational leaders" and energizing employees to deliver "extraordinary results."

> *You can design and create, and build the most wonderful place in the world. But it takes people to make the dream a reality.*
>
> **–WALT DISNEY**

Joly recognized how the enthusiasm and talent of the company's employees played a key role in Best Buy's success with customers. To that end, Best Buy invested in its workforce in several ways. They enhanced employee training—which has won praise and awards for its quality—and expanded employee benefits to include paid caregiver leave, mental health benefits, paid time off for part-time employees, and childcare backup.

The payoff was significant. Employee engagement scores hit record highs and employee turnover rates in the stores reached

85

record lows. Employees also participated in millions of hours of training annually, including new-hire orientation, product knowledge, and leadership development, both in person and online. By 2019, Best Buy was ranked number three on *Training* magazine's "Training Top 125 list," the company's third straight year in the top ten.

This positive momentum has continued since Joly stepped out of his CEO role in 2019. According to Best Buy's corporate website, "associate knowledge is the highest it's ever been, and our overall Net Promoter Score for customer satisfaction has risen consistently, which indicates that our people know what they're doing and how to do it. We know our success with customers is driven by the enthusiasm and talent of our employees. Our employees are passionate, knowledgeable and engaged in what they do—and they're hungry to know more."

It's Personal

Today's workforce is looking for more than just a paycheck. According to *Harvard Business Review*, only 38.2 percent of workers aged twenty-five to forty-five cited pay as the most important factor in their job satisfaction—even though managers most often cite compensation as the reason why employees leave. The belief that employee retention is strictly a compensation issue is clearly a false narrative. In fact, the number of employees who cite pay as the root cause of departure has declined 23 percent since 2018!

Salary and benefits alone are no longer enough to recruit, retain, and engage talent. For example, employees who were given the choice of when to work felt more than three times better about work-life balance and close to seven times better about work-related stress. Similarly, those who were allowed to choose where they work felt two times better about their work-life balance and work-related stress.

Money and perks might make people feel better in the moment, but they won't buy happiness. In the long run, it's more personal than that. Only three in ten employees rate rewards or perks (such as salary and benefits) as their top priority when choosing a job, while seven in ten customer-facing employees prioritize other elements of the job (e.g., balancing work and personal life, career growth opportunities, and job security). Good EX will get you much further along in addressing what your people need and expect from you (Figure 5.1).

Good relationships with customers also play an important role in employee satisfaction and happiness. Two in three U.S. employees agree good CX fuels good EX at a personal level. The benefits of good CX are therefore not just advantageous for the

Ranked List of Employees' Top Motivations

	U.S.	CA	UK/ IRELAND	ANZ
Being able to balance my work and personal life is my top priority in a job	26%	34%	39%	29%
Beyond salary, I'm looking for a job that provides great employee benefits	21%	17%	7%	8%
Although salary is important, it is more important that a job provides career growth opportunities	16%	15%	13%	18%
I am looking for a job that challenges me and expands my skills on a continuous basis	13%	11%	13%	16%
I am looking for a job that provides strong job security, and I am willing to sacrifice salary and benefits for more job security	11%	8%	10%	11%
Above all else, salary is the most important thing about a job	9%	10%	12%	15%
My manager is the top reason I will go to or leave the job	5%	5%	12%	5%

FIGURE 5.1

Employees Also Say That Providing a Good Customer Experience Enhances Their Own Employee Experience

89% agree having a good relationship with customers "makes my job feel more rewarding"

88% agree having a good relationship with customers "makes me feel proud of my work"

88% agree having a good relationship with customers "makes me feel happier in my role"

FIGURE 5.2: *When Customers Are Happy, Employees Feel It*

company but for its employees as well, further validating the virtuous cycle (Figure 5.2).

Think about it. The average person spends one-third of their life at work—about ninety thousand hours. That's *a lot* of time, more than people might spend with friends and loved ones. When considered that way, of course EX is personal. The environment you establish for your employees truly matters—you want them to be happy (or at least content) to be there. You want them to be engaged with their work. Businesses must therefore identify what matters most to employees and then foster their commitment and engagement around those priorities.

Generating commitment and engagement starts from the very beginning with recruitment and onboarding, followed by investment in employee career development. As discussed, B4E is about doing meaningful activities *for* your employees, not *to* your employees. It must become the new guiding light for the entire management team if talent is really a top priority. Some companies, like Best Buy, Southwest, Zappos, and Salesforce, have already followed the lighted path and reaped the rewards for doing so. Now it's your turn.

Recruitment and Onboarding

Let's consider the recruitment and onboarding journey of a new hire. Right off the bat, this journey gives the new employee a sense of what it is like working for your company. A timely and efficient recruitment process can enhance a company's reputation from both a market and candidate perspective and ensure that the very best talent is seamlessly identified, engaged, and brought into the business.

However, the challenge of finding and competing for qualified talent in a remote, tight labor market has led to rushed hiring processes that often have unintended, negative effects for new hires later down the line (Figure 5.3). Though some candidates may see this shift toward faster recruiting processes as a positive change, rushing the process can create more room for unintended missteps. These include an inability to share more about the working environment, culture, and values of the company. It also means fewer people from the company will be involved in the process, eliminating the opportunity to establish relationships right at the start.

Further, a truncated, remote process doesn't allow for an in-person interaction between the prospect and the hiring manager, which can lead to greater ambiguity of expectations and priorities, along with a different level of personal connection. Expectations become misaligned, potential employees don't always feel welcome, and the purpose and values of the company aren't always fully explained or understood.

B2C industries have the most room for improvement, with

89

RECRUITMENT

How much do you agree or disagree with the following statements about your recruitment/hiring experience?
Showing Top 2 Box "Agree"

	B2B	B2C	RETAIL
I understood the purpose and values of the company	47%	34%	35%
My company made me feel welcome and a part of the team when I first joined	46%	33%	36%
I felt taken care of and supported when I first started	45%	28%	31%
I had clear communication from leadership about priorities at my company	40%	25%	32%
During my onboarding, the focus was on customer service/customer management	36%	26%	33%
My job wasn't what I expected before starting	31%	16%	20%
I didn't get the technology needed to do my job right away	25%	16%	19%

Figure 5.3: Recruitment Experience

only 20 percent of employees stating that the onboarding process was a "great experience." They especially struggle to promptly provide new hires with the technology they need to perform their jobs. Technology is one of the weakest, yet most important, aspects of onboarding, matched only by career development. But don't get too excited yet if you are a B2B or retail organization. While you fare better, with 37 percent and 28 percent, respectively, those aren't pop-the-champagne-and-let's-celebrate types of numbers.

The culmination of this data reveals that as leaders, we are failing new hires at a time when identifying and recruiting talent is already difficult. A suboptimal recruitment and on-boarding process during the initial stages of an employee's journey is far from the best way to start building a connection with someone who will spend the majority of their time working for you.

While many of the first interactions employees have with a company are with HR or the hiring manager, other parts of the organization also play a role. Participating in recruiting new members of their own team, or within another part of the organization, should be part of everyone's job. Remember the Airbnb story? The company's "core values interview process" is a great example of how to get people involved and accountable in hiring.

Unfortunately, knowing what needs to be done does not always result in actually *doing* it. As a first step, establish and develop relationships between *cross-functional executives* to improve the recruitment and onboarding process. These relationships will affect people both within the company (employees and other internal stakeholders) and outside it (customers and other external stakeholders). As Ginger Hardage shared, "All cultures start with hiring—hire tough so you can manage easier." When you design a well-thought-out new-hire and career development strategy, everyone is better for it.

Career Development

Of course, improving employee experience can't end with hiring and onboarding. Once employees have been hired, the same cross-functional executives need to keep an eye on career development strategies. The research found that career development and achievement was the lowest-rated aspect of employee experience across each region studied. Now, take a look at Figure 5.4,

CAREER DEVELOPMENT

How much do you agree or disagree with the following statements about your career development experience?

Showing Top 2 Box "Agree"

	B2B	B2C	RETAIL
My company has technology and tools that let me track my career progression	40%	19%	25%
My company sees me as a valuable resource and cares about my advancement	37%	20%	27%
My company always connects the right data and insights on my performance before making decisions on my advancement	37%	19%	23%
I don't have as much room in my organization to move to other positions as I would like	35%	21%	23%
My company is transparent to all employees about pay and promotion decisions	35%	22%	25%
Career development of its employees is a core value/priority of my company	33%	18%	23%

FIGURE 5.4: *Career Development Experience*

which shows the top two statements that employees "agree" with.

"My company has technology and tools that let me track my career progression" was highest in B2B at 40 percent. "I don't have as much room in my organization to move to other positions as I would like" was highest in B2C at 21 percent. And "My company sees me as a valuable resource and cares about my advancement" topped retail at 27 percent. Unfortunately, B2C received the lowest percentage of "agrees" across all questions asked.

Allocating internal resources to developing and promoting employee growth helps employees recognize they are valued, an integral part of the company's success. When employees do not feel valued at work, 76 percent look for another opportunity.

> **Almost one in five employees cited career-related issues as the root cause of their decision to leave their organization.**

Even though many companies could use some upgrading when it comes to employee development, tellingly 52 percent of C-suite executives believe that their company "has a lot of training and development options to help prepare (employees) for the future," while only 36 percent of employees agree with the same statement. That leaves a significant amount of room for improvement. More importantly, a survey conducted by LinkedIn found that 94 percent of employees would stay at a company longer if that company invested in helping them learn.

In addition to greater training and development, to increase employee commitment, there must be a renewed emphasis on promoting from within through inter-role and interdepartmental movement, rewards for good performance beyond pay, and a nonpunitive approach toward employees who choose to leave. Companies that excel at internal mobility retain employees for an average of 5.4 years—nearly twice as long as companies that struggle with internal promotions and career advancement. For those companies, the average retention span is 2.9 years.

Unfortunately, many learning and development (L&D) leaders still haven't made this connection. Although 46 percent of L&D leaders said upskilling or reskilling was a top focus area for them in 2021, internal mobility and career pathing, as well as employee retention, fell sharply. If nothing else, companies should invest in employee development simply to keep talent from leaving. In short, investing in talent gives employees a reason

93

to be engaged and committed to their company's goals, giving them a reason to stick around, even when work gets challenging.

When I have this conversation with executives, I often get pushback when we start talking about the cost of talent development, especially if, after those investments, employees take their new skills elsewhere. My response is summed up nicely in Figure 5.5. If you do not make the investments in training and development, you risk people leaving anyway because, as the research shows, that is what they want from employers. That investment is a big part of what keeps them engaged and committed. Treat them well, and even if they leave someday, they will become your best brand ambassadors for life. Otherwise, if you *do not* invest in developing them and they stay, their static skills cannot evolve, even when their current position requires them to, causing the rest of their teams and customers to suffer. Ask yourself, Which is worse?

Creating better humans will always be more important than creating smarter machines.

—GARRY KASPAROV,
former world chess champion
and author of *Deep Thinking*

CFO asks CEO
"What happens if we invest in developing our people and they leave us?"

CEO says
"What happens if we don't, and they stay?"

FIGURE 5.5: An Awkward Conversation

An Unlikely Partnership

Based on how I've defined employee experience, most HR leaders quickly realize they manage some aspects of EX (like recruitment, onboarding, and talent management), have limited influence on others (like learning and development), and have zero line of sight into the rest (like technology). And if you asked those same HR leaders whether they play any role in meeting the company's CX goals? Based on the research, few would reply in the affirmative, although, as explained in Chapter 3, they know it is a top priority.

Now let's flip the corporate coin. If you were to ask the average CMO if they have any responsibility toward improving EX, would they immediately say yes? Or would they reply, "Why should I?" Interestingly enough, there appears to be a shift afoot. Nearly half (48 percent) of marketing leaders indicated that improving EX will be a strategic area of focus over the next two years. However, if you asked them if they owned CX, they would say "Well, of course"—no surprise there.

Now let's include the chief information officer (CIO). If you asked your technical leader if they owned EX or CX, what would they say? I often hear from IT leaders that they deliver the technology that impacts both EX and CX, but they aren't necessarily the ones setting the strategy or owning the processes surrounding those efforts. This is where the Experience Mindset is a game changer. Effective collaboration between various leaders such as the CMO, CIO, and CHRO will help to further enable and engage employees, right from the start and throughout their employment, to bolster the corporate brand, accelerate revenue and productivity, and ultimately, improve EX and CX in tandem.

If companies aspire to take advantage of the virtuous cycle between strong EX and CX and accelerate growth, they will need to form intentional partnerships between these C-suite

95

leaders. They must allocate money toward _experience improvements for both employees and customers, test shared metrics, hold cross-functional work groups, and create a top-down, **PEOPLE-CENTERED** corporate narrative._

Furthermore, HR must shed its "administrative expense" reputation and step into a broader dialogue as the champion of the people, the employees, and their experiences at work. The HR leaders of the future need to be bigger, broader thinkers, speaking on behalf of what employees need and want from their employers across the board (especially those in customer-facing roles). They need to be tech- and data-savvy, understand a five-generational workforce, be capable of creating flexible working arrangements, and reach across the leadership ranks to form cross-functional partnerships and work groups to design for improved EX.

At a minimum, HR, marketing, and IT must partner on this journey to develop the way forward, not just at the leadership level but within the entire company. This is not about ownership, or a political land grab; this is about improving the day-to-day lives of the people who work hard every day for your company and your customers. Today, marketing and IT have greater influence over what happens within a company than HR. Remember, only 51 percent of C-suite leaders agree that HR has a seat at the table when it comes to setting the company's vision and future success.

Contrastingly, the CIO has had a seat at the table since the late 1990s, and the CMO got a seat at the table when businesses became much more customer-focused. The only way this new operating mindset works is if the CEO sees HR as a strategic, and not tactical, piece of the company's competitive advantage. A company's vision, values, and cul-

> _Putting process before people leads to a deficit of inspiration._
>
> —BELINDA PARMAR,
> CEO of the Empathy Business,
> and STEPHEN FROST,
> principal of Frost Included

ture must come to life through its people, starting with recruitment, onboarding, and enabling career development. Otherwise, even the most eloquent mission statement is nothing more than platitudes.

Ask Questions First

Understanding what your people want and need, and then developing the corresponding processes and technology road map to meet those wants and needs, requires getting back to the basics. Generating higher employee satisfaction is a great goal to have, but you won't get there without asking your employees about their experiences on a regular basis. Still, that's only part of the equation. It also matters who asks the questions, how frequently they're asked, and which topics are covered. For example, getting the C-suite involved through "Ask Me Anything" (AMA) roundtables or setting up a Slack channel to share ideas for process improvements that then go directly to the C-suite can help build employees' connection and trust with company leaders.

Take, for example, Clearco, a Canadian financial lending firm based in Toronto. I had the pleasure of speaking with the company's cofounder and cochairperson, Michele Romanow, about seeking out and listening to employee voices. Not only does Romanow lead Clearco, but she is also the cohost of *Dragons' Den* (Canada's version of *Shark Tank*) and a two-time unicorn (with companies valued at more than $2 billion in U.S. dollars).

As Romanow explained during a webinar we did together, while Clearco was experiencing a period of hyper-growth, she wanted to ensure the company didn't lose the entrepreneurial culture they had developed over the years. Still, she realized some of the processes the company had put in place at an earlier time were not keeping up with the needs of its rapidly growing business and expanding employee base.

In response, Romanow wanted to know where there was room for improvement, but she did not want to overcomplicate that effort. So, she simply set up an e-mail inbox entitled *The stupid sh*! we do* and asked everyone to post ideas on how to (1) streamline the business and (2) eliminate preventable frustrations employees were facing.

As you can imagine, "There was no shortage of ideas."

Romanow shared two major results of the exercise. First, by asking employees for their opinions, management involved them in the process of improving their day-to-day work and the overall business. Second, the e-mail inbox allowed the leadership team to quickly and easily create a highly effective feedback loop with employees, responding to their input and further building trust. This was a valuable and effective way to uncover and resolve avoidable process and system issues before they got out of control.

The lesson was clear. Even when things are going *really well*, you have to be willing to challenge the status quo by asking the right questions. The way to do that is not always complicated, expensive, or time-consuming—it can be as simple as setting up an e-mail inbox and requesting ideas. Furthermore, if you are a leader, even a highly successful one, you may not know all the answers, *and that's okay*. By asking employees for their thoughts, concerns, and issues, you learn from them, build trust and openness with employees beyond those who report to you, allow space for new voices to be heard, and create alignment within your organization.

Simply asking employees if they're "happy" or "content" with their work environment, for example, may not reveal underlying issues that are making their jobs harder. To create surveys and opportunities for feedback from employees, businesses need to create cross-functional teams—including members of IT, HR,

CLEARCO

Cofounder and CEO Michele Romanow

Set up an e-mail inbox and asked everyone to post ideas on

THE STUPID SH*! WE DO

How to streamline the business?

How to eliminate preventable frustrations employees were facing?

INVOLVED EMPLOYEES IN THE PROCESS OF IMPROVING WORK

ALLOWED LEADERSHIP TO CREATE A HIGHLY EFFECTIVE FEEDBACK LOOP WITH EMPLOYEES, FURTHER BUILDING TRUST

marketing, customer support, and sales—that own the feedback process and connect with employees on a regular basis. These teams, which I call Experience Advisory Boards (EABs), then operationalize the data they receive from employee and customer feedback by putting the insights into action. The presence of EABs is especially key since, as discussed, executives struggle most with turning insights into actionable changes.

By asking better questions and improving data analysis, you can gauge overall satisfaction with the technology, processes, and organizational structure that support both EX and CX. Organizations that analyze data holistically will have more visibility into what happens across touchpoints. From there, insights can be analyzed beyond "what happened" to "why it happened," and opportunities for improvement can be identified.

CHAPTER TAKEAWAYS

- People look for purpose at work. They want to feel part of something great, supporting values they believe in. When they do, they are more inclined to learn new skills they can apply to their jobs and become well-rounded, developed professionals who can use their experience in meaningful

99

ways. This development is often a result of handling challenges, which they welcome.

- Money and perks might make people feel better in the moment, but they won't buy happiness. In the long run, it's more personal than that.

- At a minimum, HR, marketing, and IT will need to partner on this journey to develop the way forward—not just at the leadership level but within the entire company.

- As a whole, businesses need to do a better job providing for the people who work for them and serve their customers—or they will be stuck with unhappy employees serving unhappy customers. The real goal should be finding what matters most to your employees in order to generate their commitment and engagement.

Conversation Starter Questions

▶ Who owns employee experience today? What department do they report into? If nobody owns EX as a comprehensive function, then determine what roles touch aspects of EX (IT, HR, employee success, finance, learning and development).

▶ When was the last time your executives spent time on the front lines to experience those "moments that matter" with customers in real time?

▶ Do you have an Experience Advisory Board in place?

Chapter 6

Process: Don't Blame the People, Blame the Design

Eighty-five percent of the reasons for failure are deficiencies in the systems and process rather than the employee. The role of management is to change the process rather than badgering individuals to do better.

W. EDWARDS DEMING

IN THE EARLY 1980S, THE FORD MOTOR COMPANY WAS STRUGGLING. Between 1979 and 1982, the company had incurred billions of dollars in losses and sales were falling. Ford hired American engineer and statistician W. Edwards Deming as a consultant to help jump-start the company's growth stall and improve its product quality. But Deming, who was known for business process improvement, didn't focus on product quality at all. Instead, he aimed to find the root cause of Ford's challenges by evaluating the company's processes.

In his investigation, Deming found that "management actions were responsible for 85% of all the problems the company was having in its efforts to develop better cars." (I'm sure senior management was ecstatic when they heard that!) Deming told the leadership team that he believed both company culture and managerial operation had by far the greatest impact on employee performance and, subsequently, product quality.

Improving product quality was not about "fixing" the employees but rather *fixing the systems and processes throughout the company that supported them*. That improvement had to start at the top of Ford leadership, with then CEO Donald Petersen. As a result of Deming's help, Ford bounced back, and by 1986, only four years later, it had become "the most profitable automobile manufacturing company in America" and exceeded General Motors' earnings for the first time since 1920.

Like Deming did for the Ford company, in this chapter I'm going to dig into the second "P" in the PPTC framework: *process*.

- **Process** *is the repeatable steps or actions that, when taken, culminate in a similar result or goal in a more efficient manner.*

Although processes can be overwhelming due to the sheer volume a company might employ, they can have the most profound effect on the other three elements.

In a business environment, processes are the answer to the questions, *How do we achieve a desired outcome? How will we*

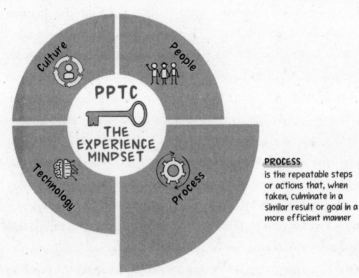

PROCESS
is the repeatable steps or actions that, when taken, culminate in a similar result or goal in a more efficient manner

leverage our people and technology in a repeatable and consistent way to maximize returns? The goal of a process should be to consistently produce the same result *regardless of who performs it.* By following set processes, organizations believe they will be able to increase productivity and profitability while reducing effort, and consistently replicate desired outcomes. At least, that's the idea.

But processes can also introduce bureaucracy and complexity if they aren't closely monitored. *If there is one thing that kills workflow, quality, and employee satisfaction, it is the breakdown of processes and the resulting wasted time.* Processes that become unnecessary, produce conflicts, or stop working altogether hinder a company's ability to improve both EX and CX. Thus, *every* process should be written in pencil, ready to be changed whenever necessary.

Overwhelmed by Process

The biggest threat to the long-term survival of most companies is neither competitors nor economic downturns. Instead, it comes from within, in the form of inertia, organizational complexity, and bureaucracy, as seen in the Ford story. As shown in Figure 6.1, the C-suite ranks "too many or redundant processes" as tied for the number one challenge to company growth.

And employees agree! As shown in Figure 6.2, employees rank "too many or redundant processes" as the third biggest internal challenge to company growth.

Research also shows that when managers remove those unnecessary steps, employees are 20 percent more likely to say they are highly motivated to provide a strong CX and 56 percent more likely to be highly engaged in their day-to-day jobs. These

What Do You Think Are the Biggest Internal Challenges for Your Company to Grow in Revenue?

RANKED BY C-SUITE	
1	Lack of growth or development opportunities for employees
	Too many or redundant processes
2	Data and technology systems are not integrated
3	Departments are too siloed and do not collaborate enough
4	Employees leave too often/can't keep top talent
5	Bad products or services or innovation
6	Outdated technology
7	Don't have the right talent
8	Poor leadership/lack of vision

FIGURE 6.1: Challenges to Company Growth, Ranked by C-Suite

correlations highlight a powerful link: *the same out-of-date processes and internal complexities that sap EX negatively impact CX.*

According to Samanage's State of Workplace Survey, workers spend more than a full day of work each week—**520 hours a year, on average**—performing repetitive tasks and services that could easily have been automated. This time adds up: "U.S. businesses are estimated to be wasting as much as $1.8 trillion annually on repetitive employee tasks." The oft said motto is true: time is money.

Bad processes are plentiful and costly, and redundancy is only one cause. Look around. The signs of a bad process are easy to spot, including:

What Do You Think Are the Biggest Internal Challenges for Your Company to Grow in Revenue?

Showing those who ranked each statement as a top 2 biggest challenge

RANKED BY EMPLOYEES	Total	US	CA	UK/ Ireland	ANZ
Employees leave too often/can't keep top talent	32%	31%	31%	32%	31%
Outdated technology	25%	24%	27%	28%	22%
Poor leadership/lack of vision	24%	24%	24%	27%	22%
Too many or redundant processes	24%	26%	23%	21%	20%
Data and technology systems are not integrated	22%	23%	18%	22%	25%
Departments are too siloed and do not collaborate enough	21%	19%	19%	22%	27%
Lack of growth or development opportunities for employees	21%	21%	23%	17%	23%
Don't have the right talent	17%	18%	21%	12%	14%
Bad products or services or innovation	12%	11%	9%	15%	13%

FIGURE 6.2: Challenges to Company Growth,
Ranked by Employees

- Unhappy and frustrated employees
- Improperly formulated tasks that need to be corrected often
- Finger-pointing and blaming between siloed departments
- Energy, time, and effort wasted on unnecessary tasks
- Customer complaints about long wait times

Choosing to overlook the impact of bad processes—and that's exactly what it is, a choice—leads to missed revenue opportunities, dissatisfied employees, and angry customers. Every year, companies lose 20 to 30 percent in revenue due to inefficiencies. The purchasing process, arguably the most fundamental to generating revenue, is broken as well: 77 percent of B2B buyers state that their latest purchase was very complex or difficult.

Technology Transformation
to Improve Processes

While leveraging technology to improve business performance is nothing new, the volume of systems and tools available has exploded, causing poor "process hygiene" to bubble to the surface, especially in relation to employee experience. Due to a lack of rigor, this abundance fails to ensure there are no broken or redundant processes, or, for that matter, any processes at all.

Digital transformation is the process of using digital technologies to create new–or modify existing– business processes, culture, and customer experiences to meet changing business and market requirements.

–SALESFORCE

But by strategically deploying the *right* type of new technology to streamline processes, businesses can significantly improve EX and, by extension, CX. When McKinsey surveyed hundreds of C-suite executives and tech leaders in 2021, they found that over the previous two years, 34 percent of technology transformations had a *significant impact* on improved employee experience (see Figure 6.3).

As a matter of fact, technological transformations impacted employee experience the most compared to other categories, such as reduced costs, realization of new revenue streams, and increased revenue from existing streams. This is a promising trend to see EX as one of the tracked categories within tech transformation metrics, especially since that spend has been historically associated with CX improvement and cost reduction.

Make no mistake, an effective technology transformation is the result of a sound strategy, one that considers the benefits or challenges that arise for the business, employees, and customers. For example, nearly 80 percent of American consumers say

Most Respondents Report Some or Significant Impact from Their Companies' Technology Transformations

Impact from technology transformation over the past 2 years, % of respondents, n=487

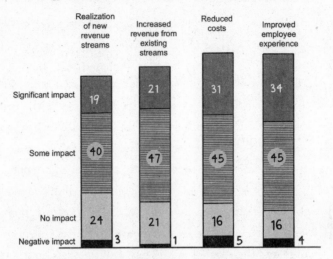

FIGURE 6.3: Impact from Technology Transformation over Past Two Years

that speed, convenience, knowledgeable help, and friendly service are the most important elements of a positive customer experience. If your tech transformation strategy seeks to improve this customer experience, it's crucial your transformation doesn't complicate processes for employees and inhibit them from providing that speedy, friendly service.

Yet, when many transformation projects are undertaken, there is a lot of pressure to finish them at lightning speed to meet arbitrary timelines with no regard for what impact it might have on other parts of the organization. The more ideal approach would be to take your time to understand what existing systems and processes might be impacted so you can adjust accordingly. If you choose the latter strategy, you obviously have a much better chance at mitigating employee and customer dissatisfaction. When you give employees time to focus on their actual work instead of spending countless hours navigating disparate systems and processes, they are more likely to have higher employee engagement, resulting in—that's right—better CX.

The Human Touch in Digital Transformation

By 2019, two-thirds of companies recognized they needed to digitize by 2020 to stay competitive. This wasn't idle talk—this recognition led to a mind-boggling $1.3 trillion in investment toward digital transformations. But most of that spend was unfortunately wasted. A reported 70 percent of that money—a full $900 billion—was spent on projects that didn't achieve their goals. How is that possible? According to *Harvard Business Review*, if people throughout a company "lack the right mindset to change and the current organizational practices are flawed, digital transformation will simply magnify those flaws."

Many organizations talk about technology or digital transformation as a way of modernizing, even revolutionizing, the technology systems used within their companies. Some have even adopted a digital-first mentality throughout their entire organization. However, *few organizations have adapted processes or provided the appropriate training to properly support employees in their use of new digital capabilities. In other words, employees need to be properly trained in the tools provided in order for them to be effective.*

Digital transformation is a two-step pursuit. Digital is the technology- and system-based side, while transformation is people- and process-based. They are tightly interconnected and both steps must happen in concert. Otherwise, impact to the business is diminished and organizational complexity and bureaucracy sneak back into everyday processes, as employees leave new digital tools untouched, reducing the likelihood of their success.

To combat regression, create a strong governance and change management practice to review and streamline processes and help break down the cross-functional silos. This practice will help ensure new and revised processes deliver the desired results as new digital capabilities are introduced into the environment.

The Silo Effect

If you look back at Figures 6.1 and 6.2, you'll see that in addition to "redundant processes," both the C-suite and employees ranked the issue that "departments are too siloed and do not collaborate enough" as another impediment to growth. Sadly, siloed departments and a lack of collaboration are all too common, and they have a damaging effect on EX and CX.

Most large companies break their businesses down into units, whether sales, marketing, customer service, IT, or otherwise. Each one of these units has separate leadership, budgets, metrics, data, systems, tools, and *processes*—in other words, they are organized across multiple silos. If some aspects of an organization's processes are designed to meet the internal needs of one of its functional silos, instead of the holistic needs of the business, the result can be lackluster experiences for both its employees and customers. For example, if a customer service

109

agent needs a manager's approval in order to provide a credit for a customer, simply to accommodate a finance department requirement, that extra step may in fact slow down the agent in resolving the issue and getting the customer what they want.

These business unit silos cause most process misalignment. While not intentional, they are the result of years and years of divisional decision making. Since each unit inevitably adjusts its processes for its own departmental goals, without much organization or coordination with the other units, the negative impact of bad processes can become compounded. Moreover, *when business units have a silo mentality, they are less likely to share data, information, or resources with anyone outside their group.*

According to CustomerGauge's "The State of B2B Account Experience," only 39 percent of B2B companies share their customer data across the entire organization, and only 61 percent share data at the departmental or divisional level. This lack of connection has an enormously negative impact on cross-company communication, collaboration, decision making, productivity, CX, and EX, especially for customer-facing departments. It is also why even processes designed with good intentions can have terrible consequences.

Customers feel the effects of broken cooperation across various divisions (Figure 6.4). For example, if a customer places an order on a website, then needs to make a change and decides to call in to the customer service line, the call center agents may be unable to make any adjustment because they aren't part of the "web team." The customer can only make the change online because the "web team" and the "customer service team" don't have the same ordering processes. Customers are similarly affected when they start a chat with a customer service bot but can't be transferred to a live person to discuss an issue because the process is set up to send customers to an FAQs page online instead. These broken or absent processes hurt overall CX but more specifically create frustrated, unhappy customers, which hurts EX in return.

CX is fairly self-contained, but companies have gotten much better at connecting customer efforts across multiple groups. Think about where CX resides. It is usually in marketing, with the CMO, and the processes around CX have been designed to remove friction and streamline engagement for customers. Where does EX reside? Well, it is a bit all over the place—it has pieces and parts in HR, others in learning and development, and others still in IT and finance. Having multiple groups involved in EX without a detailed way to uncover disconnected processes across various parts of the business only further am-

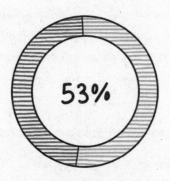

of customers say it
feels like they're
**communicating
with separate
departments**, not
one company

FIGURE 6.4: Customers Feel the Disconnection

plifies silos. These silos lead to increased complexity for people to do their job and manage their employment with you.

In any of these scenarios, it's unlikely the respective managers within each of those groups intentionally avoided a more useful process or design in favor of an ineffective one. The truth is, they probably didn't think twice about what the impact would be to their own employees, never mind to another group's employees. Think again about the Ford Motor Company: the root cause of poor product quality in this example wasn't the employees, but the bad processes created by management.

Too many organizations still have difficulty breaking down barriers between departments due to the management systems they have in place that work against that goal.

–THE DEMING INSTITUTE

When a business operates in silos, the result is inefficiency, financial waste, and missed opportunities to connect with customers and employees in meaningful ways. Active efforts must be taken to break down these silos and improve processes.

Building Bridges with SalesOps and RevOps

Given that silos between groups present significant hurdles to growth, you might think that eliminating them completely would be the way to go. However, there is value in having groups self-contained to ensure clarity in roles and expectations as well as strategic goal alignment. To that end, bridges should be built between groups to connect the various workflows and processes that require collaboration.

One way that companies have built these bridges is by establishing a Sales Operations (SalesOps) team. These teams help enhance an organization's processes with the goal of improving seller performance, revenue predictability, and forecast accuracy. Although SalesOps teams can produce incredible benefits, those benefits are mostly limited to quota-bearing employees, specifically salespeople throughout the organization. However, this function has started to shift to a broader remit. Today, 48 percent of SalesOps teams are more involved in cross-functional workstream management than they were in the past.

Revenue Operations (RevOps), a more recently developed business function, expands the operations role beyond sales. RevOps's goal is to deliver end-to-end visibility across (1) marketing, (2) sales, and (3) customer service by aligning incentives, metrics, people, data, systems, and processes to drive improved growth. Providing increased oversight and coordination between these three customer-facing business units through a RevOps team is a great place to start in eliminating unnecessary or out-of-date processes, which hinder a company's ability to grow.

There's no question that Ops teams can benefit companies in many ways, but they can also create more complexity if people are focused on fixing a single pain point versus fixing the underlying cause of broken or missing processes. These roles therefore require people who are willing to reach across the aisle to collaborate with other teams, especially if they don't have the know-how to fix all the cross-functional issues identified. This means you have to ensure you have the right talent and skills in place in either of these Ops functions if you introduce them into your own company. If you are on the fence, think about what success looks like in the future, and how best you can get there individually and as part of a broader team.

Measuring for Success

You can minimize internal resistance to interdepartmental collaboration, data sharing, and process alignment by creating shared metrics and incentives across all business functions. While you might not think incentives and metrics are process-related, they actually have the ability to change behavior, including how people perform tasks. Creating shared metrics ensures that teams prioritize multiple constituents, particularly the goals of the company as a whole, the needs of individual employees, and the expectations of customers. Any process strategy that does not prioritize these groups is an obstacle to success.

To identify which incentives and metrics to utilize, look to the data (more on that in Chapter 9). Data collection is critical to help companies identify broken and unnecessary processes for both EX and CX. As a business grows and evolves, new technologies are implemented, new products and services are launched, and, over time, complexity and bureaucracy will rear their ugly heads. That is just the nature of business. An Experience Mindset, however, insists on designing better processes for both customers and employees right from the start so that any imbalance is the exception, not the norm.

Design Thinking

Design thinking is a methodology to generate innovative solutions that reflect the needs of the user: in this case, both the customer and the employee. If you understand how your organization's existing processes affect both (good or bad), you can identify areas to improve and measure the progress you make at doing so. To put design thinking into action, think about how you can integrate process improvements for CX into process improvements for EX. This synthesis will create experiences that equally delight customers and employees in ways that would otherwise be impossible without the fusion of disparate groups, processes, and data.

For example, think of all the work needed to develop "customer journey maps," those diagrams that illustrate the steps customers go through when engaging with a company, all in the spirit of reducing friction and streamlining processes to improve Net Promoter Score (NPS) or other CX metrics. Then consider how much time and money those companies have spent improving those steps over the past few decades, and, for many, with great success.

What if those same companies decided to also create employee journey maps? These would uncover the actual day-to-day steps and processes employees must navigate to serve customers and do their jobs. The goal would be similar as well: to uncover all the employee and customer interactions where inefficiencies and broken processes affect the overall experience, then find areas of improvement that would advance EX, lead to stronger CX, and begin the growth cycle.

Designing the Journey

Sometimes we need to take a step back to find the best path forward.

In 2017, I visited a client in Australia struggling with two years of declining customer satisfaction and NPS scores. As a regulated government agency, the company assisted its citizens (the customers in this example) who needed help with construction projects or building issues. In an effort to improve those scores, the client deployed new technology and training to empower employees to better serve customers. Unfortunately, both the technology rollout and the training didn't have the positive impact on those declining scores they had hoped for.

After a few more failed improvement attempts, the agency finally decided to dig into its current processes to determine the real point of failure, since they believed they had the right technology and people in place. With the help of employees, agency executives created an entire journey map wall showing each step required for both employees and customers to open a complaint and ultimately resolve it. This journey wall stayed up for the duration of the project, which lasted several months.

As one of the executives told me, "Journey walls are essential because they illustrate the experience your customers are having with your organization. They're also particularly useful when other parts of the organization believe change isn't necessary, that the customer experience isn't so bad. The wall proves otherwise." He continued, "It gives you the truth, with no hearsay or individual opinion, and it's right there in front of you. It's very difficult for anyone to argue against that. Yes, it's a little bit confronting, but it ultimately unites the organization for the better."

Identifying an area for improvement is one thing; finding the solution and actioning the fix is another. Employees would stop and discuss what was on the journey map throughout the day and place Post-it notes with their suggestions, arranged under an identified process or task. A four-person team could then review those suggestions and test them in real time. This team, comprised of two software developers and two change management experts, sat in the room right behind the journey wall so they could discuss the suggestions being made, then design and test a fix quickly.

What they found was illuminating. There were dozens of broken processes and system limitations that were getting in the way of people doing their jobs efficiently. There were also just as many processes creating unnecessary friction for their citizen customers. One major problem quickly became obvious: the average customer spent over a year on the journey. By any standard, this duration was unacceptable.

Once the team completed its research of every step in the

process by interviewing employees and customers, they realized the metrics in place didn't allow the agency to uncover its own blind spots. They were only measuring employee inputs (for example, data entry, time on calls, and number of resolutions per week), not the effort *both* the employee and customer had to put in to complete an activity or their ultimate experience with the overall transaction.

As the team updated the journey map to unveil these blind spots, they realized there were still areas that needed new capabilities beyond what they had. For example, when a customer opened up a complaint, they had to download and print a twenty-plus-page document, sign it, and fax it back. Yes, you read that right—twenty-plus pages, over fax. Eliminating that one process by putting the form online, where it could be digitally signed, saved a significant amount of time and frustration for everyone involved.

Once they got past the initial quick fixes, they uncovered systemic process issues that unnecessarily slowed the entire complaint submission and resolution process down. They realized their current processes were not up to date—for either the employees or the customers—with the new technical capabilities

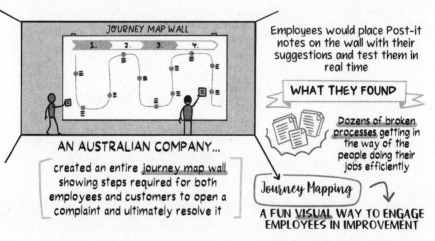

JOURNEY MAP WALL

1. 2. 3. 4.

AN AUSTRALIAN COMPANY...

created an entire journey map wall showing steps required for both employees and customers to open a complaint and ultimately resolve it

Employees would place Post-it notes on the wall with their suggestions and test them in real time

WHAT THEY FOUND

Dozens of broken processes getting in the way of the people doing their jobs efficiently

Journey Mapping

A FUN VISUAL WAY TO ENGAGE EMPLOYEES IN IMPROVEMENT

117

deployed at the agency or in line with new cross-functional training the agency had rolled out. The question then became, Where to start?

Each day, as call center employees walked into the office and headed to their stations, they passed by the journey map, posted right on the hallway wall. This visual gave them regular, easy-to-see updates on the latest changes to process and those areas still awaiting improvement.

Leadership wanted to be transparent about what they were doing and create a fun and visual way employees could suggest different methods for improvement. This approach allowed employees to participate in the process and technology fixes being deployed, which ultimately would affect their day-to-day. It also engendered a sense of pride in employees and resulted in increased employee satisfaction, which was never part of the team's goal in the first place. It was a win-win.

At the end of this journey-mapping exercise, which took about six months to complete, the agency had not only improved on all of its relevant metrics but had reduced the time from initial contact to resolution from eighteen months to just three. If the agency had not deconstructed the customers' journey, and ultimately the employees' journey, solicited and actioned feedback from employees, and updated many of its processes, its failures, and its clients' frustrations, would still be in place today.

Unleash the Power of People

In 2019, Pfizer, an American multinational pharmaceutical and biotechnology corporation, introduced a new corporate purpose that outlined a number of "bold moves." One of them was "to unleash the power of our people." One of the ways to bring that statement to life was simplification: removing needless complexity so employees could focus on meaningful work. Said another way, it's how to make work faster and easier through automation.

The entire Pfizer executive leadership team championed this simplification effort and shared in its responsibility. They recognized their employees' concerns, chief among them the bureaucracy and unnecessary processes getting in the way of them completing their work. A top-down initiative was undertaken in which the entire executive leadership team set out to address employee pain points and simplify processes and operations.

Pfizer began a large digital transformation effort. They started with scaling new ways of working: working smarter and faster with agile processes, simplifying what they called mega processes, transforming how they coach and develop talent within the organization, and scaling the data foundation and insight capabilities to improve the decision-making process.

Executives knew they had to bring everyone along for the journey if they were going to be successful. For those who were change-averse, they introduced mini road shows focused on sharing the future vision, and what provider, patient, and employee benefits there would be. Then for change advocates, they did lunch-and-learns, ideation sessions where they could not only have input but also become part of the process and take accountability for outcomes. A big part of this effort was to change the focus from activity to impact and measure people on those outcomes. Without identifying it as such, Pfizer had embarked on creating a new operating mindset, with an increased attention to EX.

Today, one symbol of this increased focus on EX is that human resources at Pfizer is now called People Experience. And as of 2021, Pfizer was proud to report that, on average, "90 percent of colleagues reported feeling engaged, as measured by

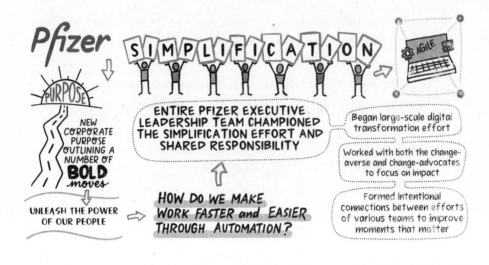

Pfizer

PURPOSE

NEW CORPORATE PURPOSE OUTLINING A NUMBER OF **BOLD** *moves*

UNLEASH THE POWER OF OUR PEOPLE

SIMPLIFICATION

AGILE

ENTIRE PFIZER EXECUTIVE LEADERSHIP TEAM CHAMPIONED THE SIMPLIFICATION EFFORT AND SHARED RESPONSIBILITY

HOW DO WE MAKE WORK FASTER and EASIER THROUGH AUTOMATION?

Began large-scale digital transformation effort

Worked with both the change-averse and change-advocates to focus on impact

Formed intentional connections between efforts of various teams to improve moments that matter

pride, willingness to recommend Pfizer as a great place to work, and intent to stay. In addition, 92 percent agreed their daily work contributes to Pfizer's purpose."

As shown with Pfizer, and throughout this chapter, an Experience Mindset requires you to design effective processes, break down silos and build bridges, and streamline workflow and operations. Intentionally creating connections between various teams helps companies improve those moments that matter. These connections then lead to superior EX and CX, as well as outcomes that are more positive for the collective stakeholders.

CHAPTER TAKEAWAYS

- Data collection is critical to help companies identify broken and unnecessary processes for both EX and CX. Analyze what both employees and customers are doing during those moments that matter and find areas where you can begin to build bridges between the internally and externally facing processes.

- The biggest threats to the long-term survival of most companies are inertia, organizational complexity, and bureaucracy. Companies that integrate what they've learned from process improvement to enhance CX and apply it toward improving EX will be able to combine the best of both worlds.

Conversation Starter Questions

- ▶ Do you have a change management team in place that regularly reviews current processes to ensure they are not creating an unnecessary burden on employees?
- ▶ Is there a recent journey map for both customers and employees that analyzes the lead-up to the "moments that matter"?
- ▶ Is your CX data shared across the entire company? Or is it only shared at a departmental or group level?

Chapter 7

Technology: Productivity and Experience, Two Sides of the Same Coin

In 30 years, a robot will likely be on the cover of Time *magazine as the best CEO. Machines will do what human beings are incapable of doing. Machines will partner and cooperate with humans, rather than become mankind's biggest enemy.*

JACK MA,
cofounder and former executive chairman of Alibaba Group

AS MENTIONED IN CHAPTER 1, THE FOURTH INDUSTRIAL REVOLUTION has started pushing digital capabilities and uses to a whole new level. Software applications now enable those technologies to penetrate every corner of daily life. Smartphones, social media, artificial intelligence, and massive amounts of user data have created a nexus of forces pushing businesses, employees, and customers into an entirely new operating dynamic. Digitizing critical aspects of a business—such as sales, marketing, customer service, and commerce—has opened up an enormous array of opportunities for increased growth, collaboration, and engagement.

Meanwhile, the democratization of technology has also been a game changer, connecting buyers and sellers from all corners of the globe with a single click. Technically advanced capabilities are no longer reserved for large multinational organizations. Research shows that 72 percent of customer interactions, on average, are now digital. Start-ups and small businesses have been able to purchase and deploy technology in a more cost-effective and efficient way, especially with the advent of software as a service (SaaS). They have the chance to automate routine tasks for greater productivity, use digital marketing technologies to increase demand, and sell outside their local communities to compete against bigger brands. All of which used to be financially out of their reach or internally impossible to manage.

Though technology holds many promises, the latest and greatest should never become the goal in itself—it's always a means to an end. In this chapter, I demonstrate the importance of technology to provide a great employee and customer experience detailing its opportunities and challenges as part of the PPTC framework.

- **Technology** *increases efficiency further by helping people perform their tasks.*

Technology's goal should be to help run the business, empower employees, and serve customers, but the tech is only as effective as the processes it enables and the people who interact with it during the course of their work. If it's not meeting that goal, then you need to either reconsider the way it was deployed or revisit its strategic value altogether.

Either way, the reality is that, too often, companies make huge investments into technology to gain strategic advantages or modernize out-of-date infrastructure and systems without considering the downstream implications beyond cost benefits. That lack of consideration means the people and processes—the two "Ps" in PPTC—become an afterthought, hindering the return on many tech investments.

The end goal for company-provided technology must be that it

123

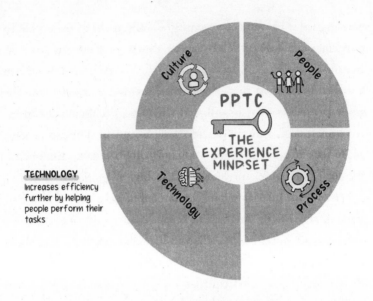

TECHNOLOGY
Increases efficiency further by helping people perform their tasks

works seamlessly together, increases productivity, and reduces the effort required to complete basic tasks for employees and customers. Anything short of that will put stress on your people, processes, and culture.

Can I Have Some Tech with My Taco?

Chipotle Mexican Grill has a reputation for ethically sourced ingredients and strong company values. Its mission is to cultivate a better world. As one of the first U.S. restaurant chains to commit to using local and organic produce, as well as more humanely raised meat without added hormones or antibiotics, it has continued its environmental consciousness by recycling used plastic gloves into trash bags and diverting 50 percent of its waste from landfills.

Recognizing the importance of EX, the company also leans into its values when it comes to its employees. Chipotle's CEO Brian Niccol understands that "if the employee experience improves, we'll have better retention and also we'll have better execution for our customers." In 2019, Chipotle announced that it would cover 100 percent of tuition costs up front for seventy-five different business and technology degrees. It since has created Emerging Leader and Mentoring programs and launched a fresh learning management system called The Spice Hub, which focuses on upskilling through gamification and immersive education.

In 2021, 90 percent of restaurant management roles at Chipotle came from internal promotions. On average, six employees were promoted per restaurant for a total of nearly nineteen thousand. In addition, the company's internal promotion rate was 77 percent for apprentice and general manager roles. "The best thing we can do is make sure that they're trained, so that they're successful in their job, and then that we give them a culture and a leader that develops them so they realize they have the growth opportunities at Chipotle," Niccol said.

These employee and sustainability initiatives have contributed to Chipotle winning numerous awards, including "Best Company for Women," "Best Company Culture," "Best Company Perks & Benefits," and "Best Career Growth," to name a few. But the company isn't resting on its laurels. Its investment in technology is squarely focused on enhancing that reputation even further.

In April 2022, Chipotle launched Cultivate Next, a $50 million venture fund. As Chipotle's chief technology officer, Curt Garner, who is leading the initiative, explained, "We are exploring investments in emerging innovation that will enhance our employee *and* guest experience, and quite possibly revolutionize the restaurant industry." In other words, Chipotle is investing in tech to improve its EX and CX equally.

Technology decisions cannot be made in a vacuum. With that in mind, in 2019, Chipotle set up an innovation hub called the

125

Cultivate Center, which tests everything from new menu items to new restaurant designs to new uses of AI and other technologies. For example, Chipotle has been experimenting with automation using a robotic kitchen assistant named Chippy.

As the name implies, the robot makes tortilla chips, helping to offset bottlenecks during peak times in the restaurant. Initially, they hoped to just use such AI technology to find better ways and times of day to make chips based on its ability to predict when a restaurant's staff might run out of them. But, as Garner shared in a CNBC interview, Chipotle then started thinking more broadly about how they could use AI to continue to reduce the crew members' more tedious and repetitive tasks.

"And," Garner continued, "we've worked with a lot of our employees to identify what are the tasks that they would love to see us bring automation to or AI, so that hopefully the role can become less complicated. And then I think there are just other places in the back of the restaurant where we have the ability to automate, whether it's on the digital make-line or other tasks."

This tech injection wasn't about trying to solve a labor problem or replace human workers. Instead, Chipotle wanted to make its employees' experiences "easier, more fun, more reward-

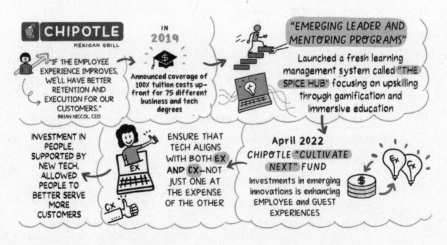

CHIPOTLE
MEXICAN GRILL

"IF THE EMPLOYEE EXPERIENCE IMPROVES, WE'LL HAVE BETTER RETENTION AND EXECUTION FOR OUR CUSTOMERS."
BRIAN NICCOL, CEO

IN 2019
Announced coverage of 100% tuition costs up-front for 75 different business and tech degrees

"EMERGING LEADER AND MENTORING PROGRAMS"
Launched a fresh learning management system called "THE SPICE HUB" focusing on upskilling through gamification and immersive education

INVESTMENT IN PEOPLE, SUPPORTED BY NEW TECH, ALLOWED PEOPLE TO BETTER SERVE MORE CUSTOMERS

ENSURE THAT TECH ALIGNS WITH BOTH EX AND CX—NOT JUST ONE AT THE EXPENSE OF THE OTHER

April 2022
CHIPOTLE "CULTIVATE NEXT" FUND
Investments in emerging innovations is enhancing EMPLOYEE and GUEST EXPERIENCES

ing, and take away some tasks that team members don't like, and give them more time to focus on the tasks that they do, such as serving guests."

Over the past five years, Chipotle's stock has gone up +924.35 (193.35 percent), and as of Q1 2022 the earnings report showed a 16 percent total revenue increase. Meanwhile, according to Chipotle's 2022 earnings release, in-restaurant sales increased 33.1 percent, while digital sales represented 41.9 percent of food and beverage revenue. CEO Brian Niccol noted, "Our investments in our people, coupled with our digital system and commitment to culinary driven by Food With Integrity, resulted in serving more guests at our restaurants with excellence."

Our north star has always been and will continue to be a relentless focus on guest experience. That combined with a design thinking approach allows us to deliver exceptional digital experiences for our guests.

—NICOLE WEST,
vice president of digital strategy
and product of Chipotle

Chipotle's example shows the importance of ensuring that tech aligns with an increase in both EX and CX—not just one at the expense of the other. As Niccol points out, it was the investment in their people, supported by new tech, that allowed them to better serve more customers. It's counterproductive to use technology to save the customer time while increasing employee effort or vice versa. Neither customers nor employees should face a greater effort than necessary to achieve their goals. Technology investments should always strike a balance.

Outdated Tech

Though the term "digital transformation" wasn't coined until late 2011, by the Capgemini consulting firm in partnership with

MIT, just nine years later it was estimated that companies would spend $6.8 trillion or more—no, that is not a typo—on digital tech and initiatives from 2020 to 2030. As the world leans increasingly toward a digital-first environment, technology that enhances—as opposed to inhibits—EX and CX will become even more critical to company success.

While I have highlighted a number of areas thus far where there is a divide between the C-suite and employees' perceptions, **the disconnect is deepest when it comes to *outdated technology***. These are systems and tools that may not be web-based or app-enabled, that feel almost homegrown or from another century (and they typically are), and that are neither integrated nor seamless.

Both customers and employees expect technology to work for their individual needs when and where it is needed and without much effort. People shouldn't feel overwhelmed by technology; instead, it should work so well that it seems like it's not even there.

Equipping employees with up-to-date and seamless tech not only affects a company's ability to provide strong CX but also individual employee success; employees who develop digital mindsets are more successful in their jobs, have higher satisfaction at work, and are more likely to get promoted.

Unfortunately, the reality is employees are not getting what they need. An average of only 32 percent of employees state that the technology their company provides is working effectively. This is a global problem—no region or country is spared, although India is doing markedly better than the rest (see Figure 7.1).

It is no surprise, then, that technology is one of the most poorly rated dimensions of EX; employees say outdated technology is tied for *the number one* top challenge to a company's growth. Further, only **TWO IN TEN** (20 percent) customer-facing employees strongly agree that their company is providing great

Employees are empowered with seamless tech	
India	70%
Mexico	48%
Brazil	44%
Argentina	34%
France	30%
Germany	28%
Singapore	26%
U.S.	24%
CAN	23%
Nordics	23%
UK/IRE	21%
ANZ	19%

FIGURE 7.1: Seamless Tech Is Not Created Equal

technology that is seamless and helps them collaborate easily (Figure 7.2).

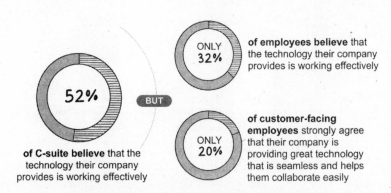

52%

of C-suite believe that the technology their company provides is working effectively

BUT

ONLY **32%** of employees believe that the technology their company provides is working effectively

ONLY **20%** of customer-facing employees strongly agree that their company is providing great technology that is seamless and helps them collaborate easily

FIGURE 7.2: The Technology Disconnect

Clearly, the C-suite doesn't understand the critical role of technology in helping people do their jobs, especially frontline employees. If that's not enough to get you interested, 44 percent of employees said "workplace technology either does nothing to make them feel happy in their job or makes their work harder. One-third of employees say their company's technology doesn't help or makes it harder to serve internal or external customers."

Let's look at some figures that clearly highlight the importance of tech to your business. As shown in Figure 7.3, *companies that provide employees with good tech report that those employees are significantly more engaged, more satisfied, and happier than those who feel their companies do NOT provide great tech.*

Don't make the mistake of thinking that improving tech is just about the individual employee's satisfaction, engagement, or happiness—it also impacts team performance. *Strong tech helps high-performing teams work more seamlessly together and collaborate more easily—both within their own teams and cross-*

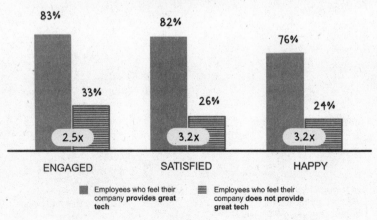

Employees at Companies That Provide Good Tech Also Report 3X Higher EX Than Those Who Work Elsewhere

ENGAGED 83% / 33% — 2.5x
SATISFIED 82% / 26% — 3.2x
HAPPY 76% / 24% — 3.2x

Employees who feel their company **provides great tech**
Employees who feel their company **does not provide great tech**

FIGURE 7.3: *Good Technology Impacts EX*

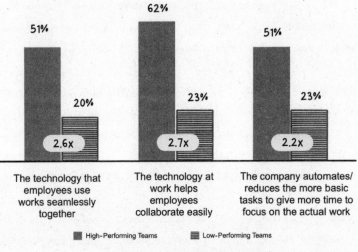

Employees Are Empowered with Seamless Tech

The technology that employees use works seamlessly together — 51%, 20%, 2.6x

The technology at work helps employees collaborate easily — 62%, 23%, 2.7x

The company automates/reduces the more basic tasks to give more time to focus on the actual work — 51%, 23%, 2.2x

High-Performing Teams   Low-Performing Teams

FIGURE 7.4: The Technology Multiplier

functionally—than low-performing teams. Further, the use of automation reduces basic tasks to give them more time to focus on high-impact work (Figure 7.4).

As work continues moving out of the office toward a more flexible model and customer experience expectations continue to rise, the role of technology will only become greater. That is why understanding these realities will assist organizations in making the case that connecting EX, CX, and IT is important. But many business leaders still seem unaware of just how important.

The Deepening Disconnect

Fifty-two percent of C-suite executives believe the technology their companies are providing IS working effectively. Don't miss the subtlety here: this stat highlights the fact that only 48 percent of the C-suite agree the tech they are providing employees ISN'T working effectively.

131

That's not just bad news; **that's a crisis.**

While you may have a number of theories as to why leaders are failing so hard here, consider the following facts about IT leaders and the deepening disconnect.

- While 84 percent of IT leaders say that improving employee technology is crucial, only 21 percent say their current technology maximizes employee engagement, and only 25 percent report that it maximizes productivity.
- Only 50 percent of IT leaders claim they are increasing investment in EX.
- Over half (55 percent) of organizations are finding it difficult to integrate user experience (UX), up from 48 percent a year prior.
- Forty-two percent of companies say the inability to keep up with ever-changing processes, tools and systems is what makes it most difficult to integrate end-user experiences.

These findings show that even IT is aware of the less-than-optimal employee tech experience, and yet only a small percentage are working to rectify it.

The problem is further exacerbated by the fact that *the more senior a leader is, the less likely it is that they are using the same tech that many of the employees are, especially those on the front lines, such as sales and service*. Meaning, they are not only out of touch with what employees think about the current technology, but they are also out of touch with its potential limitations and even opportunities. Unless they spend time in the call center or log in to the CRM or customer service system, they won't fully appreciate how outdated and disjointed systems slow their people down, and how that impacts their organization's ability to grow.

132

The Connected and Integrated Workforce

When the COVID-19 pandemic hit in 2020, many companies found themselves flat-footed, trying to run as fast as they could to modernize after ignoring some glaring issues for years. For all intents and purposes, employee technology needed the most work. Suddenly, employees had to operate from kitchens and living rooms around the world, with only 40 percent of IT leaders and CIOs saying their department had the right tools, policies, and procedures in place to support a remote workforce. In a work-from-anywhere, hybrid world, the ability to walk over to talk to someone, or ask for help, is much more difficult. Employees are left scrambling to be responsive to customer demands and remain effective in their jobs without the right technology needed to do so.

The irony of course is that there are more than enough technology options out there today to do pretty much anything you could dream of, whether you're working from home or in an office, or whether your work is cloud-based, on-premise, or a hybrid of the two. So then why do businesses struggle to properly equip their employees?

Companies that have invested in new tech but whose employees are still frustrated by the technology likely have an integration problem, not a technology problem, per se. People are not trained on the new tech, so they don't use it. New processes, or lack thereof, get in the way of improved productivity and efficiencies. And yet, even with those realities, there appears to be no slowing down on purchasing new technology. Worldwide, IT spending is projected to total $4.4 trillion in 2022, a 4 percent increase from 2021. Software spending alone is expected to grow 9.8 percent to $674.9 billion in 2022.

> The EY 2022 CEO Outlook Survey found 47 percent of the 2,000 CEOs surveyed are relying on information technology, more than any other strategy, to compete in the economy ahead. Similarly, almost half of CEOs (47 percent) see technology as key to customer engagement and maintaining or improving margins.

It may look good on a slide in an executive's presentation deck when IT deploys a new CRM, mail, finance, or expense system, but managers often underestimate the degree to which introducing new systems may incite employee uncertainty and resentment, especially if it is not a seamless experience. Furthermore, if you reduce or cut training, wait to integrate new tech with existing systems, or ignore broken processes—all in the name of reducing costs—how can you expect the employee experience to improve?

That approach is not just shortsighted but may lead to an actual deterioration in EX. *If you've touted some new technology as a way to fix the ills of the past and improve employees' day-to-day work lives, and then it doesn't, what does that say about your company's planning and leadership?*

> "Poor leadership and lack of vision" was ranked number five by employees and number eight (out of eight) by the C-suite as a top challenge to growth.

Integrate Your Systems

To implement helpful, streamlined, and simplified technology in your business, start by recognizing that the average enterprise operates a library of more than nine hundred unique applications to help run the business. That's stunning, but what is shocking is that only *29 PERCENT* of those applications are integrated with other applications. Even assuming that a sizable percentage of those nine hundred average apps are used in the back office to run the company's operations, that still leaves hundreds of applications that aren't integrated with others, creating system and data silos.

When one of your employees gets a service call, why do they need to log in to the billing system, log in to the CRM system, and then log in to a half dozen other apps, just to properly serve that customer? Think about the last time you called in to a company's customer service department. It's possible you were transferred multiple times to get the right department, then you had to repeat yourself ad nauseam to explain the problem to different people, or you needed to tell them what product or service you were even calling about in the first place. It's maddening!

The reason that happens? *Systems are not seamlessly integrated, processes between different groups are not established, nothing about the experience for the customer or the employee is frictionless, and leadership isn't willing to do the work or spend the time to get it fixed.* At least, that would be what the data implies. Otherwise, the argument would be they are just flat-out unaware or don't care.

To be clear, this scenario isn't reserved only for customer service departments. I had a conversation with a midsize company who explained it took three weeks to close their quarterly books because of the multiple systems that were required to pull sales, shipping, and inventory data together. They recognized there must be a more efficient way to approach the process, so they kicked off a project to simplify the process in under a week.

The project included soliciting suggestions and feedback from the accounting team, enlisting IT to help integrate disparate sys-

135

tems, and streamlining processes. The result? Six months later, they were able to close the books in three days. The CEO and investors were happy, but more importantly, the employees tasked with closing the books each month were happy. Not only had they been actively engaged in the project, but ultimately, the results made their jobs easier.

Again, executives don't want to make life difficult for their customers or employees. But difficulties arise when there isn't a clear understanding of why the dissatisfaction exists. To create an Experience Mindset, a change management team must be put in place, even if it is just one person to catch these scenarios before they become a terrible experience for everyone, costing companies time and money.

It's Like Magic

Automation is a huge part of any process improvement and employee effectiveness discussion, and it is a critical piece of the entire PPTC framework. Ninety-three percent of organizations see automation as a means to create better CX. Highly automated organizations are typically enjoying a 10-percent-plus uplift in EX, new customer acquisition, commercial performance, and ease of resolution.

In the future, customers will not just value efficiency most in their experience, but they will be willing to pay more for it. This fact should squash any concerns about ROI. While improving the experience for customers is good, *automation should ultimately improve the experience and reduce effort for BOTH customers and employees.*

Research shows that only 33 percent of employees agree that their company automates basic tasks, allowing them to focus on actual work, while 52 percent of the C-suite agree. Again, while the twenty-percentage-point difference should be an area of concern, the bigger issue is that the C-suite is fine with employees wasting time doing what automation could easily accomplish.

Using automation can ensure a process is followed consistently every time, eliminating the unknown human variable. It frees employees to focus their unique human traits—including imagination, improvisation, novelty, interpersonal relations, and empathy—on "exceptional" challenges, one-off events, and complex human interactions during those moments that matter, rather than mundane, routine tasks. The use of automation can create better-connected employee experiences (Figure 7.5).

In short, *automate wherever possible to minimize effort and maximize efficiency for employees and customers without sacrificing experience.*

Use of Automation Initiatives to Create Better-Connected Employee Experiences

30% of organizations have implemented automation initiatives to create better-connected employee experiences

44% are currently implementing automation initiatives to create better-connected employee experiences

20% are planning to implement automation initiatives to create better-connected employee experiences

FIGURE 7.5: Automation Is Your Friend

137

Technology Is a Team Sport

Designing, developing, and supporting a company's technology road map has historically been the remit of CIOs or IT leaders. However, as more business units deploy their own technology and silos remain fiercely protected, creating a seamless tech experience throughout the company requires a new approach. CEOs need to get all the various business unit leaders across the company to participate in technology-related planning in a more holistic way. Now is the time to build those bridges between groups and develop a new operating mindset.

The responsibility to determine what tech is best for your business cannot rely solely on IT. They of course need to be involved, but they typically don't have a day-to-day line of sight to frontline employees' issues outside of maintaining work-issued hardware and software as well as tech support. They may, for example, help employees when their computers are down or a system is experiencing a glitch. But they rarely, if ever, have conversations with employees about how to make the systems they use more effective, what applications need to be integrated, and what systems they spend the majority of their time using.

Some companies are waking up to the importance of interdepartmental collaboration. Of the IT professions surveyed, 57 percent now collaborate more closely with the HR department. Almost two-thirds (64 percent) of CIOs say they work more closely with the CHRO. With those stats in mind, think about your own company: Does your CIO make it a regular practice to pull HR into the technology assessment process? Does IT include sales, customer service, and marketing leaders in request for proposal (RFP) discussions? Do they meet with other groups to get a pulse on employee satisfaction and usage?

If your answer is *no* to any or all of these questions, then

138

your employees probably aren't as happy as you think they are with the technology and systems you have deployed. Interweaving CX and EX technology needs assessment (TNA) will lead to mutually beneficial outcomes for everyone. Spend the time surveying stakeholders, prioritizing needs, identifying common features and functionalities, and then documenting those requirements. That way, there's a greater chance that process integration and application integration happen *before* new systems and tools roll out into the hands of employees and customers. Ultimately, every discussion related to technology should happen with IT in the room. It is the IT department—and particularly the CIO—that ensures all stakeholders benefit from a technology solution, not just one silo.

Invest Equally

If IT does not include a conscious sense of balance between EX and CX tech investments, whatever choices they make will ultimately unbalance the company's Experience Mindset. Note, I am not referring to a balanced spend; I'm referring to a balanced experience or effort improvement. For example, say IT develops a new portal where customers can pay a bill, open a ticket, or change the nature of the service they are receiving. At the same time, IT must also ensure that there is a corresponding way for employees to handle each of those requests, one that is similarly easy to use and just as frictionless as on the customer side. Can you say with assurance that your IT exhibits this type of balance?

There is no "fail-safe" switch to automatically keep CX from being dominant. No automated system will ever maintain such a balance and synergy. Rather, the only way to maintain a balance between the tech investments made for customers and employees is dynamically using human beings to constantly monitor the situation, and to meet and negotiate the strategy and tactics for keeping technology aligned with an Experience Mindset.

CHAPTER TAKEAWAYS

- Executives, managers, people leaders: spend time in the call center, go on sales calls, and log in to the CRM and customer service systems so you can have a firsthand appreciation of your employees' experiences using technology at work.
- Take an inventory of what tech is currently deployed to determine where you can reduce redundancy. Whenever you find two or more apps that essentially serve the same purpose, ask yourself: Do I need them all? Then choose the best to keep.
- Don't stop there: *integrate* systems with the other apps you've culled out to save. After identifying areas for improvement, consider potential technology solutions that could apply. These may include automation, application program interface (API), and data integration. Whatever you decide on, updated processes must then be deployed.

Conversation Starter Questions

As an IT leader, if you do not have the luxury of an innovation hub like Chipotle's Cultivate Center, you can still analyze the current state of your company's technology. Go on a listening tour and meet with employees from all over the organization to ask the following questions:

- What part of your job would be easier if it was automated?
- What are the bottlenecks you encounter serving our customers?
- What processes are slowing you down?
- What systems do you need access to in order to do your job?
- What applications should be integrated?
- What data do you need access to?

Chapter 8

Culture: An Era of Experience

A genuine culture built on fundamentals like trust and aimed at the goal of business for good is more than enough, but only if it genuinely outweighs the traditional business motives of driving revenue, growth, and profit.

MARC BENIOFF,
founder and CEO of Salesforce

AS THE OLD ADAGE GOES, "CULTURE EATS STRATEGY FOR BREAK-fast." Often misattributed to Peter Drucker, this famous quote highlights the fact that even with the best strategic plan in place, your company will never change its approach to EX and CX unless you have the company culture to support this shift. A company culture that supports an Experience Mindset understands the intrinsic connection between what it does internally for employees and how that manifests itself in the experiences of its customers during those moments that matter. It uses an experiential approach to decision making, ensuring those efforts gain greater alignment between people, processes, and technology.

That's why I chose to add *culture* to the PPT framework, giving us PPTC.

- **Culture** *refers to the beliefs and behaviors that determine how employees and management interact both internally and externally with other stakeholders.*

CULTURE
refers to the beliefs and behaviors that determine how employees and management interact both internally and externally with other stakeholders

PPTC
THE EXPERIENCE MINDSET

Culture

People

Technology

Process

It's true that companies can replicate a competitor's products or services, especially in a commoditized market. However, it is flat-out impossible to replicate another company's culture. That's not to say you can't mimic best practices, like how a competitor handles pay equity or diversity and inclusion, but you will never have the same people and operating mindset—there is no getting around that.

Culture starts at the top with the CEO, but it needs to be embraced by everyone in the organization: individual contributors, middle managers, and the C-suite. Every stakeholder must believe in the company's mission and live those values in the way they work as well as how they treat their fellow employees, customers, and greater stakeholders. Leadership and management styles matter here, especially when communicating the strategic direction of a company and inspiring employees to participate in the journey.

There are too many important aspects of company culture to cover in just one chapter. The focus here is on those that relate to EX, CX, and growth. You'll learn why culture is the *number*

143

one driver of good EX *and* good CX, and how growth begins and ends with a healthy company culture. While a great culture accentuates positive behaviors and traits that lead to improved performance, *a dysfunctional one encourages qualities that hinder even the most successful organizations.*

You Might Have a Culture Problem

Resistance to cultural change can be catastrophic. When executives make statements like "That's not the way we do it here," "We tried that in the past and it didn't work, why would it work now?," and "Our employees won't get on board," they are setting the company up for failure. These shortsighted pronouncements will develop into an internal inertia that brings any hope for change to a screeching halt.

Sometimes leadership hesitates to embrace a new way of business, and sometimes individuals and teams fail to wholeheartedly adopt an organizational culture change. Effective change requires everyone to embrace uncertainty and maintain a positive outlook about the coming changes. Our research found that 43 percent of EX executives cite employees' resistance to cultural transformation as the biggest obstacle to improving both employee and customer experiences, whereas 31 percent of CX execs said the same.

To change a business's culture, you need a set of processes—social operating mechanisms—that will change the beliefs and behavior of people in ways that are directly linked to bottom-line results.

—RAM CHARAN

For an Experience Mindset to flourish, your stakeholders must believe in what the company is doing. Everyone has to rally around common goals. There will always be stragglers, but if the majority of your orga-

nization isn't on board, you have a serious culture problem to solve. Excitement should always be brewing over what might be accomplished today and the possibilities that lie ahead. When the culture has lost its way and needs to get back on track, an active effort must be made to *change* the culture through a company-wide initiative.

Start with the Culture

In 1993, after passing on the top job three times, RJR Nabisco CEO Lou Gerstner Jr. agreed to take the helm at a floundering IBM. Despite being the world's largest computer manufacturer and one of the country's leading companies, with three hundred thousand employees and $60 billion in sales, "Big Blue" was reeling from losses of $5 billion the previous year. Its stock price had dropped from $43 in 1987 to $13 in the 1990s. The company was on the verge of collapse.

Gerstner was an industry outsider, a CEO who had no

145

knowledge of computers whatsoever, making him an unlikely choice, especially from the perspective of IBM's employees (many of whom were "lifers"). Gerstner knew he needed to establish trust to make an impact, not only with his leadership team but with IBM's employees and customers. To that end, he spent time early in his tenure with both sets of stakeholders to better understand what they felt had caused IBM's predicament.

What Gerstner found was an organization filled with people who were committed to IBM, who had built industry-leading products for decades but had grown averse to taking risks. They were focused on internal competition, processes, and fiefdoms instead of customers, collaboration, and external competitors. Meanwhile, IBM's customers felt the company was no longer meeting their needs but simply sticking to the status quo, forcing them to consider alternative solutions.

While it wasn't his intention to tackle culture at first, after conversations with lifer employees, Gerstner realized he needed to begin his turnaround strategy there: "You can quickly figure out, sometimes within hours of being in a place, what the culture encourages and discourages, rewards and punishes. Is it a culture that rewards individual achievement or team play? Does it value risk taking or consensus building?" In Gerstner's opinion, "culture isn't just one aspect of the game—it is the game." If he hadn't started with its troubled culture, IBM's fortunes might have taken a very different turn.

IBM had been a product-led organization since its founding in 1911, an approach that had proven highly successful. While it was still a product leader in a number of categories in the early 1990s, there was a deeply embedded bureaucracy and resistance to change that kept it from innovating further, putting the company's future in jeopardy. "This codification, this rigor mortis that sets in around values and behaviors, is a problem unique to—and often devastating for—successful enterprises," Gerstner wrote.

If Gerstner was going to be successful, he needed to rally employees around the guiding principles established by the founders eighty years prior, such as having respect for others, providing great customer service, being known for excellence, and managers leading effectively. Previous leaders had paid lip service to the importance of teamwork, Gerstner explained, but "everyone's pay was based on individual unit performance." By tying employee compensation to the performance of the whole company rather than to an employee's particular division, he aligned everyone's incentives. But that wasn't enough. "People don't do what you *expect* but what you *inspect*," Gerstner wrote. This realization led him to change the company's performance metrics to force teams to break down silos and collaborate across fiefdoms. When he arrived, the company evaluated performance based on product quality and category market share. By shifting the emphasis to collaboration and customer satisfaction, employees would be incentivized to stop isolating themselves.

Likewise, the company proclaimed its devotion to customers above all, but "no one in the field could make a pricing decision without a sign-off from the finance staff." In short, talk is cheap. Gerstner understood that the culture would always reflect the actual incentives. "If you want to out-execute your competitors," Gerstner wrote, "you must communicate clear strategies and values, reinforce those values in everything the company does, and allow people the freedom to act, trusting they will execute consistent with the values."

IBM's employees had lost sight of the fact that their real competition lay outside IBM, not across the hall. While this may seem obvious, many companies are guilty of creating and celebrating internal competition in this way. Establishing a new

147

CEO LOU GERSTNER

"CULTURE ISN'T JUST ONE ASPECT OF THE GAME — IT IS THE GAME."

"If you want to out-execute your competitors, you must **communicate clear strategies and values**, reinforce those values in everything the company does, and **allow people the freedom to act**, trusting they will execute consistent with the values."

MANAGEMENT DOESN'T CHANGE CULTURE. MANAGEMENT INVITES THE WORKFORCE ITSELF TO CHANGE THE CULTURE.

operating mindset required employees and the C-suite to unify around overall company goals.

Nodding your head as your manager tells you what to do is one thing. Committing to *how* you are going to support what is being asked of you is another. Under Gerstner, every employee was required to make three personal business commitments to fulfill company goals. Then, they were genuinely held accountable for those actions. Performance against these commitments was tied directly to recognition and compensation. This new approach created not only an understanding of what was expected of each employee but also garnered greater engagement. Employees felt they had a say in how their performance was being measured and a real shot at meeting expectations.

While more common today, it was unusual in the early 1900s for a company to be vocal about diversity and equality. However, IBM's founding chairman, Thomas Watson Sr. was. IBM had enacted an unequaled list of progressive workplace programs and policies, from hiring people with disabilities, starting in 1914, to the arrival of professional women and equal pay for equal work in 1935.

When IBM wanted to build manufacturing facilities in North

Carolina and Kentucky in 1953, the states were still segregated. Thomas Watson Jr., who was IBM's president at the time, wrote a letter to his managers, stating, "It is the policy of this organization to hire people who have the personality, talent and background necessary to fill a given job, regardless of race, color or creed."

Understanding the importance of reconnecting with the company's founding values, Gerstner took a close look at his senior executive team. He decided it didn't reflect the diversity of the market for talent or of IBM's customers and employees. To rectify the imbalance, Gerstner launched eight diversity task forces made up of middle- and senior-level executives to address the unique concerns of their respective constituencies. "We made diversity a market-based issue. . . . It's about understanding our markets, which are diverse and multicultural."

Even as IBM began to fix these and other internal challenges, Gerstner wanted to tackle customer issues that had cropped up as a result of the company's past, siloed focus. One of IBM's founding principles, conceived by Thomas Watson Sr., had been to "deliver superior customer service." To emphasize this point to the public, they placed full-page ads in U.S. newspapers that, as Thomas Watson Jr. described, said, "IBM Means Service." Watson Jr. further explained, "Hopefully cutting-edge equipment, hopefully all sorts of pioneering efforts, hopefully Nobel Prizes. But the service is something that most companies forget."

As IBM grew larger over the years, this principle had become harder to follow, and execution had been inconsistent at best. The company was no longer anticipating what customers might need from it in the future. It was too fixated on what customers were currently doing. Gerstner anticipated that the cultural changes happening *inside* of the company would result in IBM becoming more responsive to what was happening

149

outside the company, including getting closer to the needs of its customers.

"Management doesn't change culture," Gerstner wrote. "Management invites the workforce itself to change the culture." Greater alignment between employees had to start at the top with how the business was run. At the end of Gerstner's reign as IBM's chairman and CEO, the company employed sixty-five thousand more people and had turned a huge profit, making up for more than the $13 billion in losses notched up in the two years prior to his arrival.

The Five Key Elements

In 1993, IBM was in the middle of an existential crisis. Revenue was down, the stock was in a slump, internal issues hampered innovation and collaboration, employees weren't focusing on what was truly important, and customers were going elsewhere. Something had to change. Gerstner decided that "something" was the culture. And he was right.

Fast-forward to 2022, and culture has become the new business topic du jour. Organizational culture and the impact of the pandemic on culture were the topics of 53 percent of company earnings calls analyzed by Accenture between January 2020 and April 2022. Much of the culture discussion centers on attracting, retaining, and reskilling talent, especially in light of the fact that "1-in-5 global employees see themselves leaving their positions in the next year." Executives have had to respond quickly to the risk associated with finding the right talent, or losing top talent, as the world recovers from a pandemic and customer and employee expectations are rapidly changing.

In a Boston Consulting Group (BCG) study of forty digital

transformations, "companies that focused on culture were 5x more likely to achieve breakthrough performance than companies that neglected culture." Meanwhile, the Accenture study found that "one in two CEOs are investing to unlock talent to drive their business transformations." This raises the question: Where should companies start in assessing the health of their culture?

As part of our research, we conducted a regression analysis to understand what parts of employee experience affect customer experience and, ultimately, company culture. The analysis identified five key elements of EX as clear, statistically strong drivers of CX: *trust, C-suite accountability, alignment, recognition,* and *seamless technology* (Figure 8.1). Though these elements alone do not create a healthy company culture, they directly contribute to developing one.

For purposes of this chapter, I'll focus on the first four of these cultural elements, since seamless technology was covered extensively in Chapter 7. Although each of these elements has

Five Key Elements

 TRUST: Company culture is inclusive, promotes diversity, and provides a space where employees feel listened to and empowered to be themselves.

 C-SUITE ACCOUNTABILITY: HR has a seat at the table for discussions on the overarching company vision, and the C-suite acts on employee feedback, helping to ensure EX is prioritized at the highest levels of the company.

 ALIGNMENT: Employee values and the company vision are aligned.

 RECOGNITION: Internal resources are allocated to develop and promote employee growth. Employees feel valued and integral to the success of the company.

 SEAMLESS TECHNOLOGY: Ensure that company-provided technology—both hardware and software—work seamlessly together, increase productivity, and reduce the effort required to complete basic tasks.

FIGURE 8.1

been touched upon throughout the book, looking at them in greater depth will show that all five are intertwined—each one builds on the other to establish strong EX. Together, they play a significant role in supporting an engaged and healthy culture, further solidifying a great employee experience. In turn, CX is strengthened as well.

Trust

Company culture is inclusive, promotes diversity, and provides a space where employees feel listened to and empowered to be themselves.

Working for Salesforce has been a master class in the power of having a strong culture. Salesforce consistently is named a "great place to work" around the globe, and that is because Salesforce has built a culture of trust by being incredibly intentional about its values, its behavior, and the experiences it delivers. The focus on culture starts at the top with our founder and CEO, Marc Benioff, who has put trust as our number one value alongside customer success, innovation, equality, and sustainability.

Trust is an important component of company culture because it improves communication, teamwork, commitment, and productivity. Two types of trust are key: trust that an employee has in their organization and trust that the organization has in an employee. According to the 2021 Edelman special report, "The Belief-Driven Employee," some 78 percent of employees said they trusted their coworkers, followed by their direct manager (77 percent), chief executive (71 percent), and head of human resources (70 percent). And across all examined markets and sectors from the study, employees who feel trusted and empowered are one and a half times more likely to say they are top CX supporters within a company.

Empowering employees demonstrates management's trust in their capabilities, increasing employee confidence in what they can accomplish on their own and as a team. In return, such empowerment instills greater trust in leadership and coworkers, boosts employee motivation, fosters greater creativity and collaboration, improves retention, and reduces risk aversion, which ultimately results in a better bottom line.

> Psychological empowerment is positively associated with a broad range of employee outcomes, including job satisfaction, organizational commitment, and task and contextual performance, and is negatively associated with employee strain and turnover intentions.

Trust is also a key element for an inclusive workplace culture. Companies thrive when people do. Being inclusive is more than getting diverse talent into the company; it allows everyone, once they are employees, to have a voice and feel heard. Research by McKinsey reveals that an inclusive culture is increasingly a competitive advantage for organizations. It helps companies increase the likelihood of retaining top talent, encourages employees to support one another, and boosts performance levels (Figure 8.2).

Competitive Advantage of Inclusive Culture

Elite organizations are turning the "Great Attrition" into the "Great Attraction" with inclusivity

47%
increased likelihood
of employees staying
with an organization
if it's inclusive

90%
increased likelihood of employees
going out of their way to help a
colleague if they work in an inclusive
organization

7x
increased likelihood of employees
saying their organization is high
performing if it's inclusive

Figure 8.2

Prospective employees look for a company culture that is inclusive, promotes diversity, and provides a space where employees feel listened to and empowered to be themselves. Those attributes have a disproportionate impact on employee engagement and satisfaction. People want to feel like their work matters, and a supportive culture, with trust at its core, is the best way to make that happen.

C-Suite Accountability

HR has a seat at the table for discussions on the overarching company vision, and the C-suite acts on employee feedback, helping to ensure EX is prioritized at the highest levels of the company.

Lack of C-suite accountability and ownership for EX deepens the C-suite/employee disconnect. For leaders to be accountable, they need to be committed to the business and its people. Leading others isn't something to take lightly. As the saying goes, people don't leave bad jobs; they leave bad bosses. Further, they will sometimes leave good jobs and good companies because of poor leadership. And the way a company is managed and led is a direct reflection of its culture.

If you are an executive leader, accountability is part of the job description. Part of being accountable is being willing to ask questions, being open to suggestions, and acting on feedback, particularly concerning the employee experience. Nearly half of C-suite executives (49 percent) feel that their company excels in acting on employee feedback, compared to just 31 percent of employees (Figure 8.3).

A culture is defined by the worst behavior tolerated.

—ADAM GRANT

As I outlined extensively in Chapter 3, managers are at a loss

Perceptions of EX Prioritization
Employee Versus C-Suite

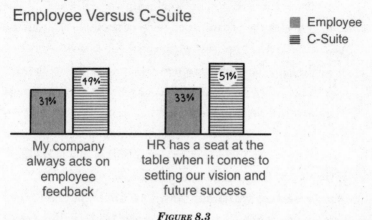

Figure 8.3

about who owns EX. And if nobody owns EX, who will respond to employee feedback? Who will share the lessons learned from employees? Who will advocate for needed changes to EX? There must be direct accountability or nothing will get done. Establishing this accountability requires a collective effort. Some companies create one or more of the following:

- **Experience Advisory Board (EAB):** As I mentioned briefly in Chapter 5, an EAB is a group of individuals from different parts of the company, with a preference toward customer-facing employees versus managers or back operations people. Members of the board are given alternative channels of communication (such as Slack or other collaboration tools) to ensure that ideas, suggestions, and issues that come from the EAB can be easily captured and to allow for further collaboration outside the board. The idea behind an EAB is to break down the barriers of traditional silos or reporting line systems and brainstorm ideas, ideate, and then feed suggestions directly to executive leadership.

- **Center of Excellence (CoE):** A CoE is a team of representatives from management, lines of business (LOB), and IT. The CoE provides the organization with best practices around a particular area of interest when there is a knowledge deficit or skills gap. For example, a new CoE may be set up to manage the adoption and integration of a new CRM system, meet regularly to develop a needs assessment, interview employees who will use the system, and keep communication between groups open. An important goal of a CoE is to eliminate inefficiency and help achieve excellence.

- **Employee Resource Group (ERG):** An ERG is a group of employees who join together in their workplace based on shared characteristics or life experiences. ERGs generally help provide peer-to-peer support, enhance career development, and contribute to personal development in the work environment. ERG members typically have a pulse on what is going on in the business around their specific area and can provide CEOs with an on-the-ground perspective.

- **Voice of the Employee (VoE):** VoE is a structured process in which companies directly solicit and gather employees' stated needs, wants, expectations, and performance experience about the systems, technology, and processes they have been provided. The voice can be captured via direct observation, surveys, interviews, focus groups, and data, or from internal groups, such as the aforementioned EABs, CoEs, and ERGs.

Uncovering what employees want and need may seem like a daunting task, but it doesn't have to be, and it is crucial to developing a supportive culture. Any or all of these groups or processes can provide a more formal and structured way to de-

156

velop greater accountability between the C-suite and employees. Without at least one of these, or a similar group or initiative, you risk losing connection with your employees. When the connection between employees and leadership is lost, so is accountability.

Alignment

Employee values and the company vision are aligned.

An engaged workforce is aligned with the values and vision of the organization. The employees are enthusiastic about their work and find purpose and meaning in what they do each day. They care about the future of the organization and are likely to perform better on business-critical key performance indicators such as CX.

Employees want alignment with the company's values. But in order to achieve this alignment, companies need to spell out the core beliefs guiding the organization. More important, management must live by those values in a visible way. Otherwise, even the best value statements are worthless.

Seventy percent of employees say alignment is the greatest hurdle to achieving company strategy. Your people won't know what to prioritize or why unless leadership sets clear goals with milestones and assigns success metrics that everyone can align around. Goals connect employees to the company's mission or vision, and progress toward a meaningful goal is the top motivator for employees.

This is where the C-suite needs to do a better job communicating, not only with direct reports but everyone in the organization. Companies that align employees around long-term goals experience heightened EX and better execution.

Recognition

Internal resources are allocated to develop and promote employee growth. Employees feel valued and integral to the success of the company.

People don't join companies to stay in the same role, title, and pay bracket forever. They all seek an environment where they will be recognized and rewarded for good work. When people find a place where they feel like they understand what is expected of them to succeed and are given the tools to be successful, it will never be "just a job" to them. It will be a place where they will build a career, learn new skills, and make lifelong friends.

Recognizing employees for a job well done is a low-cost, high-impact motivator that significantly boosts engagement. In response, employees will feel truly motivated to work hard and stay with the company. The management consulting company Korn Ferry found that recognition was deemed "one of the most meaningful rewards" by employees and reduced employee turnover while increasing productivity, and this, in turn, created a positive work environment. Retaining talent and making employees feel valued is imperative.

> *What you appreciate appreciates.*
>
> –LYNNE TWIST, author of *The Soul of Money*

■

Culture is a living, breathing organism, requiring daily care and nurture—it can never be taken for granted. These five elements require constant attention to foster a culture that drives growth. If any element isn't addressed, the employee experience will falter. If every element is neglected for a long period of time, the system collapses.

When Culture Goes Wrong: Volkswagen

Martin Winterkorn, who took over as Volkswagen's CEO in 2007, planned to "transform his company into the world's largest automaker by selling more than 10 million cars a year." That would have equaled three times VW's sales when Winterkorn arrived. While there is nothing wrong with setting ambitious, high-growth targets, if the culture makes people feel the only way to reach those goals is to engage in unethical behavior, then there's obviously a problem. And, oh boy, was there a problem.

In 2015, VW, the world's third largest employer at the time, admitted that it "rigged about 11 million of its diesel vehicles world-wide with software to dodge government emissions tests." That admission sparked the biggest scandal in the company's history, ultimately costing the legendary carmaker more than $37 billion in vehicle refits, fines, and legal costs. The fallout was intense and resulted in the most in-depth investigation of a company in German economic history.

Regulators across the world opened investigations. VW halted sales of its 2015 models. The CEO faced charges and resigned. Five other VW executives were also charged with conspiracy and fraud. Hundreds of employees were caught in the cross fire. VW stock plunged.

While it's impossible to cover all the ins and outs of the scandal, investigators found that VW's engineers felt they couldn't openly push back on management or admit failure without fear of retribution, including termination. Poor decision making ensued as engineers believed they could only meet the company's aggressive growth goals by cutting corners and cheating the system.

VW's cutthroat management style ultimately led to managers lying about illegal emissions instead of fessing up when their vehicles couldn't meet clean air standards. When the deceit was exposed in 2015, the new chairman, Hans Dieter Pötsch, and new chief executive, Matthias Müller, held a press conference at which Pötsch explained, "There was not one single mistake, but rather a chain of errors that was never broken." He continued, "There were weak spots in parts of our processes."

The roots of the deception were the "misconduct and shortcomings of individual employees, insufficient internal processes to detect such fraud, and a mind-set in some areas of the company that tolerated breaches of rules," Pötsch said. Müller's response was different: "The crisis was an opportunity for VW to make long-needed structural changes. Since the start of this year, the VW group's executive board has brought in six new members, and top management has been changed at seven of VW's 12 brands," he said. Without this type of cultural renaissance, the company's future was at risk.

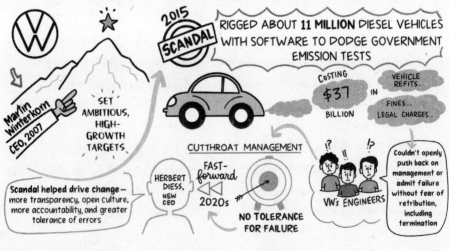

Fast-forward to the 2020s. While it's still too soon to see the results of this large-scale, 650,000-person cultural transformation, progress has been made. During a virtual shareholder meeting in September 2020, Volkswagen chief executive Herbert Diess said the scandal helped drive change: "Our objective is more transparency, a more open culture of discussion, more accountability, and greater tolerance of errors."

New leadership is now in place, and a regulatory oversight board had been supervising the business for a number of years, at the request of U.S. regulators, to reestablish compliance with the EPA and the Clean Air Act. The board has made a number of suggestions to improve the organization and its culture. It has also created a risk-based compliance program and a training program to improve workplace culture.

VW appointed dedicated compliance officers for various groups such as marketing and sales. The company also set up systems for employees who needed advice regarding compliance, HR, and legal issues. VW then used the questions collected from each of those areas to help design future training programs for employees.

The Wall Street Journal reported that Volkswagen "established a group compliance committee and a human-resources steering committee. It also said it launched a global framework to oversee its integrity and compliance program and introduced a code of conduct across its brands. The company also published the results of an employee survey on ethics and compliance."

In addition to legal issues, in the wake of the scandal, the Volkswagen brand also took a big hit. When the emissions scandal broke, VW pulled all ads relating to its "clean engines." Over the span of a mere seven days, the brand fell from third to thirty-first in a list of thirty-two car manufacturers. And despite the CEO stepping down and issuing a number of apologies, Volkswagen was named "one of the most hated brands on the planet."

Consumer Reports estimated that as many as 11 million vehicles and at least 1.2 million of its diesel vehicles in the UK were rigged to cheat emissions tests worldwide. This means VW opened the door for millions of customers to lose trust in the brand overnight—and it will take them years to gain it back. Still, they were determined to win back their customers' trust. They started by setting aside a provision of some €6.5 billion to cover the necessary service measures and other efforts to turn their image around.

VW's first ad campaign after the scandal broke said, "We have broken the most important part in our vehicles: your trust. . . . Now our number one priority is winning back that trust." The ad went on to promise to individually contact every affected customer as a way to reestablish trust and rebuild its relationship with those affected by the scandal.

By attempting to create a competitive advantage at all costs, Volkswagen fostered the perfect environment for this malfeasance. Employees felt they had no voice. Middle managers were discouraged from pushing back on unrealistic C-suite expectations. VW's C-suite created a toxic culture—and the entire company paid the price.

The External Effect of Culture

There is a tendency to narrow the conversation about the impact of a great culture to employees—those "internal customers"—without considering how that culture influences and affects those people outside the company. Does it matter what your customers or other outside stakeholders think of your culture? Indeed it does. Research shows there are a handful of a company's behaviors that influence a customer's decision to buy from a company (Figure 8.4):

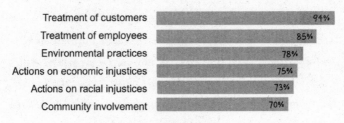

What Customers Say Influences Their Decision to Buy from a Company

Treatment of customers	94%
Treatment of employees	85%
Environmental practices	78%
Actions on economic injustices	75%
Actions on racial injustices	73%
Community involvement	70%

Figure 8.4

- Treatment of customers and employees
- Environmental practices
- Actions on economic and racial injustices
- Community involvement

This is not to say these behaviors are the only reasons a customer might decide to purchase from a company, but they signal that customers pay attention to company culture. Notice in Figure 8.4 how customers consider the treatment of employees nearly as important as how they themselves are treated.

Culture isn't just an aspect of management; it is the *essence* of management. When approached correctly, culture influences employees to make the right decisions, even when nobody is looking. They do the right thing not because they are told to but because the culture teaches them what is expected. When that is the case—when you can nurture a corporate culture based on a clear operating mindset—you can preserve and guide an organization through centuries of change. Obviously, this kind of cultural transformation toward an Experience Mindset will not happen overnight, nor will it be easy. It takes vigilant leadership, commitment, and patience. But change is possible, as the research makes clear, and the effort will be more than worthwhile.

163

Why Employee Experience
at Salesforce Now?

Salesforce is one of the world's best workplaces, named on *FOR-TUNE's 100 Best Companies to Work For* for fourteen years and a *World's Best Workplace* by Great Place to Work since 2017. That's because, from the very beginning, our founders had a unique vision: to create a different kind of technology company, one that's values-driven and committed to making the world a better place. This focus on our values, our culture, and taking care of our people will never change.

But we recognized that to remain a world's best place to work, employee experience needs to evolve. What's gotten us here will not take us to where we need to be and to where we want to go in the future, especially given ever-changing workplace dynamics (i.e., the employer–employee contract or a competitive labor market). Creating exceptional experiences is all about continuous improvement and iteration. We needed to approach creating employee experiences in a more structured, formalized, personalized, and innovative fashion.

Enter our newly formed employee experience (EX) team.

This team's mission is to continuously identify employee needs and use them to refine and iterate on the experiences we deliver to our people. Why is this so important? Because our employees are the most important way we deliver meaningful experiences to our customers and partners. If our employees' needs aren't met first, it's unlikely they'll deliver for our customers.

So before hiring for and building out our EX team, we started with the people that know our customers best: our customer success group (CSG). We looked at these CSG teams to learn how they approach similar work. Just like our CSG teams seek to create easy and seamless customer experiences, our EX team exists to design and deliver simple and personalized employee experiences that feel uniquely Salesforce—all in an effort to drive better business outcomes.

These simple, personalized experiences are critical to employees' success. After all, outside of the workplace, employees are interacting with technologies and apps that know them as individuals and meet their needs—but at work, the experience can be very different. This digital divide between personal and professional lives distracts from employees' ability—and desire—to drive the innovation and customer success that lead to growth.

To help address this, our EX team is made up of those who specialize in service design, a practice that draws on human-centered design to better orchestrate experiences for customers and employees, using empathy as a starting point. In fact, service design can be thought of as a mindset, a methodology, *and* a set of tools to craft services that not only consider the user— aka the customer or employee—but all of the people, systems, and interactions involved in that particular ecosystem.

And here at Salesforce, that ecosystem is vast. Our EX team sits within our employee success (ES) team, and they actively work across the ES organization to build the service design mindset and capability. In addition, the team has a global scope across all our functions, partnering with leaders across organizations to apply service design methods for either completely new or reimagined experiences. This holistic approach has helped the team expand their reach and ensure the work lands in the right way, considering a service from multiple angles so that the outcome is useful, efficient, and desirable.

At Salesforce, we know our employees have a choice in where they work. And we know that if we want to continue to retain them and attract top talent, we have to continue to create and evolve the greatest employee experience.

165

- A company's culture is the supporting mechanism for every decision and every strategy.
- For a positive culture to flourish, your stakeholders must believe in what the company is doing. Everyone has to rally around common goals. There will always be stragglers, but if the majority of your organization isn't on board, you have a serious culture problem to solve.
- Prospective employees look for a company culture that is inclusive, promotes diversity, and provides a space where employees feel listened to and empowered to be themselves. People want to feel like their work matters, and a supportive culture is the best way to make that happen.

Conversation Starter Questions

- ▶ What is your mission and vision statement?
- ▶ When was the last time you revisited your employees' alignment with the current goals of your business?
- ▶ Do you feel like the company is living up to its commitments to employees, both at the C-suite and individual contributor level?
- ▶ Do your employees feel like the company is living up to its commitments to them, both at the C-suite and individual contributor level?

Chapter 9

Using Metrics to Understand and Improve CX and EX

Measurement is fabulous. Unless you're busy measuring what's easy to measure as opposed to what's important.

SETH GODIN

IT'S BEEN SAID TIME AND AGAIN, BUT IT BEARS REPEATING: YOU can't improve what you can't measure. In many contexts, CX is fairly easy to measure. Market research metrics, such as NPS, are accepted benchmarks for measuring CX. And per the research in Chapter 3, many companies are good at measuring CX with agreed-upon KPIs. But while companies have gotten much better at capturing and analyzing customer data, their ability to do the same for employee data is lacking. Even if they've become good at measuring employee engagement and satisfaction, leaders are still missing a major piece of the EX puzzle. They need to—objectively and honestly—consider employee perspectives, via data, on a regular basis (though the insights they are likely to find will be quite disconcerting).

Very few businesses measure this totality of EX, moving beyond annual surveys toward more formalized KPIs, including Employee Net Promoter Score (eNPS), Glassdoor.com ratings,

167

attrition and retention tracking, and employee health indexes. And even fewer connect the dots to gain the benefits of CX and EX working in concert.

Leaders have little to no understanding of how to measure employee and customer *effort* during those moments that matter, and they struggle to show the direct link between improved employee engagement, customer satisfaction, and growth. Sadly, most businesses fail to measure, let alone manage, the quality of these key interactions between employees and customers.

While there is not a predefined, single metric that will allow you to track the virtuous cycle, it's not impossible to measure EX and CX together. It will, however, take some work to define what works best for your organization and current reporting capabilities. The metrics mentioned in this chapter are a starting point. Pick a few you may already have in place, or that would be easy to implement, gather baseline numbers, and begin to test a hypothesis of leverage points between them. An easy place to start would be to identify metrics that provide insights into the effectiveness of PPTC, not in totality but in specific areas so you can quickly analyze the data for insights. Then you can look for ways to make adjustments where necessary.

Problem-Solving Through Metrics

When businesses realize they're falling short in delivering great employee and customer experiences, they tend to make the same mistake: they set out to "fix" the problems without really knowing why they are coming up in the first place. Without data, companies don't have the ability to determine causes. Unfortunately, that doesn't stop many of them from moving forward with important strategic decisions. By focusing on symptoms before diagnosing causes, they overlook the actual problems that, inevitably, continue to cause trouble in measurable or, worse, hidden ways.

Unfortunately, most C-suite executives focus on *output* metrics—such as KPIs—rather than *input* metrics, leading indicators of your eventual output metrics, which have a better chance of uncovering systemic problems. They ask questions like:

- What are our highest-volume products?
- How many customer calls is the call center handling daily?
- What percentage of our calls are resolved during first contact?
- What is our average sales win rate?
- How many leads is marketing generating daily/weekly/monthly?
- How many customers are we gaining/losing quarterly?

Such outcome metrics are important to establish a baseline against which progress can be measured, budgets determined, and resources allocated. But they mask potential performance variations (regions, teams, channels) and underlying issues, and they assess the business from a backward-looking lens. This approach cannot provide the full picture of what is working or not working without further data and analysis.

For example, instead of asking how many customer calls the call center is handling, what if they asked, "What are the top three reasons customers are calling in?" That would allow executives to find ways to resolve those issues proactively prior to a customer even picking up the phone, starting a chat, or sending that e-mail. As a result, overall call volume would be reduced, along with effort for the customer and the employee.

EX would be improved for the call center agents as they

would no longer have to answer the same questions over and over. CX would be better since customers wouldn't have to deal with long hold times and getting bounced around from agent to agent to resolve their issue. Without balancing both input and output metrics, it will be difficult to sustain long-term strategic success.

Setting the Right Metrics

While a number of output-based metrics are being tracked by the C-suite to monitor progress toward long-term corporate goals, as shown in Figure 9.1, they are not being linked to the CEO's personal annual bonus or long-term incentive plan.

In other words, even though executives claim that providing a good employee experience is a top priority to the overall company and understand the bottom-line importance of CX and EX, they have yet to tie employee and customer metrics to their compensation.

If your KPIs are not aligned with how people, including the C-suite, are compensated, the full benefits of improving the con-

Despite Rising Interest in ESG (Environmental, Social, and Governance), Strategy Is Still Primarily Driven by Business Metrics

Question: Are the following non-financial-related outcomes included in your:

a) company's long-term corporate strategy?

b) personal annual bonus or long-term incentive plan?

■ Company's long-term corporate strategy   ▨ Personal annual bonus or long-term incentive plan

Customer satisfaction metrics		71%
	39%	
Employee engagement metrics		62%
	16%	
Automation and digitization goals		54%
	23%	

FIGURE 9.1: Customer and Employee Metrics Key to Long-Term Strategy

nection between EX and CX will continue to be overlooked. For example, if your customer service agents are rewarded based on how quickly they get customers off the phone, their decision-making process is unlikely to be focused on the best customer outcome. Instead, those agents will focus on behaviors that satisfy the respective KPI. That results in poor CX even if all the metrics you use claim things are going great. Simultaneously, such incentives set employees up for negative experiences with unhappy customers each time they rush to get off the phone. That makes for poor EX, too.

The unintended consequence of a misaligned metric is the wrong behavior and a poor experience for both sides. *The appropriate metrics must be aligned to balance what is good for the employee, what is good for the customer, and what is good for the company as a whole.* But even the right metrics may not accurately capture EX and CX, as sometimes employees must deviate away from a "good" KPI to deliver a great customer experience. For instance, employees must never be penalized for doing what they believe is right for the customer, even if it increases a "call handle time." Allowing this leeway empowers employees to create a better experience for customers while enjoying a better experience themselves—they can finally do their jobs properly without worrying about the impact on their productivity metric, as we saw with Zappos in Chapter 1. Any measurement must allow for employee autonomy during those moments that matter.

KPIs are, of course, important and necessary to any business, but you have to be aware of what you are tracking and why. As shown in the PPTC framework, processes, both good and bad, can have significant impact on long-term success. So, it is important to consider introducing *process effectiveness metrics* to the mix as an additional way to long-term success and operational transformation.

171

The Importance of Process Effectiveness Metrics

Process metrics provide valuable information on the effectiveness at each stage of an identified business process. Analyzing them can guide you directly to the glitch in the process that brings that whole process down. Some areas where these metrics can be highly effective include time (how long does the process take?), cost (how much money or labor expense is used to complete the process?), and quality (what is the defect rate of product output?).

Once you've established process metrics, you must tie them into a new set of key KPIs, such as customer satisfaction (CSAT), NPS, employee engagement, and productivity. These KPIs need to supply real business value, helping you understand the overall performance and health of the business. This information allows you to make critical adjustments where necessary to achieve stated goals and not just hit arbitrary numbers on an executive dashboard.

Say, for example, you have been making significant investments in training your call center agents. While agent satisfaction scores have improved, as they feel increasingly capable of using the new systems and tools, the CSAT score has actually declined slightly. After further analysis, you determine from a process metric that the handoff time between first-level support and technical support is twice as long as expected due to a recent staffing change. While call center reps are now better trained and equipped, a separate issue (staffing) inhibited customers from having an improved experience.

The staffing change was not updated in the system, so the existing process wasn't able to accommodate the call volume. This breakdown between the two parts of the call center was delaying call resolution, resulting in poor customer satisfaction. *Without simultaneously monitoring employee-based metrics, customer-based metrics, and process metrics, you would not have been able to determine what was causing the declining CSAT scores. This is why I suggest you start with PPTC—as you can see, an underlying broken process can derail improvements you are making elsewhere.*

CX Metrics That Matter

While technology is useful to help design, monitor, and manage CX initiatives—such as journey mapping, capturing customer feedback, website tracking, or A/B testing—if used mindlessly, technology may overcomplicate the process of improving experience. The demand for data is clearly there. The CX management market in the United States reached $2.9 billion in 2021 and is expected to grow 15.3 percent per year from 2022 to 2030. But simply tracking every metric clouds decision making with unnecessary detail, wasting time and effort and distracting leaders from the higher-impact items hidden in the data. There are more than fifty KPIs or metrics that can provide insight around CX, but four in particular are essential, which I outline in the following sections. Each gives a different piece of the CX picture, helping you identify opportunities for improvement.

Net Promoter Score (NPS)

In 2003, Fred Reichheld, a partner at Bain & Company, created a way of directly measuring the impact of customer experience: the Net Promoter Score (NPS). NPS measures how well an organization generates loyalty, indicating with a single number whether or not you're delivering on the promises you make to customers. In other words, NPS *measures the likelihood of new and repeat business*.

To do so, a company's customers are asked how likely they are to recommend the company to friends, family, or business associates on a scale of 1 to 10. Customers who give you a 6 or below are called *detractors*; those who give a score of 7 or 8 are called *passives*; and those who give 9 or 10 are *promoters*. To calculate NPS, you subtract the percentage of detractors from the percentage of promoters.

The percentage of passives is not included while calculating the score. The score is displayed as a number (not as a percentage) within the range of –100 to +100. For example, with 100 respondents, in which 50 percent of them are promoters and 20 percent of them are detractors, your NPS score would be 30 (50 promoters –20 detractors = 30).

CX drives more than two-thirds of customer loyalty, outperforming brand and price combined, and an NPS promoter has a customer lifetime value that's 600 percent to 1,400 percent higher than a detractor. NPS is therefore undoubtedly a key metric. Any NPS above zero is considered good, since a positive number means that your customers are more loyal than otherwise. A score above twenty, meanwhile, is considered "favorable," a score above fifty, "excellent," and one over eighty, "world-class." Beyond simply assessing the health of your brand and measuring overall customer satisfaction, NPS is useful for forecasting business growth, sales, and cash flow.

| NPS = % promoters – % detractors |

What Is a Good NPS Score for My Business?

The common questions I get when discussing NPS scores are: What industries are strong in NPS (B2B and B2C)? and What are the average scores in "my" industry? As you can see in Clearly-Rated's 2022 annual industry benchmark study (Figure 9.2), B2B service firms reported the following NPS scores based on overall satisfaction with the services provided (sample focused on clients working with firms in the United States and Canada). You will also notice the NPS calculation in action. Across industries, there is a wide variance of NPS scores, from as low as 23 for commercial printing to 60 for clients of design services.

It's important to note that only three industries met the minimum global standard for "excellent" service, which is classified as 50 NPS (remember, 80 is considered "world-class"). These industry benchmarks demonstrate that the quality of service provided by B2B firms is still below the threshold for what clients might consider satisfactory, much less excellent.

Design Services Leads B2B NPS Scores

	Average score	% Promoters	% Passives	% Detractors	Net Promoter Score
Architecture	8.21	50%	36%	14%	36
B2B Software	8.38	56%	33%	11%	45
Banking	8.36	54%	34%	12%	43
Building Services	8.18	54%	34%	12%	35
Commercial Construction	8.16	47%	38%	15%	33
Commercial Printing	7.83	39%	46%	15%	23
Commercial Real Estate	8.09	47%	36%	17%	30
Design Services	8.71	67%	27%	7%	60
Engineering (not technology-related)	8.44	57%	31%	12%	46
HR Services	8.22	49%	38%	13%	37
Insurance	8.31	53%	36%	11%	42
IT Service	8.32	57%	30%	13%	44
Management Consulting	8.24	48%	41%	11%	37
Manufacturing	8.49	58%	31%	11%	47
Marketing/Creative Agency	8.39	51%	40%	9%	42
Other B2B Services	8.30	52%	36%	12%	40
Software Development	8.39	56%	33%	11%	46

FIGURE 9.2: NPS for B2B Service Providers in 2022

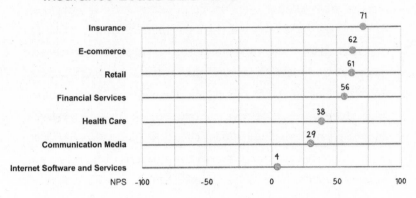

Insurance Leads B2C NPS

	NPS
Insurance	71
E-commerce	62
Retail	61
Financial Services	56
Health Care	38
Communication Media	29
Internet Software and Services	4

NPS scale: -100, -50, 0, 50, 100

FIGURE 9.3: 2022 NPS Benchmarks for B2C

Now let's look at NPS averages of B2C industries (Figure 9.3). These industries prove that an average NPS score over 50 is achievable.

Since a single negative experience is all it takes to turn a potential promoter into a detractor, brands have learned to pay due attention to each customer interaction and act quickly to embrace change.

Customer Satisfaction Score (CSAT)

An experience with a business stands out in the customer's mind for three months. If they were satisfied by that experience, they'll keep coming back. *So, if your goal is to gauge customer satisfaction regarding a particular product or service interaction, CSAT might be the best metric to track.* First, you have to survey customers to determine their satisfaction. Next, calculate your CSAT by dividing the positive responses—your satisfied customers (a rating of 4 or 5 on a 5-point scale)—by the total number of responses. Then multiply the result by 100. For example, if you have 50 responses and 30 are positive, your CSAT would be 60 percent.

$$CSAT = (positive\ responses \div total\ number\ of\ responses) \times 100$$

CSAT is popular for taking the pulse of customer interactions, such as when customers speak with a call center agent, interact with the brand online via a self-serve portal or website, or make a purchase. Customer service and marketing executives often use this metric to validate the effect of changes to CX or make the case for increasing budget and head count.

Customer Effort Score (CES)

CES reveals how much effort your customers are required to put into their interaction with your company to get their needs met. The Corporate Executive Board (CEB), now part of the Connecticut-based technology research and consulting firm Gartner, introduced CES in 2010. The idea is simple yet powerful: on a scale of 1 to 7 (with 1 representing the highest level of disagreement), customers are asked a question such as "How easy was it for you to solve your problem today?" or "How much effort did you personally have to put forth to handle your request?" The thinking is that "effort is the strongest drive to customer loyalty."

From there, CES is calculated by the percentage of customers who at least "somewhat agree (those who give a 5 or above) that the company made it easy to resolve their issue." The CES is equal to the sum of the scores given by the customers in total divided by the number of responses. So, let's say you received 50 survey responses and the total sum based on the 1-to-7 scoring is 150. The CES would be 3, which is 150 ÷ 50. A CES of 5 is considered a good score.

$$CES = (total\ sum\ of\ scores) \div (number\ of\ responses)$$

Customer effort is 40% more accurate at predicting customer loyalty as opposed to customer satisfaction.

—GARTNER

CES is an especially powerful metric when monitored on a regular basis. Customer service organizations, for example, use CES—along with operational measurements such as repeat calls, transfers, and channel switching—to uncover high-effort pain points in customer interactions.

Customer Effort Index (CEI)

If you want to dig even more deeply into how hard your customers work in order to work with you, consider creating your own Customer Effort Index (CEI). You might ask customers questions like:

- How many times did you have to interact with our business to accomplish your goal?
- How many of our various channels did you interact with?
- How many times did you have to talk to someone in the contact center to get something simple done?

These additional questions could be used to generate a custom CEI. You could then connect that score to the service agent involved in the interaction to more accurately measure that employee's individual performance. This would give you a fuller picture than other blended output metrics that might hide what's really going on. Such information would allow you to provide training where necessary and reward improvement when merited. You could also correlate your CES with your CEI to provide further valuable insights.

What Is the Best Metric to Use?

Among the many options for tracking CX, NPS remains the leader in providing an overall picture of customer satisfaction. While the results are based on only one question, that simplicity allows NPS to also be less intrusive for those customers being surveyed. In B2B companies, 41 percent prefer NPS, followed by CSAT at 26 percent and CES at 11 percent. That being said, financial services, wholesale, energy/ utilities, and CPG are still utilizing CSAT almost as frequently as NPS (Figure 9.4).

Most large organizations with revenue of more than $1 billion have more than 50 CX metrics–some as many as 200–all owned and managed by different people in different parts of the organization.

—GARTNER

B2B Experience Metric Adoption by Industry

	NPS	CSAT	CES
Telecommunications	48	28%	13%
Financial Services	37	32%	14%
IT Services	46	32%	9%
Logistics	41	32%	12%
Manufacturing	43	27%	16%
Industry Services	48	28%	10%
Computer Software	42	32%	11%
Professional Services	44	25%	13%
Wholesale	33	22%	22%
Energy/Utilities	44	41%	11%
Consumer Packaged Goods	36	28%	18%

FIGURE 9.4

EX Metrics That Matter

When Doug Conant became the CEO of Campbell Soup in 2001, the company had already lost half its market value. As shared in *Harvard Business Review*, "Sales were declining, and the organization was reeling from a series of layoffs." Looking for the source of this decline, Conant discovered a Gallup survey showing that Campbell's employee engagement levels were the worst in the Fortune 500. Conant realized that if he was going to save the company, he needed to face this reality head-on and find a way to fix it.

Conant's first order of business was to set new expectations with his executive leadership team. He did so by creating a culture-building program around the Campbell Promise: "Campbell valuing people. And people valuing Campbell." Conant wanted to telegraph that he was putting people first and that he expected his C-suite team to do so as well.

> *To win in the marketplace . . . you must first win in the workplace. I'm obsessed with keeping employee engagement front and center.*
>
> **–DOUG CONANT,**
> president and CEO of
> Campbell Soup Company

With a relentless focus on improving Campbell's workplace culture, Conant dramatically increased employee engagement. Ten years after his arrival, another Gallup survey found that "Campbell Soup's employee engagement scores outshone those of the other companies surveyed, and included a spectacular 17-to-1 engaged-to-disengaged employee ratio. (In 2001, the ratio was a nightmarish 1.67-to-1.)" This dramatic progress led to many honors for the company, which won Gallup's "Great Workplace Award" for four consecutive years.

Conant's EX improvement efforts had a huge effect on the

180

THE EXPERIENCE MINDSET

company's bottom line. Over his tenure, total shareholder return went from a negative to exceeding industry and stock market benchmarks by multiples. And while S&P 500 stocks lost 10 percent of their value over the past decade, by 2009, Campbell's stock increased by 30 percent. "Keeping employee engagement front and center triggered the engagement-profit chain," Conant said, "and helped Campbell's to deliver stellar returns."

Organizations whose employees are largely satisfied with their experience are 48 percent more likely to meet organizational customer satisfaction goals, 89 percent more likely to meet innovation goals, and 56 percent more likely to live up to the company's reputation. But the sad fact of the matter is that only 19 percent of employees feel truly satisfied and inspired. To increase your employees' satisfaction and inspiration, you must first understand what's actually going on inside your organization. Then, since different groups often capture unique employee satisfaction and productivity data, it's prudent to develop a comprehensive, cross-functional data collection, aggregation, and analysis strategy. As noted, when employees are engaged, committed, and loyal, EX can influence and support key operational objectives by improving productivity and the bottom line.

Choosing your KPIs is the first step toward measurable EX improvement. The question then becomes, How do you choose the right ones that align with your business goals? There are a number of commonly used metrics to track EX at a basic level, but not beyond employee engagement and satisfaction, which might be a result of this concept just beginning to take hold in the C-suite. As mentioned, there are fifty-plus metrics in CX being used today in some form or fashion; yet for EX, the metrics are still maturing to go beyond "talent management" and into actual employee experience. And though each business is different regarding objectives, size, activity, and process, there is a starter list of indicators to consider when defining your KPIs, no matter how your company operates or what industry you're a part of.

Employee Net Promoter Score (eNPS)

If you are already using NPS to track CX, introducing Employee Net Promoter Score (eNPS) should be a no-brainer, an easy addition to the executive dashboard. As described on the NPS website, companies should align their approach to collecting and acting on employee feedback with their approach to collecting and acting on customer feedback. The idea is to "explicitly tie together their customer system and their employee Net Promoter System by measuring Net Promoter Score and Employee NPS (or eNPS)."

As with NPS, eNPS is measured by a single question: "On a scale of zero to ten, how likely is it you would recommend this company as a place to work?" The answer immediately reveals employee sentiment, making ongoing measurement much more feasible. A simple metric tracked regularly is much more valuable (and actionable) than a once-a-year employee survey, which is what is used. This makes eNPS an excellent leading indicator for spotting potential problems with EX before they start cropping up in higher attrition and bottom-line results.

Note that the eNPS question does not refer to whether or not employees would recommend the company's product or service. It simply measures whether your employees think the company is a great place to work. Similar to NPS, eNPS results will fall into the same three categories: promoter (rated a 9 or 10), passive (rated a 7 or 8), or detractor (rated 6 or below). The percentage of passives is not included while calculating the score.

| eNPS = % of promoters − % of detractors |

For example, with 100 respondents, in which 50 percent of them are promoters and 20 percent of them are detractors, your eNPS score would be 30 (50 promoters −20 detractors = 30).

Importantly, *this number is not equivalent to the number of employees who recommend working at your company*. In this example, that would have been 50 percent of your respondents (the 50 promoters). Instead, the eNPS offers a more nuanced picture of the overall employee experience in your company by subtracting the number of employees who are having a negative experience. That means the focus is on the *unhappy and passive employees who could potentially have a destructive impact on overall company culture*. While passives are not included in the equation, if they are indifferent about their jobs, it's possible they could slide into becoming detractors, unless you get to them ahead of time and change their mind for the positive. You can't just wait around until they're ready to leave.

If your eNPS is negative, you have more detractors at your company than promoters. That means the majority of your workforce feels disengaged or passive and is likely looking for an exit. If that's the case, you have a serious problem. The research shows that more than half of employees are not very happy, satisfied, or seeing a long-term fit at their company, to the point that one in five plans to leave in the next year.

Just as with NPS, you must collect eNPS data regularly: quarterly at a minimum and ideally on a monthly basis. You might choose to survey different departments, regions, or offices

183

as a way of quickly identifying outliers within various segments. Doing so will help ensure you don't have some employee groups that are happy and others that aren't; the latter might get lost in a company-wide or regional survey, which shows averages.

Tracking your findings over time will uncover unexpected problems and blind spots. For example, if you notice a downward trend over a short period, you are more likely to immediately understand and address it than if it had gone unnoticed for a long time. Maybe a certain region is struggling and there's a specific issue with leadership that can be addressed before it spirals out of control.

Of course, unexpected findings don't have to be negative. In fact, positive surprises can be helpful, too. Say you uncover a particular business unit that has extremely happy employees; you can investigate to learn why and apply what you learn across the entire company.

Your eNPS can also be followed up with more comprehensive surveys to identify what is driving detractors, why your promoters are so happy, and, finally, why your passives are so indifferent. The goal of gathering data isn't to just check a box saying that you do employee surveys—it's to zero in on opportunities for improvement and then actually follow through. However, keep in mind eNPS has its limits. The score is based on an extremely broad question that does not provide actionable insights you can act upon. But it can be used as one data point, among many, to help you start a conversation at the executive level about current employee sentiment.

Turnover and Retention Rates

Another metric to consider is your turnover and retention rates, which reveal your company's ability to hold on to talent. This metric measures the length of a typical employee's tenure at your company. The cost implications of losing talent are significant, including the monetary cost of replacing employees. Studies have shown the cost of replacing an individual employee can range from one-half to two times the employee's annual salary—a significant blow to many companies' bottom line. How significant? U.S. businesses are losing $1 trillion every year due to voluntary turnover.

But the cost of talent retention goes beyond employee replacement; it is a top challenge to company growth across markets and industries. "Employees leaving too often, can't keep top talent" was tied for the number one challenge to company growth by employees and number four (out of eight) ranked by the C-suite.

Retention of talent matters if you want to remain competitive, so use this data to determine why employees chose to leave to see if you can diagnose the hole in your bucket. For example, if new hires are quitting at a faster rate in their first three months on the job, your onboarding process may need work.

Unlike eNPS, which allows for real-time employee surveying, turnover and retention is a lagging indicator. Once someone leaves, the opportunity to save them has, by definition, passed. These are useful indicators, but measuring turnover and retention doesn't let you off the hook for understanding whether employees are happy *before* they go, and if there was something you could have done to keep them.

$$\textbf{Turnover Rate} = \frac{\text{total number of employees that left}}{\substack{\text{total number of employees at the} \\ \text{beginning of the period}}} \times \textbf{100}$$

Just as with CES, a high retention rate isn't necessarily ideal. Low turnover indicates good EX, but it can also alert you to a lax performance review process. You must strike a balance between keeping top talent and developing promising talent while dismissing those who are underperforming. A good rule of thumb is to benchmark your *voluntary* and *involuntary* turnover and retention rates against other companies in your industry.

Employee Satisfaction Index (ESI)

Also similar to CX, *satisfaction* is a leading indicator of good EX. That's why the next metric to consider is the **Employee Satisfaction Index (ESI)**. It is a broader indicator of employee satisfaction than eNPS because it encompasses expectations as well as enthusiasm. Just like with eNPS, the main goal of using the ESI is to get a number for comparison over time and between different parts of the company. The difference between eNPS and ESI is that the eNPS measures loyalty and centers around one question. By comparison, the ESI is derived from *three* questions:

1. How satisfied are you with your current workplace?
2. How well does your current workplace meet your expectations?
3. How close is your current workplace to the ideal one?

Employees answer each of the questions on a scale of 1 to 10, where 1 is the lowest and worst possible rating and 10 is the highest and best possible rating. The ESI value is then calculated according to the equation below. The ESI is scored between 1 and 100; the higher the score, the better.

| ESI = (question mean value ÷ 3) x 100 |

Since the ESI is calculated on just three questions, companies typically include them as part of a larger employee survey with substantially more questions to create a wider understanding of employee satisfaction. *Keep in mind that the goal of ESI, and other such metrics, is not just to gauge the current attitudes of employees but to use the findings as a way to start a broader conversation between managers and employees.*

To do so, ask additional questions that dig deeper into those main three so you can gain greater clarity into why your employees gave the score they did. For example, a follow-up to the first question—"How satisfied are you with your current workplace?"—might be "Does a flexible workweek make you more satisfied?" or "Do you have the training you need to do your job?" These tee up two great conversation starters for managers to have with their teams about work-from-home options and trainings employees might not be aware of.

Glassdoor Ratings

Glassdoor allows employees to anonymously review their employers as well as offer insights into CEO approval ratings, salary reports, benefit reviews, and more. Though there are a number of online rating systems that reveal EX within a company, Glassdoor is specifically useful for employers. It allows them to read honest reviews that show the level of employee satisfaction and the positive experiences they have or have not developed within their organization.

Reviews are evaluated using a rating algorithm and companies are given 1 to 5 stars, 5 of course being the best. For larger companies, tracking this rating can provide unique insight into not only how current employees feel but how those who have left felt about their time with the company, often with shocking candor. (We used Glassdoor ratings as one of the data sources for the Forbes Insights–Salesforce research covered in Chapter 3.) As Glassdoor explains, "This approach gives job seekers and employers what they've asked for—the freshest perspective on what it's really like to work inside any company, according to employees."

Measuring Culture

Unfortunately, according to Forrester Research, cultural strength metrics remain the least often tracked KPIs for analyzing EX success (at only 17 percent). Not surprisingly, you can see this misalignment in employee satisfaction levels: there is nearly a twenty-point gap between how satisfied employees are with their work culture and how important they think it is. (Of course, as we've seen, this is the case with most of the initiatives that employees rate as being especially important.)

A word of caution: metrics drive behavior, both good and bad. Don't make the mistake of committing the company to changes in those attributes that impact culture without first adjusting measurements and rewards (remember IBM). If your people are still being rewarded for the old way of doing things, then no matter how much you communicate the reasons for and benefits of a new approach, nothing will change.

You're Not Done Yet

I'm not suggesting you track all of these metrics, especially all at once; these are options for you to consider and discuss with your teams to uncover hidden opportunities. The trick is to measure both CX and EX metrics in concert and not in isolation, looking at the respective counter metric to begin to better understand the connection between them. Regardless of which metrics you choose to measure and manage your CX and EX initiatives, don't stop there. The key is to understand what these signals are actually telling you and then act on that understanding to improve the way your business operates. Operational excellence is all about getting a clear understanding of the ways people experience your organization and ensuring that KPIs are aligned with the company's goals. When it comes to employees, you must share the results of these surveys and explain what is being done to fix any issues that have been uncovered in the process. Otherwise, you will lose the goodwill of people taking the time to fill out the surveys. You must be transparent about the results and act on what you find.

Getting better at not just gathering but truly understanding this data will reduce the likelihood that managers and employees end up working toward a metric instead of an outcome. *Improvement is an ongoing journey, not a destination*. The metrics you track should be tailored to your company's goals and selected to obtain the insights you need—not just the metrics you are comfortable with or are currently using.

This is not an overnight process. You must commit to these metrics—capturing, analyzing, and acting on them—over the long term. Too often, business leaders convince themselves that unexpected data isn't correct or that it must be an outlier because it doesn't align with what they think is going on. If you aren't willing to believe in, and act on, the data you gather when it doesn't match your perception, why go through all the trouble of measuring things in the first place? Kill the metrics and save yourself time, money, and headaches. Just know that you'll also be killing your ability to improve EX and CX in the process.

These metrics will help you ensure that you are not only developing your own Experience Mindset but helping the entire organization develop with you. It's of course an ongoing process—metrics are not the "end"—but measuring your progress, or lack thereof, allows everyone involved to keep working toward a set goal. However, this only works if leaders, including the CEO and the entire C-suite, are on board with an operating mindset that is oriented toward the experience of both employees and customers. In the next chapter, we take a look at what it would be like to work for such a leader, and what it would be like to work for the exact opposite.

CHAPTER TAKEAWAYS

- When businesses realize they're falling short in delivering great employee and customer experiences, they tend to make the same mistake: they set out to "fix" the problems without really knowing why they are coming up in the first place.
- The unintended consequence of a misaligned metric is the wrong behavior and a poor experience for both sides. *The appropriate metrics must be aligned to balance what is good for the employee, what is good for the customer, and what is good for the company as a whole.*
- Since different groups often capture unique employee satisfaction and productivity data, it's prudent to start with a comprehensive, cross-functional data collection, aggregation, and analysis strategy before you get too far down the EX metric road.

Conversation Starter Questions

- Are you tracking both input and output metrics?
- Do you have any cross-functional metrics shared between employees and customers?
- Are metrics aligned with corporate goals and executive compensation?
- What employee data are you currently capturing? Are you analyzing the data on a regular basis?

Ripped from the Headlines

*What you are about to read is based on true events.
Names, places, and events have been changed,
fictionalized, and altered for anonymity, but make no
mistake—stories just like this take place every day.*

WILLIAM WATERBRIDGE WAS GENERALLY CONSIDERED THE GREATEST executive of his generation. And for good reason. For decades, his company had produced industry-leading shareholder returns unlike any other.

He began his career in the 1970s as a salesman for a small Midwest parts manufacturer, which went by the grandiose name of Universal Distribution Corporation (UDC). His beat was notoriously slow and the few customers he had were surly and demanding. Yet, through sheer force of will—not to mention a huge personality—Waterbridge managed to turn his region into one of the most profitable for the company.

Not surprisingly, the young man quickly rose through the ranks of UDC: first through sales leadership, then marketing and customer service, and eventually into senior management. Within eight years, he had become the youngest vice president in the company's fifty-year history.

Two years later, UDC's largest customer abandoned the company, causing it to slide into Chapter 11. Still VP at the time, Waterbridge popped up as a bidder on the debt. He bought the moribund company, mostly for its patents and customer list, for pennies on the dollar.

The legend of William Waterbridge was born.

Through a breathtaking run of acquisitions, along with the poaching of top technical talent to refresh its product offerings, within a decade of Waterbridge's purchase, UDC had become one of the most talked-about companies in manufacturing. It turned out Waterbridge was just getting started.

In order to take the business to the next level, he first took UDC private, then, four years later, public again. His timing was perfect: UDC jumped to a valuation of $9 billion. It also put the first billion dollars into Waterbridge's pocket.

Meanwhile, Waterbridge implemented a radically new and innovative business philosophy that would, in time, become legendary, known as the "Waterbridge Way."

The "W-Way," as it came to be called, was manically focused on profits, return on assets, and shareholder returns. There was no question: it was a product-led philosophy, and UDC followed suit. It wasn't unusual for Waterbridge to say that profits should not be the *first* priority—they should be the *only* priority.

His argument was simple. Companies survive on revenues and thrive on profits. Maximize profits and that money can be used to reinvest in R&D, logistics, and product development. Increased profits means increased stock value, which makes the company's investors happy (and wealthy). Meanwhile, if the company thrives, there will be endless numbers of potential new employees who would love to work for such a high-flying organization.

The W-Way worked. Indeed, it was so successful for so many years that UDC soon joined the Fortune 100, then the Fortune

193

50. At that point, the company had a market cap of nearly a trillion dollars. William Waterbridge was being lionized as the business leader of his generation.

The shadow of Waterbridge's celebrity and success extended beyond his office at UDC. As the years went by, many C-level executives passed through the company's ranks. When they eventually left, they were recruited to lead many of the nation's greatest companies in transportation, finance, pharmaceuticals, and aviation. Being designated as the latest "Waterbridge Wonder" was the ultimate golden ticket to power and success.

However, while performance was strong for shareholders, not everything was perfect at UDC. Almost from the beginning of Waterbridge's tenure, there were rumors of disenchantment in the rank and file. With so much focus placed on profit and productivity, employees felt overwhelmed. A number of them used social media to regularly post about exhausted customer service personnel, burnout, and even mental breakdowns.

Confronted with this fact by a reporter at a company press conference, Waterbridge, with typical unflappability, calmly replied, "We are a great company precisely because we work very hard, every single day, delivering for our shareholders. If employees can't keep up with the high expectations and hard work we demand of them, then they are welcome to leave. And I'll shake their hand as they go."

When union organizers managed to get enough signatures for a union vote at one of UDC's plants in Ohio, Waterbridge sent out a message stating that unionization was not acceptable at the company. When the workers went ahead and voted for the union, Waterbridge laid them off and shut the plant down—over a Zoom call. He cited underperformance and a lack of potential profits as the reason for the closure. He then went a step further and canceled all of the employees' benefits at that time as well. There was an outcry in the media, but Waterbridge was unfazed; he offered no apology for his tactics during his next "stellar" earnings call with investors.

UDC had an official retirement age of seventy-three. But, as Waterbridge approached that milestone, it was generally assumed he would simply ignore it. Instead, at his seventy-second birthday party, Waterbridge shocked the business world by announcing that he would leave the company in twelve months to the day, take his $200 million severance payment, and become an advisor to private equity firms and CEOs.

Within minutes of the announcement, every executive office, newsroom, and even the halls of Washington, DC, were buzzing with speculation about the impact of the news. Who could replace such a business giant? What did it mean for the company? The economy?

It took a few days for the shock to fade, but when it did, the betting on Waterbridge's replacement began. It centered on two up-and-coming executives at UDC—Bruce Penrose and Dee Fernandez—not least because they were the last ones standing as most of the company's senior execs had already left for other companies. Waterbridge famously promoted from within at the C-level, and he was unlikely to change for his last act.

The considerable media coverage and general speculation even led the president of the United States to be quoted as saying, "We're just as curious in the White House as everyone else in the world as to who will now captain Universal Distribution. Those are big shoes to fill."

As for Penrose and Fernandez, they maintained a low profile and pretended to focus on their jobs. On the rare occasions when they were ambushed by a reporter, they only spoke platitudes: the other was a great candidate, they were humbled even to be considered, and they would be honored to follow the great William Waterbridge.

They also stayed away from each other as much as possible.

They were civil at executive board meetings and other company gatherings. But privately, Penrose told his team to get ready for some big changes, while Fernandez quietly worked on her budget and met with customers and employees to get input on next year's strategy.

A private encounter was inevitable. And it happened at Dulles International Airport when the two managers, heading toward their respective gates, found themselves standing next to each other awaiting the next interterminal train.

Penrose grinned and thrust out a hand. "Crazy enough for you, Dee?"

Fernandez met the handshake. "It's going to only get crazier, Bruce. Are you up for it?"

Penrose winked. "Born for it. I figure this is the Old Man's final test. And I intend to ace it."

The train pulled into the station, the open doors beckoning.

Dee nodded. "Well, good for you, Bruce. May the best *person* win."

Bruce Penrose smiled knowingly. "I think *he* already has."

Dee Fernandez decided to wait for the next train.

In the weeks that followed, the betting line among Vegas bookmakers, which had been even until then, made a strong shift to Penrose. They obviously had some insider information.

A week later, in her hotel room at Davos, at the end of a troubled sleep, Dee bolted upright in bed. She had remembered Bruce Penrose's words at the airport. Maybe he wasn't just talking himself up; maybe he knew something she didn't?

For the next few hours, sitting there in the darkness, Dee racked her brain, trying to think if there was anything that could have tipped Waterbridge's scale toward Penrose. Then, as the clear Swiss dawn light slipped through the curtains, it hit her: the last executive board meeting.

Each attendee in turn had described the status of their operating group. As usual, Penrose had put on a show—charts, handouts, perfectly curated slides—and equally as usual, everything was going just *great* at all of his plants around the world. It was all so obviously fraudulent that Dee had to fight the urge to laugh. She assumed everyone else at the meeting felt the same way about Penrose's theatrics. But then she noticed that Waterbridge was listening intently.

That annoyed her even more than Penrose's antics. Didn't the Old Man see through all of this? Didn't he understand that his ass was being kissed? Dee felt the anger—and frustration—rising in her chest. What could she do to present herself as the antithesis of this showboating blowhard?

Simple, she thought: *transparency*. Surely the boss would appreciate the truth for once. It might engender even more trust between her and him.

And so, when it came time to make her presentation, Dee gave an unsparingly factual update on the operations under her command. Through it all, Waterbridge nodded in agreement, a good sign, she told herself. She felt that she had chosen the right strategy.

But right before the end of her presentation, she went for broke. "One more thing, Mr. Waterbridge," Dee said. "We've detected a growing restlessness among some of our employees, especially those in our plants and customer-facing roles like sales and field service. They feel overworked and unsupported with the systems and tools required to do their jobs. We've already lost a number of our best people, who have gone to competitors, including Consolidated Industries. I fear that if this problem isn't addressed, sir, we could be facing the same union organizing that we saw a few years ago.

"Perhaps instead of the stock buyback we've been discussing

today, we should instead take some of that money and invest it into making our employees' work experiences better. Happier employees will pay in happier customers."

Dee then realized the room had gone silent. Waterbridge stared at her emptily. After what seemed like years, Joe De-Mint, the COO, cleared his throat and announced, "Very *emotional* speech, Dee; thank you. Next presentation."

Sitting now on the edge of the bed, her face in her hands, Dee realized what she had done: she had violated the W-Way. That explained the Old Man's empty look. He didn't care about employees (they were replaceable) and he didn't care about customers (there were always more where they came from). All that mattered was profits and shareholder value. Everything else was a meaningless distraction . . . and anyone who didn't understand that had no place running William Waterbridge's company.

Dee didn't attend any keynote speeches or breakout forums at Davos that day. Instead, she stayed in her room typing out her résumé and contacting headhunters. When she returned to the office two days later, she set about finding her replacement; she believed it was only a matter of time before she was shown the door.

A few weeks later, when William Waterbridge called an all-hands meeting, virtually and in person at UDC headquarters, to announce his replacement, Dee stayed in her office waiting for the inevitable. Bruce Penrose was the new CEO. Waterbridge remained chairman.

If Penrose had assumed he would need to fire Dee, he misjudged his counterpart. By the time Penrose finished with all of the congratulatory handshakes and back pats and had returned to his office, there was already a prepared letter waiting on his desk announcing Dee's resignation, effective immediately.

"Good," said Penrose, tossing the letter in the trash. He

turned back to his computer to begin answering all of the congratulatory e-mails and requests for media interviews.

When Dee walked out of UDC for the last time, she already had a pocket full of job offers. Most were for positions much like the one she was leaving: executive vice president, group general manager, even COO. She had dismissed them all. She was never going to be at the mercy of a tyrannical boss again, and she wanted to take her time before making any rash decisions.

It was three weeks later, when she had decided it was time to get out of her leggings and sweatshirt and attend her kids' baseball game—the first complete game she'd been able to attend in some time—that Dee opened her laptop again. Amid the hundreds of unanswered e-mails—letters of condolence, lunch offers, interview requests, and spam—her eyes stopped at an unlikely note, with the subject "CEO offer."

It was from a company she knew: the second-tier competitor she had referenced during her fateful presentation, Consolidated Industries. Based in the middle of the United States, Consolidated had been around seemingly forever, eking out a profit as a discount brand. They had built a solid business without much innovation and with little change over the past few decades.

Known as having good enough products at cheaper prices, they were not viewed as a company that added much value beyond that. They mostly picked up scraps from bigger competitors, especially UDC, when customers needed better pricing. But over the previous year, they had also been poaching some of UDC's top talent as they tried to move the business to the twenty-first century.

She opened that e-mail first.

It was from the founder, Martin Yettle, written in a style as out-of-date as the company. It said only, "If you're free, how about we talk about you joining Consolidated as president and CEO." Dee smiled at its casual yet direct tone, and then moved on to the next message.

But later, as she did her third walk of the day around the neighborhood, she found herself musing about the offer. Isn't that what you wanted, she asked herself, to be CEO? Yeah, she silently replied, but not at some low-price, second-rate company that seems stuck in the Stone Age.

That night, she replied to Yettle's offer and arranged a visit. "No promises," she told the founder, "but I'm open to hearing what you have to say."

"I guarantee you'll love it," said Yettle. "We're like family here."

Hanging up, Dee said aloud, "Well, that would be nice for once."

Two days later, on the flight home from the interview, Dee took out a pad of paper and found herself charting out how to turn Consolidated into a real market leader and viable competitor to her former employer. All the ingredients are there, she told herself. They just need to be brought into modern times. And she knew how to do it.

In the taxi on the way home, she called Yettle and took the job. Yettle promised to back her on any initiative she undertook. "I ain't a second-guesser," the founder said. "I figure you know how to do your job."

"But, sir, you are the *founder.*"

"That's right. And this founder needs a long vacation."

Dee hung up and sat back in disbelief.

A week later, she flew to Indianapolis and made her way to an old industrial park on the outskirts of the city. Consolidated's facility was a large, faceless structure—not a great start. But as Dee made her way to the lobby, she noted that not only was the lawn precisely mowed, but bright flowers had been planted around the front steps. She also noticed that the building was freshly painted. There was a sense of pride everywhere she looked on Consolidated's campus. She nodded approvingly, noting that the fancy new glass-and-steel buildings at UDC were never this well maintained. She was already getting a good feeling about the company.

Inside, the lobby was worn but neat, the receptionist friendly and helpful. When Dee announced her name, the young woman clapped her hands. "Oh hi, Ms. Fernandez! It's nice to meet you. Everyone's waiting for you in the cafeteria." As she was being walked to her meeting, Dee asked the receptionist who took care of the flowers in front of the building. "They are so beautiful," she said. The receptionist explained a group of employees volunteered their time on weekends to maintain the grounds. Dee had never heard of such a thing.

The rest of the day went the same way. She found worn but nicely maintained offices and manufacturing floor, friendly employees, a slightly awestruck ("So you really worked for William Waterbridge? What's he like?") executive team. However, she also noticed a lot of the operational infrastructure was from the twentieth century and needed to be updated. When she finally returned to her hotel room, Dee took a small bottle of champagne out of the refrigerator and called home.

"Well?" her husband asked without even saying hello.

"Not what I'm used to, but I like it. I can do something here. Start packing. I'll look for a place and check out the schools."

"Are you sure you'll be happy? It's much smaller than UDC."

"Yeah, but it's not just a chance to be a CEO. I can finally do the things that were shot down under the W-Way."

"Okay," her husband said. "You certainly sound happier than I've heard you in a very long time. Should I tell the kids?"

"Yes. Tell them it's on."

For the next two months, Dee was never in her office. Rather, she spent her time visiting various departments, meeting with employees on the factory floor, and checking out distribution warehouses. She was inspired by the way people there were always willing to help one another. She also met with customers to get a feel for their relationship with Consolidated.

There were many questions, but even more listening. Every day at lunch, usually at a local diner, she sat down with different company executives to hear their points of view. The meals were casual but highly informative. Dee managed to learn about the company's operations, power structure, and employee morale. She also developed a taste for chicken-fried steak.

What she discovered from her executives was that while the company was doing moderately well, thanks to a handful of popular products and low prices, the employees were becoming worried. They feared that Consolidated was losing even more ground to its bigger and faster-moving competitors. Talk around the office was the company might not be around in a few years, either through bankruptcy or as the victim of an unfriendly acquisition by a company like UDC.

They also cared about their customers, but they noticed many of them were now, with sadness, looking elsewhere to more dynamic and innovative vendors; the employees felt they didn't have a way to respond accordingly without investment in upgraded technology, additional services, and new value-driven products. This was an even greater concern. Consolidated wanted to keep providing personal care to its customers and preserve the family atmosphere they loved. But, despite the employees' best efforts, customer satisfaction numbers were beginning to fall.

Moreover, right now, the employees were especially worried that Dee was going to charge in, fire long-term employees, and try to impose the dreaded Waterbridge Way on their beloved company.

Regarding this last concern, Dee was caught by surprise. She had spent her entire career at UDC, and though she often fought the W-Way in practice, she had always assumed that Universal's huge, enduring success was the product of that operating philosophy. After all, everyone thought William Waterbridge was a business genius, right?

Dee spent a long weekend barely leaving her corporate apartment, ordering food delivery, and working through this paradox. Was there a different "Way"? she asked herself. And wasn't that the implication of what she had said at that executive board meeting that had cost her the top job at UDC?

Dee called an all-hands meeting of Consolidated employees for 11 a.m. Tuesday morning. It wasn't difficult to do, as nearly all of the employees were in the same building. She took the stage—an old high school orchestra riser—and looked out at the thousand employees before her. When they had arrived, they had greeted one another with smiles, handshakes, and hugs—but now they looked at her nervously, with concerned expressions.

"Folks," she began, "I know you've been worried that I'm going to bring the ways of my previous employer here to Consolidated. I want to assure you that nothing could be further from the truth.

"Rather, I intend to keep what has made this company not only a great supplier to our customers but also a wonderful place to work, one that each and every one of you takes pride in.

Whether it's tending the flowers outside the building or the un-solicited help I've seen you give each other. If we are going to keep our customers, we need to provide you with the technology and tools to scale our service and support levels up to those of our competitors—even higher—while *not* losing that personal care that is synonymous with this company."

She looked out at the crowd, scanning their reaction. So far, so good. She continued, "But you also need new innovative prod-ucts to sell. Our competitors are teaching us that every day. So we will invest in new product development to leapfrog our com-petition in a few key categories, and we will do so with your in-put and guidance.

"I will make this commitment to you right now: we will match our biggest competitors when it comes to industry-leading products and serving our customers, but we will do so without compromising what makes this company such a special place to work."

Her words were met with sustained applause. "You will learn more about this in the weeks and months to come," she contin-ued when it had quieted down, "but for now, let me lay out the immediate steps."

Dee spent the next hour talking about the systems, training, and development opportunities she intended to put in place at Consolidated. She spoke of new organizational structures as well, such as cross-departmental councils to coordinate the implemen-tation and maintenance of this infrastructure. These would help gain real-time feedback on the changes being made. She prom-ised to maintain Yettle's open-door policies, and the company's amazing culture, but with a particular emphasis on ideas about improving both employee and customer experiences.

She also spoke directly to the factory employees, expressing her gratitude for all of their hard work in making sure the Consolidated name became synonymous with quality. Later that day, she met with the product design team, telling them they had her trust and promising to provide them with the budgets they needed to stay innovative. But in return, she explained, she expected risk-taking and creativity, not just slightly improved iterations of existing products.

When Dee left the office that day, she saw only grins on her managers' and employees' faces. She had given them what they had dreamed of but increasingly despaired over ever seeing happen.

That night, after a full day, Dee called her husband on the phone.

"How did it go?" he asked.

"Good. Everyone seemed happy with my plan."

"Then why do you sound so glum?"

"Because I've raised their expectations on something I've never attempted. If it doesn't work, I'll have ruined their beloved company. And if I do set this company on the right path, I'm not sure how to pay for it."

"Isn't this why you wanted to be a CEO? I have faith that you'll make it work."

"Well, I'm glad somebody on this call does."

In the end, Dee did find the money. Using her name as a draw, she took Consolidated into a secondary offering that raised $60 million. She first used that money to put into place a comprehensive customer relationship management system. The system provided her sales and service employees with data at their fingertips to enable them to customize orders, discount prices, and offer add-on features.

Ultimately, it empowered those employees: they could now make all the decisions necessary to deal with each customer's needs in a single phone call, without having to pass that call on to other departments and managers for approvals. The result was that customer satisfaction and NPS scores stopped declining, and again rose—to unprecedented levels.

Some of the money also went to building a robust website that enabled 50 percent of customers to perform their entire transaction on their own, talking to customer service reps only for custom requirements. Dee then set a goal of 75 percent self-service. She also created employee user groups that were solicited for new service and product ideas. And she armed every field service employee with the most advanced technology to help them do their job more efficiently. Employees were stunned to find they'd even been given new ergonomic chairs and desks.

Money was also spent on the manufacturing line for newer equipment, safety improvements, and better lighting; developing online manuals and FAQs for customers; and supporting R&D in new product development.

At first, the results were not spectacular, as employees had to acclimate to all these changes. But as they became accustomed to the new systems and processes, the interdepartmental councils, and a C-suite that was actually hungry for and receptive to even the most radical new ideas, the company's morale returned. Consolidated was even named the "Best Place to Work" in Indianapolis for the first time in the company's history.

Customers had a similarly improved experience. They found that the service they had always loved at Consolidated now offered the speed, flexibility, and accuracy they expected from big-name competitors, like UDC. Given a choice, they came back to the smaller, more personal company. Revenues and profits rose. Employees were happy. Customers were happy. Shareholders were happy. And Dee finally enjoyed a full night's sleep.

Three years into Dee's tenure, Consolidated's available cash had grown to nearly ten times what it had been when she arrived. When a brief stock market downturn occurred, she was approached by a group of underwriters who tried to convince her to have the company buy back its stock to reduce the float and drive up the per-share price. She listened politely, even when one of the underwriters said, "This is what Bill Waterbridge would do."

She sent them on their way. And instead of a buyback, she opened a new office to accommodate a slew of new employees and created a new recognition and rewards program. She also increased benefits to include reimbursement for employee development via certification programs and paid tuition at local universities and colleges. These opportunities and benefits were open to every employee.

Further, Dee announced that employees would henceforth enjoy one day off per month to perform community service. Employees were soon working as volunteers and board members at nonprofits throughout the region.

Privately, Dee told her board of directors that she intended to rally the company around a greater purpose, *not* just profits. She also gave the board a challenge: How could they reimagine manufacturing in a more sustainable way? Could they set a goal to be carbon neutral by 2030?

After the board meeting, one of the directors said to her, "It sounds a little crazy, but I've learned not to argue with your success."

Energized by the response from employees and the community with this new program, Dee initiated a program she had been pondering for a long time: Consolidated paid to send its customer service personnel to meet their major customers in person. The program was a runaway success. Some employees even became close personal friends with their customers . . .

all but guaranteeing that neither would ever leave Consolidated.

■

Over the next decade, Consolidated enjoyed the fastest growth rate, the second highest profit margins, and the highest levels of employee loyalty and engagement in its industry. It also won numerous awards for innovation and was making progress on its sustainability goals.

During this period, Dee devoted her time to advancing customer experience and employee satisfaction in synchrony. She introduced advisory boards that invited customers and employees to share feedback and suggestions on what Consolidated could be doing better. She also recruited top industry talent (which had become easier with Consolidated's growing success). Dee was rapidly becoming, if not a household name in the local community, certainly one that earned respect in the business world.

Occasionally, Dee read the business pages for news about UDC, but mostly for rumors of new products and to compare their quarterly financials and profit margins against Consolidated's. In the process, she began to notice that UDC was struggling. Revenues were still strong but in a slow decline. The company was trying to pivot from a product-led organization to one that was more customer-focused. This shift had cut into the company's profitability, without showing any real gains in customer satisfaction.

Indeed, even with all the investment targeted at them, UDC's customers seemed unhappier than ever. Surveys showed that while those customers were being offered even more deals, discounts, and perks, they felt that it was never enough. They also found encounters with company service personnel to be endless, inconclusive, and increasingly unpleasant.

Meanwhile, there had been strikes at three of UDC's plants that Dee used to run: two of them at facilities in states where UDC had moved to escape unions. Employees were complaining of poor working conditions, long hours, and warehouse injury rates twice that of their closest competitor.

Bruce Penrose was still at the helm as CEO. He had responded to the complaints according to the tenets of the "Waterbridge Way," replacing half the employees with robots and automation, not just to cut costs but to eliminate the people making the most noise. Penrose sent a memo alerting these staff members that their time at UDC had come to an end—and to leave their badges and company equipment at the office that Friday. This led not only to a lot of negative media coverage but to the departure of the man who had replaced Dee. He told the media, "Life is too short. I just can't do this anymore. The Waterbridge Way is not my way."

Dee hired him as her new COO.

UDC was still the largest company in the industry by far. And Penrose continued to run it with an iron fist, as he had been taught by his mentor. But the company was obviously no longer the confident world dominator it had been under its founder. It seemed to have lost its edge: new products were late, upgrades of existing products overpromised, and employee turnover was rising. New recruits were increasingly hard to find, and customer satisfaction levels seemed to have plateaued no matter how much money UDC threw at the problem. Meanwhile, the company was losing 1 percent of market share each year, and its stock was down 40 percent from two years earlier.

At the annual trade show, Dee and Penrose were slated to sit on the same panel about the future of the industry. The two had not seen each other since their encounter at the airport a decade before. In public, Penrose called Consolidated "my little competitor" and wished Dee good luck with her "turnaround projects," even though Consolidated had doubled in size while Universal had seen almost no growth in four of the past five years. In private, he never mentioned her name. Across the industry, there was considerable anticipation at the upcoming meeting of these two old rivals.

However, Penrose bowed out of the panel at the last minute. There were rumors that Waterbridge was asked by the board to come back as chairman to shake things up at UDC. Dee discounted them, and besides, she was too busy meeting with new customers attending the show to give it a second thought.

A week later, after she returned to the office, her secretary rushed in, her hand over her mouth. "Ms. Fernandez," she said with amazement, "William Waterbridge is on the line to speak with you."

As she waited for the buzz on her phone, Dee shook her head in astonishment. This was the phone call she once wanted more than anything in the world.

She picked up the receiver. "Mr. Waterbridge."

"Dee?"

"Yes, sir."

"Dee, I'm letting you know that Bruce Penrose is leaving Universal and I have come back as interim chairman while we search for his replacement."

"I see."

"I'm not going to go into details, Dee. You understand. The reason I'm calling is to see if you might be interested in coming back to assume the CEO title. You have the experience, unmatched knowledge of our culture, and, it goes without saying, we have always gotten along well together. Are you interested? Shall we meet?"

Dee didn't respond for what felt like ten minutes. Here was her chance to run one of the world's largest distribution companies, to put her personal stamp on it and see her novel ideas writ large.

But then Dee shook her head to clear her mind. She thought of her employees at Consolidated. She loved them—and they seemed to return that love with hard work and dedication. Together, they had turned the company into a small but mighty adversary to UDC. And she thought of Yettle's trust in her, so different from William Waterbridge and his ruthless W-Way.

"Well, Fernandez?" asked the irritated voice on the other end of the line.

"Mr. Waterbridge, thank you for the kind offer—and for being a mentor to me all of those years. But I'm happy where I am—and I think I'll stay."

Author's Note

*In the beginner's mind there are many possibilities; in
the expert's there are few.*

SHUNRYŪ SUZUKI,
author of Zen Mind, Beginner's Mind

TODAY'S ENTERPRISES ARE MORE COMPETENT THAN EVER BEFORE.
The best of them have implemented the most sophisticated information systems to achieve efficiencies that were previously
impossible, even unimaginable. Product time to market is faster,
customer satisfaction reaches new heights almost yearly, and
more employees are enjoying the flexibility provided by remote
work and other benefits.

The biggest threat facing business today seems to lie in
workers' unhappiness. Yet, for years, the underlying nature, the
propellant, of that threat remained elusive. Numerous polls and
studies, many of which I was a part of, underscored this unhappiness, even among employees at companies that offered a modern buffet of benefits.

Having read this book, I hope you, too, now understand what
I found in my research, the causes and effects that got us to
where we are today. For a half century, when companies were

faced with the two variables that defined their businesses—CX and EX—they focused on the former and assumed the latter could be mollified with the changes in modern corporate culture. Indeed, so deep was this belief that three generations of managers were inculcated with the mindset that the customer was not only first, but *everything*.

Yet, as discussed throughout this book, CX and EX are *inextricably bound* together; you could say that they, in fact, share the same destiny. Company managers and C-suite leaders can no longer continue to improve the quality of their customers' experience without an *equivalent* improvement in their employees' experience. That customer satisfaction is plateauing (and will soon begin to decline) because organizations haven't given commensurate investment and attention to the satisfaction of their own employees.

Ultimately, what is required is change, a true shift in the *mindset* of the people who run these companies, or who will someday. People like you. It's time to reconsider your point of view, to consider almost starting anew. As Zen monk Shunryu Suzuki explains, you must move away from a limiting "expert's mind" and toward a limitless "beginner's mind." By removing the myopic obsession with customer experience—which many "experts" consider the be-all and end-all of growth—you can provide your employees with what they want and need most. By empowering employees, EX improves, but, as you've learned, so does CX. And if CX and EX have a positive effect on each other, growth is bound to follow. It's the virtuous cycle in continuous motion. As discussed, this does not mean you leave considerations on CX behind, but instead create a balanced effort to elevate both employees' and customers' experiences.

The lessons throughout this book are meant to help you do just that: improve the experiences of ***both your customers and***

214

your employees. The goal is growth, of course, but it's impossible to achieve without being open to new approaches that allow you to focus on *all* of your people—those who work for you and those who buy from you. If you can do that, and do it well, you will find yourself in a much better position in the future.

Mahalo,
Tiffani

Acknowledgments

I NEVER PLANNED TO WRITE A SECOND BOOK. BUT AFTER A KEYNOTE presentation in Vancouver and a quick meeting with the Salesforce CMO at the time, Stephanie Buscemi, I found myself on this amazing two-year journey of research, hundreds of conversations, and dozens of *aha* moments that ultimately led to *The Experience Mindset*. I had plenty of support along the way, and I'd like to thank the incredible people who were there for me throughout.

The entire Salesforce Ohana that helped make this happen: Sarah Franklin, Kexin Chen, Fatima Sy, Ivy Wright, Amanda Benz, Alice Avery, Dan Farber, Conor Donegan, Pip Marlow (for the continued ANZ support), and Kelly Smith. I'd also like to thank the Future Forum team and the Office of Innovation and the Market Strategy and Insight team, led by our fearless leader, John Taschek—there is no better group of people to help me be better at what I do every day. I've had the chance to work with the best executive leadership team led by Salesforce CEO Marc Benioff, and I'd like to give a special shout-out to our CFO, Amy Weaver, who is always willing to talk things through with me. . . . I am forever grateful to all of you.

The research team: The Forbes team led by Brian McLeod. The Edelman (Zeno DXI) Data and Intelligence team led by Antoine Harary. The retail case study was the brainchild of Lalith Munasinghe, founder of Talenteck and professor at Barnard College, Columbia University, and Kate Gautier, Stanford MBA. They (and their team) brought EX + CX = Growth "causation" to life in a real case study.

My publishing team: This amazing group helped me take my ideas from a vision board to a second book. Thank you to my publisher, Portfolio, and the team I worked with: Adrian Zackheim, Kim Meilun, and Margot Stamas. You were willing to listen to my crazy ideas and make them happen! Thank you to my agent, Jim Levine, who believed in a first-time author with an idea, and here we are on a second book! And thank you to my amazing publicist, Mark Fortier, who has been on this journey with me the longest and has had the greatest impact on so much of what I get to do each day.

My collaboration team: Getting me to write and not talk takes a village. What do I want to say? Moreover, how do I want to say it? Dave Moldawer, the Bookitect, kept me focused on the task at hand and not what I was excited about on any given day. Then came the fun part (ha-ha)—writing the book. Putting thousands of words on paper, making it tell the best story, and keeping it short isn't easy.

Thankfully I had Mike Malone in my corner again—our weekly Zoom calls were a highlight—and I often found myself asking . . . who writes at 1 a.m.? We do! Then there were the final touches to clean up what my tenth-grade English teacher would have been so disappointed about. Thank you, Zach

Gajewski—you never gave up, you were able to keep me calm, and you were such a joy to work with. Jane Cavolina, you have been there for me on both books, tracking down all those endnotes and making sure I didn't say anything I couldn't back up. My sketch artist extraordinaire, Tanmay Vora, who is incredible at turning my words into memorable images for both books, my podcasts, and anything else I send his way. Patricia Rush for pulling together all my research into something usable; there is nobody better to navigate a very long list of web links and make sense of it all. I also want to thank Jim MacLeod for putting up with endless edits on creative projects. And last but definitely not least, my sounding board, Marie Meoli (who knows my stuff better than I do)—you are always willing to follow my crazy ideas to wherever they take us, and you are the best plus-one ever! Mahalo to all of you.

My thinking partners: Stepping into the new territory of EX was a bit uncomfortable for me, but there is no better group of people to have helped me navigate how best to frame this story. The entire Thinkers50 community, who always answered the call or e-mail when I needed guidance, especially Liz Wiseman, Rita McGrath, Laura Gassner Otting, Tasha Eurich, Roger Martin, Nancy Duarte, Hubert Joly, Nick Ferrazzi, Vala Afshar, Tom Peters, Stuart Crainer, and Des Dearlove.

My hoaloha: I can't thank my friends enough for all they do to support me. Especially my chosen sister, Lori Newman— you're always there to pick me up when I need it most and celebrate my accomplishments the loudest. I couldn't have survived these past few months without you—I love you. Susan McGarry (aka Suki), I am so grateful to call you a friend. Thank you for being there in my darkest moments to shine a light back on my heart. Shay, you're always there to remind me what two girls from Hawaii can accomplish . . . on the mainland. The Channel Chicks, who have been by my side for twenty-plus years. And so many others (Stephanie, Savannah, PJ, Sherri)—I can't name you all, but you know who you are. Thank you for being in my life; I am grateful.

My family: This book is dedicated to my mom. Finishing this book was bittersweet. I turned in my manuscript the day she got sick and used the last thing she said to me before she passed away as the dedication of this book. She is the star of the fictional story at the end of the book—Dee, the CEO protagonist. She was strong, independent, and a force all the way to the end. I will miss her every day. And to IDLR, my life partner . . . I could not do what I do each day without your support. There is nobody I'd rather have by my side to dance through this thing called life—you bring sunshine and laughter to each and every day and I love and appreciate you, always.

Appendix:
Research Methodology

1. "The Experience Equation: How Happy Employees and Customers Accelerate Growth," Forbes Insights in association with Salesforce: This study, conducted in 2020 (in the early days of the COVID-19 lockdown), set out to test if employee experience was actually the missing link to improving customer experience and delivering higher revenue growth.

2. "The Experience Advantage: Transforming Customer and Employee Experience for the Future of Work," by Salesforce and Edelman DXI: This second, more comprehensive research project began in partnership and surveyed more than 4,100 global C-level executives and employees across 12 global markets to "identify the key elements of employee experience that drive customer experience and increase revenue."

Henceforth, when I refer to data from these studies—I will be skipping between them—I will append, in parentheses, the number above as the source of the data.

METHODOLOGY

Study One: "The Experience Equation"
[United States ONLY; Forbes Insights and Salesforce]

1. RESEARCH: Forbes Insights used publicly available data from the American Customer Satisfaction Index and Glassdoor ratings as well as three-year compound annual growth rate (CAGR) information to analyze the correlation between employee experiences, customer experiences, and revenue growth across 263 companies.

2. SURVEY: In June 2020, Salesforce surveyed 300 U.S.-based senior executives about the importance of CX and EX and how these executives seek to improve them to affect revenue growth and business outcomes. All respondents represented companies with at least $20 million in annual revenue. Two-thirds of companies surveyed had more than $500 million in annual revenue. Seventy-eight percent of executives were C-suite members.

3. INTERVIEWS: Forbes Insights conducted interviews with a select group of executives in July and August of 2020. These executives work at companies that fall into the same firmographics as the companies surveyed. Taken in concert, these information sources paint a compelling picture of the ways in which great employee and customer experiences together power growth—and suggest how companies can design effective EX- and CX-centered growth strategies.

222

Study Two: "The Experience Advantage"
[Salesforce and Edelman DXI]

Salesforce 2021 findings in partnership with Edelman DXI leveraged two key sources of data: a proprietary survey conducted during the late summer of 2021 and a proprietary retail case study conducted in partnership with Columbia and Stanford Universities.

The survey had 3,500 employee and 626 C-suite respondents across 12 markets spread across America (AMER); Europe, the Middle East, and Africa (EMEA); Asia Pacific (APAC); Australia and New Zealand (ANZ); and 3 sectors.

All respondents had to belong to one of the following groups or sectors:

- **Brick-and-Mortar Retail Employees:** *n = 1,501 global //* **C-suite:** *n = 254 global*
  Employees working in a retail or restaurant environment who directly interact with customers (for example, retail stores across industries, pharmacies, fast casual dining, and so on)

- **B2C Customer Service Employees:** *n = 1,500 global //* **C-suite:** *n = 254 global*
  Those working directly with consumers—primarily in an office setting—in industries such as financial services, banking, insurance, telecom, airlines, travel companies, hotels, and so on

- **B2B/B2G Manufacturing and HLS Employees:** *n = 500 global //* **C-suite:** *n = 118 global*
  Those working in client services in manufacturing or health/life sciences industries

As part of this work, Salesforce then commissioned a first-of-its-kind retail study with Dr. Lalith Munasinghe, professor at

223

Barnard College, Columbia University; and Kate Gautier, a doctoral researcher at Stanford University and cofounder of Talenteck Research Labs. The survey and case study together illustrate the material and measurable impact of EX on CX and growth, showing how the pandemic catalyzed long-emerging trends, providing an opportunity to reimagine how we think about experience and to supercharge growth.

The retail case study gave us access to proprietary company data from a major U.S. retail chain, including three years of employee and financial data from more than one thousand stores. Collecting the retail data over a long time span is what enabled us to control for different variables and focus on the direct link between various factors of employee experience and how they impact revenue.

The proprietary survey that was conducted in the summer of 2021 plus access to three years of proprietary company data from a large U.S. retailer laid the foundation for the findings in the Experience Advantage White Paper.

Notes

Introduction

xvi **An increased focus:** Kate Gautier et al., "Research: How
Employee Experience Impacts Your Bottom Line," *Harvard
Business Review*, March 22, 2022, https://hbr.org/2022/03
/research-how-employee-experience-impacts-your-bottom-line.

xvi **Companies with high customer experience:** "The Experience
Equation: How Happy Employees and Customers Accelerate
Growth," Forbes Insights in association with Salesforce, 2020,
https://www.salesforce.com/form/conf/forbes-ex-cx-growth.

xvi **nine in ten C-suite executives:** "The Experience Advantage:
Transforming Customer and Employee Experience for the Future
of Work," Salesforce and Edelman DXI, 2022, https://www
.salesforce.com/form/pdf/the-experience-advantage.

xvi **"If you treat your employees right":** Shep Hyken, "How
Southwest Airlines Keeps the Romance Alive with Its Customers,"
Forbes, March 18, 2018, https://www.forbes.com/sites/shephyken
/2018/03/18/how-southwest-keeps-the-romance-alive-with-its
-customers/?sh=2a0307101656.

xvi **"If you take care of your":** Richard Branson, "Put Your Staff 1st,
Customers 2nd, & Shareholders 3rd," *Inc.*, March 4, 2016, YouTube
video, 3:39, https://www.youtube.com/watch?v=NPiCYoX-S_I.

xvi   **"Employees who believe":** Anne M. Mulcahy, "Motivation," Anne M. Mulcahy (website), https://storyofmulcahy.wordpress.com /motivation.

xvii   **"the sole purpose":** Milton Friedman, "The Social Responsibility of Business Is to Increase Its Profits," *New York Times Magazine*, September 13, 1970.

xvii   **"the purpose of business":** P. F. Drucker, *Management: Tasks, Responsibilities, Practices* (New York: Harper and Row, 1973), 61.

Chapter 1. Customer Experience

1   **Innovation breeds a lot:** Peter Johnston, "Chewy CEO Sumit Singh on Innovation as a Motivator for Success," National Retail Federation, January 17, 2022, https://nrf.com/blog/balancing -growth-and-customer-centric-culture-with-chewy.

2   **88 percent of customers:** "Nearly 90% of Buyers Say Experience a Company Provides Matters as Much as Products or Services," *Salesforce's State of the Connected Customer*, 5th ed., (report) May 10, 2022, https://www.salesforce.com/news/stories /customer-engagement-research/.

3   **up from 84 percent:** Conor Donegan, "State of the Connected Customer Report Outlines Changing Standards for Customer Engagement," Salesforce, June 12, 2019, https://www.salesforce .com/news/stories/state-of-the-connected-customer-report -outlines-changing-standards-for-customer-engagement.

3   **through a "branding lens":** Tony Hsieh, "How I Did It: Zappos's CEO on Going to Extremes for Customers," *Harvard Business Review*, July–August 2010, https://hbr.org/2010/07/how-i-did-it -zapposs-ceo-on-going-to-extremes-for-customers.

4   **average call duration:** Astrid Eira, "88 Call Center Statistics You Must Read: 2021 Data Analysis & Market Share," FinancesOnline, updated November 8, 2022, https:// financesonline.com/call-center-statistics.

4   **longest Zappos customer service call:** Richard Feloni, "A Zappos Employee Had the Company's Longest Customer-Service Call at 10 Hours, 43 Minutes," *Business Insider*, July 26, 2016, https://www.businessinsider.com/zappos-employee-sets-record-for -longest-customer-service-call-2016-7.

4   **special customer service line:** Jenny Gross, "Retail Therapy: Zappos Offers to Listen to Pandemic Worries," *New York Times*, May 31, 2020, https://www.nytimes.com/2020/05/31/business /zappos-coronavirus.html.

5   **the company located a stash:** Gross, "Retail Therapy."

5   **"stronger brand loyalty":** "Front-Line Training," Zappos Insights, https://www.zapposinsights.com/training/school-of-wow /front-line-training.

6   **Figure 1.1:** Qualtrics XM Institute, "Q2 2020 Consumer Benchmark Study," cited in "ROI of Customer Experience," August 18, 2020, via eMarketer, https://www.insiderintelligence.com /content/customer-experience-2021.

6   **improve CX by 1 percent:** Maxie Schmidt-Subramanian, "Improving Customer Experience by One Point Can Drive More Than a Billion Dollars in Revenue," Forrester, January 13, 2020, https://www.forrester.com/blogs/improving-customer-experience -by-1-point-can-drive-more-than-a-billion-dollars-in-revenue -in-2019.

6   **CX leaders had three times:** Holly Briedis, Anne Kronschnabl, Alex Rodriguez, and Kelly Ungerman, "Adapting to the Next Normal in Retail: The Customer Experience Imperative," McKinsey and Company, May 14, 2020, https://www.mckinsey .com/industries/retail/our-insights/adapting-to-the-next-normal -in-retail-the-customer-experience-imperative.

6   **Figure 1.2:** Briedis, "Adapting to the Next Normal in Retail."

13   **"One thing I love":** Jeff Bezos, "2017 Letter to Shareholders," Amazon.com, April 18, 2018, https://www.aboutamazon.com/news /company-news/2017-letter-to-shareholders#.

13   **Amazon now allows customers:** "Amazon Offers Free Returns with No Box, Tape, or Label Needed," Amazon.com, January 5, 2022, https://www.aboutamazon.com/news/operations/free -returns-with-no-box-tape-or-label-needed.

13   **keep some returned items:** Katie Tarasov, "How Amazon Plans to Fix Its Massive Returns Problem," CNBC, April 10, 2022, https://www.cnbc.com/2022/04/10/how-amazon-plans-to-fix-its -massive-returns-problem.html.

14   **a mission to be "Earth's most customer-centric":** "Who We Are," Amazon.com, https://www.aboutamazon.com/about-us.

14   **accounted for roughly 23 percent:** Danielle Inman, "Retail Returns Increased to $761 Billion in 2021 as a Result of Overall Sales Growth," National Retail Federation, January 25, 2022, https://nrf.com/media-center/press-releases/retail-returns -increased-761-billion-2021-result-overall-sales-growth.

14   **Amazon's total retail e-commerce sales:** Daniela Coppola, "Worldwide Retail E-Commerce Sales of Amazon from 2017 to 2021," Statista, October 7, 2021, https://www.statista .com/statistics/1103390/amazon-retail-ecommerce-sales-global.

14   **"you've got to start":** "Steve Jobs Insult Response—Highest Quality," December 1, 2016, YouTube video, 1:55, https://www.youtube.com/watch?v=oeqPrUmVz-o.

15   **"catering to customer convenience":** "How COVID-19 Has Pushed Companies over the Technology Tipping Point—and Transformed Business Forever," McKinsey and Company, October 5, 2020, https://www.mckinsey.com/business-functions/strategy-and-corporate-finance/our-insights/how-covid-19-has-pushed-companies-over-the-technology-tipping-point-and-transformed-business-forever.

15   **Fifty-one percent of growing SMBs:** Eric Bensley, "New Report: 71% of Growing Small and Medium Businesses Survived the Pandemic by Going Digital," Salesforce, September 13, 2021, https://www.salesforce.com/news/stories/growing-smbs-survived-the-pandemic-by-going-digital.

15   **77 percent of information technology:** "Top 10 Enterprise Technology Trends Reported by 100+ IT Leaders," Salesforce EMEA, April 19, 2022, https://www.salesforce.com/eu/blog/2020/01/enterprise-technology-trends-report.html.

15   **customer experience software market:** Alan Webber, "Worldwide Customer Experience Software Forecast, 2022–2026," IDC, March 2022, https://www.idc.com/getdoc.jsp?containerId=US48955722.

Chapter 2. Employee Experience

19   **Your top employees:** Tiffani Bova, "A New Way to Think with Roger Martin," *What's Next!*, May 3, 2022, YouTube video, 32:40, https://www.youtube.com/watch?v=3dRL1VfCSLE.

19   **2.6 billion people:** "More Than 2.6 Billion Worldwide Told to Observe Lockdowns," Medical Xpress, March 24, 2020, https://medicalxpress.com/news/2020-03-billion-worldwide-told-lockdowns.html.

19   **Eighty-one percent of the global:** "Coronavirus: Four Out of Five People's Jobs Hit by Pandemic," BBC News, April 7, 2020, https://www.bbc.com/news/business-52199888.

20   ***employees, not customers*:** Cydney Roach, "Employees Now Considered the Most Important Group to Companies' Long-Term Success. What Are the Implications?," Edelman, May 20, 2021, https://www.edelman.com/trust/2021-trust-barometer/spring-update/employees-now-considered.

20   **"This shift in power":** Roach, "Employees Now Considered the Most Important Group."

NOTES

20   **"company's ability to win":** "2019 Edelman Trust Barometer
        Special Report: Institutional Investors," Edelman, December 4,
        2019, https://www.edelman.com/research/2019-edelman-trust
        -barometer-special-report-institutional-investors.

21   **In August 1983, William B. Johnson:** Jay P. Pederson, "The
        Ritz-Carlton Hotel Company, L.L.C.," *International Directory of
        Company Histories*, vol. 40 (New York: St. James Press, 2001),
        455–57.

21   **became the first service-based company:** "The Malcolm
        Baldrige National Quality Award," Ritz-Carlton, http://news
        .ritzcarlton.com/the-malcolm-baldrige-national-quality-award.

22   **first in Employee Net Promoter Score:** "Ritz-Carlton
        Competitors," Comparably, https://www.comparably.com
        /companies/ritz-carlton/competitors.

22   **"We hired people":** Tiffani Bova, "Driven by Purpose and
        Delivering Excellence with Horst Schulze," August 1, 2019, in
        What's Next! with Tiffani Bova, podcast, 34:05, https://
        whatsnextpodcast.libsyn.com/driven-by-purpose-and-delivering
        -excellence-with-horst-schulze.

24   **all future Apple Store managers:** Carmine Gallo, "How the
        Ritz-Carlton Inspired the Apple Store," *Forbes*, April 10, 2012,
        https://www.forbes.com/sites/carminegallo/2012/04/10/how-the
        -ritz-carlton-inspired-the-apple-store-video/?sh=69d0c
        1463449.

26   **70 percent of employees:** Naina Dhingra et al., "Help Your
        Employees Find Purpose—or Watch Them Leave," McKinsey and
        Company, April 5, 2021, https://www.mckinsey.com/business
        -functions/people-and-organizational-performance/our-insights
        /help-your-employees-find-purpose-or-watch-them-leave.

28   **56 percent of employees:** "2019–2020 Top Insights for the
        C-Suite: How to Excel at Strategy and Execution; A Strategy
        Perspective," Gartner, https://www.gartner.com/en/insights
        /top-insights/strategy-2020.

29   **members say that providing a good:** "The Experience
        Advantage: Transforming Customer and Employee Experience
        for the Future of Work," Salesforce and Edelman DXI, 2022,
        https://www.salesforce.com/form/pdf/the-experience
        -advantage.

29   **post-pandemic workforce policies:** Jack Kelly, "The Great
        Disconnect Between Bosses and Workers," *Forbes*, April 2, 2022,
        https://www.forbes.com/sites/jackkelly/2022/04/02/the-great
        -disconnect-between-bosses-and-workers/?sh=236a89531411.

30 **"Eighty-seven percent of surveyed":** "Findings on the Relationship Between Customer Centricity and Employee Experience," Gartner, July 27, 2020, G00706020.

31 **"intentional goal of spreading":** "The Productivity-Pay Gap," Economic Policy Institute, updated August 2021, https://www.epi.org/productivity-pay-gap/.

32 **Figure 2.1:** "The Productivity-Pay Gap."

32 **20 percent engagement:** Ryan Pendell, "The World's $7.8 Trillion Workplace Problem," Gallup, June 14, 2022, https://www.gallup.com/workplace/393497/world-trillion-workplace-problem.aspx.

32 **they have "clear expectations":** Jim Harter, "U.S. Employee Engagement Slump Continues," Gallup, April 25, 2022, https://www.gallup.com/workplace/391922/employee-engagement-slump-continues.aspx.

33 **who are *"extremely satisfied"*:** Harter, "U.S. Employee Engagement Slump Continues."

33 **This lack of engagement:** Pendell, "The World's $7.8 Trillion Workplace Problem."

33 **Figure 2.2:** Harter, "U.S. Employee Engagement Slump Continues."

34 **Lost employees are expensive:** Society for Human Resource Management, "The Cost of Replacing an Employee and the Role of Financial Wellness," Enrich.org, January 15, 2020, https://www.enrich.org/blog/The-true-cost-of-employee-turnover-financial-wellness-enrich.

34 **organizations that are the best:** Jim Harter, "Employee Engagement on the Rise in the U.S.," Gallup, August 26, 2018, https://news.gallup.com/poll/241649/employee-engagement-rise.aspx.

35 **"that such transactional approaches":** Leena Nair et al., "Use Purpose to Transform Your Workplace," *Harvard Business Review*, March–April 2022, https://hbr.org/2022/03/use-purpose-to-transform-your-workplace.

35 **cutting $1.5 billion per year:** A. B. Brown, "Unilever Finds Short-Term Sustainability Costs Lead to Long-Term Savings," SupplyChainDive, February 22, 2021, https://www.supplychaindive.com/news/unilever-supplier-sustainability-costs-savings/595388.

35 **they reinvested three-quarters:** Dennis Carey, Brian Dumaine, and Michael Useem, "CEOs Are Suddenly Having a Change of Heart About What Their Companies Should Stand For," *Business Insider*, September 5, 2019, https://www

.businessinsider.com/kraft-heinz-unilever-ceo-investments
-economy-2019-8.

36 **"a purpose beyond reducing"**: Carey, Dumaine, and Useem,
"CEOs Are Suddenly Having a Change of Heart."

36 **"Unilever Sustainable Living Plan"**: "Unilever Celebrates 10
Years of the Sustainable Living Plan," Unilever, May 6, 2020,
https://www.unilever.com/news/press-and-media/press-releases
/2020/unilever-celebrates-10-years-of-the-sustainable-living-plan.

36 **"lead their companies"**: Carey, Dumaine, and Useem, "CEOs
Are Suddenly Having a Change of Heart."

36 **"92% of those"**: Carey, Dumaine, and Useem, "CEOs Are
Suddenly Having a Change of Heart."

37 **"But we can do everything possible"**: "Strategy and Goals,"
Unilever, https://www.unilever.com/planet-and-society/future
-of-work/strategy-and-goals/.

37 **shareholder return of 290 percent**: Afdhel Aziz, "Paul Polman
on Courageous CEOs and How Purpose Is the Growth Story of the
Century (Part 1)," *Forbes*, May 25, 2020, https://www.forbes.com
/sites/afdhelaziz/2020/05/25/paul-polman-on-purpose-courageous
-ceos-and-the-growth-story-of-the-century-part-1/?sh=197e189
c1dfd.

38 **"management by wandering around"**: Shelley Dolley, "The
Heart of MBWA," *TomPeters!* (blog), February 27, 2013, https://
tompeters.com/2013/02/the-heart-of-mbwa.

38 **Sixty-nine percent of employees**: Lindsay Kolowich Cox, "11
Eye-Opening Statistics on the Importance of Employee Feedback,"
Hubspot Blog, https://blog.hubspot.com/marketing/11-employee
-feedback-statistics.

38 **Sixty-one percent of employees**: Bruce Temkin, "Employees
Around the World Want to Be Listened to and Treated Better,"
Qualtrics XM Institute, January 27, 2022, https://www
.xminstitute.com/blog/employees-listen-treat-better.

38 **Employees most committed**: "PWC Report: The Keys to
Corporate Responsibility Employee Engagement," Engage for
Success, February 2014, https://engageforsuccess.org/csr-and
-sustainability/pwc-report-the-keys-to-corporate-responsibility
-employee-engagement.

39 **Eighty-one percent of employees**: "Close the Employee
Experience Gap," EY, March 2021, 7, https://assets.ey.com/content
/dam/ey-sites/ey-com/en_gl/topics/workforce/ey-closing-the
-employee-experience-gap.pdf.

39 **"We are treating"**: Alan Murray and David Meyer, "CEOs Weigh
In on the Post-Pandemic World of Work," *Fortune*, April 27, 2021,

https://fortune.com/2021/04/27/ceos-weigh-in-on-post-pandemic
-world-of-work-ceo-daily.

Chapter 3. The Big Research Findings

41   **Your people come first:** "Paying It Forward: The Southwest
ProfitSharing Plan," Southwest, https://southwest50.com
/our-stories/paying-it-forward-the-southwest-profitsharing-plan.

42   **we dug up data:** All research in this chapter comes from these
studies, unless otherwise noted: "The Experience Equation: How
Happy Employees and Customers Accelerate Growth," Forbes
Insights in association with Salesforce, 2020, https://www
.salesforce.com/form/conf/forbes-ex-cx-growth, and "The
Experience Advantage: Transforming Customer and Employee
Experience for the Future of Work," Salesforce and Edelman DXI,
2022, https://www.salesforce.com/form/pdf/the-experience
-advantage. The methodology behind the studies and additional
information about geographies, survey respondent demographics,
time frame, and scope are detailed in the appendix.

43   *Forbes* **named Southwest:** "Awards and Recognition," Southwest
Media, 2020, https://www.swamedia.com/pages/awards-and
-recognition/.

44   **ranked Southwest as number one:** Kelly Yamanouchi,
"Southwest No. 1 in Airline Quality Rating," *Atlanta Journal-
Constitution*, May 3, 2021, https://www.ajc.com/news/business
/southwest-no-1-in-airline-quality-rating/E7ASWIIQB5CRPLW
COCNXZTARYM//.

46   **"place a high priority on EX":** KPIs, or key performance
indicators, are the metrics by which you gauge business-critical
initiatives, objectives, or goals.

54   **workers' real wages increased 4.7 percent:** "Working People's
Real Wages Fall While CEO Pay Soars," Executive Paywatch,
AFL-CIO, https://aflcio.org/paywatch.

Chapter 4. The Experience Mindset

61   **When a company's founding:** Fred Reichheld, *Winning on
Purpose: The Unbeatable Strategy of Loving Customers* (Boston:
Harvard Business Review Press, 2021), 68.

61   **a Medium article entitled:** Brian Chesky, "Don't Fuck Up the
Culture," Medium, April 20, 2014, https://medium.com/@bchesky
/dont-fuck-up-the-culture-597cde9ee9d4.

68   **Everything starts with:** "Employees Are the Essence of
Corporate Advantage," Zurich, September 30, 2021, https://www

.zurich.com/en/knowledge/topics/future-of-work/employees-are
-the-essence-of-corporate-advantage.

71 **eight times more likely:** Jonathan Emmett, Asmus Komm,
Stefan Moritz, and Friederike Schultz, "This Time It's Personal:
Shaping the 'New Possible' Through Employee Experience,"
McKinsey and Company, September 30, 2021, https://www
.mckinsey.com/business-functions/people-and-organizational
-performance/our-insights/this-time-its-personal-shaping-the
-new-possible-through-employee-experience.

71 **"I believe [free education]":** Richard Pérez-Peña, "Starbucks to
Provide Free College Education to Thousands of Workers," *New
York Times*, June 15, 2014, https://www.nytimes.com/2014/06/16
/us/starbucks-to-provide-free-college-education-to-thousands-of
-workers.html.

72 **Schultz retired in 2017:** "Starbucks' Schultz to Remain Interim
CEO Until March," Reuters, June 6, 2022, https://www.reuters
.com/business/retail-consumer/starbucks-schultz-remain-interim
-ceo-until-q1-2023-2022-06-06/.

72 **"establishing a new tone":** Heather Haddon, "Howard Schultz,
Returning to Starbucks, Seeks New Start with Baristas," *Wall
Street Journal*, March 19, 2022, https://www.wsj.com/articles
/howard-schultz-returning-to-starbucks-seeks-new-start-with
-baristas-11647694802.

72 **"The most serious challenge":** Andy Serwer, "Starbucks Fix:
Howard Schultz Spills the Beans on His Plans to Save the Company
He Founded," *Fortune*, January 18, 2008, http://archive.fortune
.com/2008/01/17/news/newsmakers/starbucks.fortune/index.htm.

73 **"satisfy the evolving behaviors":** "A Message from Howard
Schultz: The Next Chapter of Starbucks Reinvention," Starbucks
Stories and News, July 11, 2022, https://stories.starbucks.com
/stories/2022/a-message-from-howard-schultz-the-next-chapter-of
-starbucks-reinvention.

73 **pressure to meet drive-through time quotas:** Michael
Sainato, "'Coffee-Making Robots': Starbucks Staff Face Intense
Work and Customer Abuse," *Guardian*, May 26, 2021, https://www
.theguardian.com/business/2021/may/26/starbuck-employees
-intense-work-customer-abuse-understaffing.

73 **mobile orders had become:** Grace Dean, "Former Starbucks
Workers Say the Chain's Mobile Ordering Is Out of Control,"
Business Insider, June 26, 2021, https://www.businessinsider.com
/starbucks-mobile-ordering-app-barista-pandemic-coffee
-customers-online-digital-2021-6.

74 **"A long-standing policy":** Clint Rainey, "What Happened to Starbucks? How a Progressive Company Lost Its Way," *Fast Company*, March 17, 2022, https://www.fastcompany.com /90732166/what-happened-to-starbucks-how-a-progressive -company-lost-its-way.

74 **"the lack of contact":** Heather Haddon, "Howard Schultz Says Starbucks Is Seeking Fresh Blood in CEO Search," *Wall Street Journal*, updated June 6, 2022, https://www.wsj.com/articles /howard-schultz-says-starbucks-is-seeking-fresh-blood-in-ceo -search-11654488060?mod=latest_headlines.

74 **"I am not in business":** Heather Haddon, "Starbucks's Schultz, Back as CEO, Prioritizes Baristas over Stock Price," *Wall Street Journal*, April 4, 2022, https://www.wsj.com/articles/starbucks -suspends-buybacks-to-invest-in-operations-as-schultz-returns -11649055660.

75 **Starbucks also announced a plan:** Amelia Lucas, "Starbucks to Hike Wages, Double Training for Workers as CEO Schultz Tries to Head Off Union Push," CNBC, May 3, 2022, https://www.cnbc .com/amp/2022/05/03/starbucks-to-hike-wages-double-training-for -workers-amid-union-push.html.

75 **there was a caveat:** Andrea Hsu, "Starbucks Says Employees Getting New Benefits, but Not at Stores That Are Unionizing," NPR, May 3, 2022, https://www.npr.org/2022/05/03/1095909869 /starbucks-union-ceo-howard-schultz-workers-united-labor -benefits.

75 **"The work of our Reinvention":** "A Message from Howard Schultz."

Chapter 5. People: The Heartbeat of Business

80 **Instead of focusing on productivity:** Ashish Kothari, "Battling Burnout: A Conversation with Resilience Expert Dr. Amit Sood," McKinsey and Company, December 7, 2021, https://www.mckinsey .com/industries/healthcare-systems-and-services/our-insights /battling-burnout-a-conversation-with-resiliency-expert-dr-amit -sood.

80 **Leavitt's Diamond Model:** H. J. Leavitt, "Applied Organization Change in Industry: Structural, Technical, and Human Approaches," University of Akron, Cummings Center Special Interest, June 1962, http://collections.uakron.edu/digital /collection/p15960coll1/id/21949.

80 **"Sometimes we may aim":** Leavitt, "Applied Organizational Change in Industry."

83   **CEOs say that customer experience:** "The CEO View of CX," Walker, 2016, 8, https://f.hubspotusercontent10.net/hubfs/8834760/Reports%20and%20Case%20Studies/WALKER-CEO-View-of-CX.pdf.

83   **"there were zero buy":** "The Heart of Business with Hubert Joly," July 1, 2021, on *What's Next! with Tiffani Bova*, podcast, https://podcasts.apple.com/us/podcast/the-heart-of-business-with-hubert-joly/id1262213009?i=1000527494718.

84   **"all hands on deck":** Gary Peterson, "Cutting ROWE Won't Cure Best Buy," *Forbes*, March 12, 2013, https://www.forbes.com/sites/garypeterson/2013/03/12/cutting-rowe-wont-cure-best-buy/?sh=3c6dd75133ba.

84   **encouraged in-person collaboration:** Kim Bhasin, "Best Buy CEO: Here's Why I Killed the 'Results Only Work Environment,'" *Business Insider*, March 18, 2013, https://www.businessinsider.com/best-buy-ceo-rowe-2013-3.

84   **"thoughtful, purposeful way":** James Covert, "Best Buy Cutting 2,000 Managers," *New York Post*, February 26, 2014, https://nypost.com/2014/02/26/best-buy-cutting-2000-managers/.

84   **Joly led the company through:** Brian Sozzi, "Former Best Buy CEO: Companies Should 'Pursue a Noble Purpose and Good Things,'" Yahoo! Finance, March 13, 2020, https://www.yahoo.com/now/former-best-buy-ceo-companies-should-pursue-a-noble-purpose-and-good-things-155902345.html.

86   **Best Buy was ranked:** John Vomhof Jr., "Why Best Buy's Employee Training Program Is World Class," Best Buy, March 5, 2019, https://corporate.bestbuy.com/why-best-buys-employee-training-program-is-world-class/.

86   **"associate knowledge is the highest":** Vomhof, "Why Best Buy's Employee Training Program Is World Class."

86   **38.2 percent of workers:** Laura Gassner Otting, "How to Re-Engage a Dissatisfied Employee," *Harvard Business Review*, May 19, 2022, https://hbr.org/2022/05/how-to-re-engage-a-dissatisfied-employee.

86   **belief that employee retention:** "2021 Retention Report: The COVID Edition," Work Institute, 12, https://info.workinstitute.com/en/retention-report-2021.

86   **Salary and benefits alone:** Ryan Pendell, "Employee Experience vs. Engagement: What's the Difference?," Gallup, October 12, 2018, https://www.gallup.com/workplace/243578/employee-experience-engagement-difference.aspx.

86 **those who were allowed:** "Future Forum Pulse: Summer Snapshot," FutureForum, July 19, 2022, https://futureforum.com /pulse-survey.

87 **Only three in ten employees:** "The Experience Advantage: Transforming Customer and Employee Experience for the Future of Work," Salesforce and Edelman DXI, 2022, https://www .salesforce.com/form/pdf/the-experience-advantage.

87 **Two in three U.S. employees:** "The Experience Advantage."

87 **Figure 5.1:** "The Experience Advantage."

88 **Figure 5.2:** "The Experience Advantage."

89 **the challenge of finding:** "The Experience Advantage."

90 **onboarding process was a "great experience":** "The Experience Advantage."

90 **While you fare better:** "The Experience Advantage."

93 **76 percent look for:** "The Experience Advantage."

93 **LinkedIn found that:** "The Transformation of L&D," LinkedIn Learning, 2022, https://learning.linkedin.com/content/dam/me /learning/en-us/pdfs/workplace-learning-report/LinkedIn -Learning_Workplace-Learning-Report-2022-EN.pdf.

93 **upskilling or reskilling:** "2021 Workplace Learning Report," LinkedIn Learning, https://learning.linkedin.com/content/dam/me /business/en-us/amp/learning-solutions/images/wlr21/pdf /LinkedIn -Learning-Workplace-Learning-Report-2021-UK -Edition-.pdf.

94 **Creating better humans:** Garry Kasparov, "Creating Better Humans Will Always Be More Important Than Creating Smarter Machines," Forum Network, November 10, 2017, https://www .oecd-forum.org/posts/22213-creating-better-humans-will-always -be-more-important-than-creating-smarter-machines.

95 **improving EX will be a strategic area:** "Predictions 2022: CMOs Emerge as Emboldened Business Leaders," Forrester, October 26, 2021, https://www.forrester.com/blogs/predictions -2022-b2c-cmo -trends.

96 **only 51 percent of C-suite leaders:** "The Experience Advantage."

96 **Putting process before people:** Belinda Parmar and Stephen Frost, "People or Process: Which Does Your Company Put First?," World Economic Forum, September 15, 2016, https://www.weforum .org/agenda/2016/09/empathy-index-human-resources-business.

Chapter 6. Process: Don't Blame the People, Blame the Design

101 **Eighty-five percent of the reasons:** The Deming Institute (@DemingInstitute), "Later in life, Dr. Deming upped his

estimate . . . ," Twitter, February 10, 2022, 1:22 p.m., https://
twitter.com/DemingInstitute/status/1491840004124860441?s=20&
t=9bKEWMmdw83ZelB6j7jFrw.

101 **"management actions were":** "Dr. William Edwards Deming
Remembered—Part Two," Doug Williams Group, May 11, 2018,
https://thedougwilliamsgroup.com/dr-deming-remembered
-part-two.

102 **"the most profitable automobile":** "Dr. William Edwards
Deming Remembered—Part Two."

102 **exceeded General Motors' earnings:** John Willis, "Deming to
DevOps (Part 1)," IT Revolution, October 16, 2012, https://
itrevolution.com/deming-to-devops-part-1.

103 **the C-suite ranks "too many or redundant":** "The Experience
Advantage: Transforming Customer and Employee Experience
for the Future of Work," Salesforce and Edelman DXI, 2022,
https://www.salesforce.com/form/pdf/the-experience-advantage.

103 **third biggest internal challenge:** "The Experience Advantage."

103 **when managers remove:** "Findings on the Relationship
Between Customer Centricity and Employee Experience," Gartner,
July 27, 2020, G00706020.

104 **workers spend more:** Samanage, "U.S. Businesses Wasting Up
to $1.8 Trillion Annually on Repetitive Employee Tasks,
Samanage Survey Says," Samanage, February 23, 2016, https://
www.prnewswire.com/news-releases/us-businesses-wasting-up-to
-18-trillion-annually-on-repetitive-employee-tasks-samanage
-survey-says-300224177.html.

104 **"U.S. businesses are estimated":** "U.S. Businesses Wasting Up
to $1.8 Trillion Annually on Repetitive Employee Tasks,
Samanage Survey Says."

105 **Every year, companies lose:** Nick Candito, "How Inefficient
Processes Are Hurting Your Company," *Entrepreneur*, December 8,
2016, https://www.entrepreneur.com/article/286084.

105 **77 percent of B2B buyers:** "The B2B Buying Journey," Gartner,
https://www.gartner.com/en/sales/insights/b2b-buying-journey.

106 **Digital transformation is the process:** "What Is Digital
Transformation?," Salesforce, https://www.salesforce.com/ca
/products/platform/what-is-digital-transformation/.

106 **34 percent of technology transformations:** "Seven Lessons on
How Technology Transformations Can Deliver Value," McKinsey
and Company, March 11, 2021, https://www.mckinsey.com
/business-functions/mckinsey-digital/our-insights/seven-lessons
-on-how-technology-transformations-can-deliver-value.

106 **impacted employee experience:** "Seven Lessons on How Technology Transformations Can Deliver Value."

107 **positive customer experience:** Tom Puthiyamadam and José Reyes, "Experience Is Everything. Get It Right," PwC, 2018, https://www.pwc.com/us/en/services/consulting/library/consumer -intelligence-series/future-of-customer-experience.html.

108 **digitize by 2020:** Jackie Wiles, "Gartner Top 3 Priorities for HR Leaders in 2019," Gartner, December 12, 2018, https://www .gartner.com/smarterwithgartner/top-3-priorities-for-hr-in- 2019.

108 **a mind-boggling $1.3 trillion:** Behnam Tabrizi et al., "Digital Transformation Is Not About Technology," *Harvard Business Review*, March 13, 2019, https://hbr.org/2019/03/digital -transformation-is-not-about-technology.

108 **full $900 billion:** Steven ZoBell, "Why Digital Transformations Fail: Closing the $900 Billion Hole in Enterprise Strategy," *Forbes*, March 13, 2018, https://www.forbes.com/sites/forbestechcouncil /2018/03/13/why-digital-transformations-fail-closing-the-900 -billion-hole-in-enterprise-strategy.

108 **"lack the right mindset":** Tabrizi et al., "Digital Transformation Is Not About Technology."

110 **39 percent of B2B companies:** "The State of B2B Account Experience," CustomerGauge, August 2021, 74, https:// customergauge.com/ebook/b2b-nps-and-cx-benchmarks-report.

110 **Customers feel the effects:** Conor Donegan, "State of the Connected Customer Report Outlines Changing Standards for Customer Engagement," Salesforce, June 12, 2019, https://www .salesforce.com/news/stories/state-of-the-connected-customer -report-outlines-changing-standards-for-customer-engagement.

112 **Too many organizations:** John Hunter, "Break Down Barriers Between Departments," Deming Institute, August 29, 2016, https://deming.org/break-down-barriers-between-departments.

113 **48 percent of SalesOps:** "State of Sales Report," Salesforce, September 22, 2020, https://www.salesforce.com/news/stories /the-fourth-state-of-sales-report-shows-how-teams-adapt-to-a-new -selling-landscape.

116 **"Journey walls are essential":** Tiffani Bova, "The Secrets to a Successful Customer Journey Transformation," Salesforce, September 22, 2017, https://www.salesforce.com/au/blog/2017/09 /the-secrets-to-a-successful-customer-journey-transformation.html.

118 **"to unleash the power":** Albert Bourla, "A Letter from Our Chairman & CEO," Pfizer, https://www.pfizer.com/sites/default

NOTES

/files/investors/financial_reports/annual_reports/2019/chairman
-ceo-letter/index.html.

119 **removing needless complexity:** "Simplicity Is Designed to
Enable Colleagues at Pfizer to Remove Needless Complexity and
Focus on Meaningful Work," Pfizer, https://www.pfizer.com/sites
/default/files/investors/financial_reports/annual_reports/2019
/our-bold-moves/unleash-the-power-of-our-people/simplicity-is
-designed-to-enable-colleagues-at-pfizer-to-remove-needless
-complexity/index.html.

119 **how to make work faster:** "Pfizer's Digital Strategy and
Transformation," *Bio-IT World*, July 20, 2021, https://www
.bio-itworld.com/news/2021/07/20/pfizer-s-digital-strategy-and
-transformation.

119 **digital transformation effort:** "Pfizer's Digital Strategy and
Transformation."

119 **Executives knew they had to bring:** "Pfizer's Digital Strategy
and Transformation."

119 **change the focus from activity:** "Pfizer's Digital Strategy and
Transformation."

119 **"90 percent of colleagues":** "Pfizer 2021: Environmental, Social &
Governance Report," Pfizer, 37, https://www.pfizer.com/sites
/default/files/investors/financial_reports/annual_reports/2021
/files/Pfizer_ESG_Report.pdf.

Chapter 7. Technology: Productivity and Experience, Two Sides of the Same Coin

122 **In 30 years, a robot:** Sherisse Pham, "Jack Ma: In 30 Years, the
Best CEO Could Be a Robot," CNN Business, April 24, 2017,
https://money.cnn.com/2017/04/24/technology/alibaba-jack-ma
-30-years-pain-robot-ceo/index.html.

122 **72 percent of customer interactions:** "2022 Connectivity
Benchmark Report," MuleSoft, February 7, 2022, 8, https://www
.mulesoft.com/lp/reports/connectivity-benchmark.

124 **"if the employee experience":** Danny Klein, "Chipotle's Focus
Turns to Career Advancement for Workers," QSR, April 27, 2022,
https://www.qsrmagazine.com/fast-casual/chipotles-focus-turns
-career-advancement-workers.

125 **management roles at Chipotle:** Klein, "Chipotle's Focus Turns
to Career Advancement for Workers."

125 **Chipotle winning numerous awards:** "Chipotle Awards,"
Comparably, 2022, https://www.comparably.com/companies
/chipotle/awards.

125   **"We are exploring":** "Chipotle Announces $50 Million New Venture Fund, Cultivate Next," Chipotle, April 19, 2022, https://ir.chipotle.com/2022-04-19-CHIPOTLE-ANNOUNCES-50-MILLION-NEW-VENTURE-FUND,-CULTIVATE-NEXT.

126   **how they could use AI:** "Chipotle Goes Automated," CNBC, March 16, 2022, https://www.cnbc.com/video/2022/03/16/chipotle-goes-automated.html.

126   **"ability to automate":** Klein, "Chipotle's Focus Turns to Career Advancement for Workers."

126   **"easier, more fun":** "Chipotle Goes Automated."

127   **Our north star:** Lisa Jennings, "Nicole West Grows Chipotle's Digital Sales with Relentless Focus on Customer Experience," *Nation's Restaurant News*, January 18, 2022, https://www.nrn.com/people/nicole-west-grows-chipotle-s-digital-sales-relentless-focus-customer-experience.

127   **"Our investments in our people":** "Chipotle Announces First Quarter 2022 Results," Chipotle, April 26, 2022, https://ir.chipotle.com/2022-04-26-CHIPOTLE-ANNOUNCES-FIRST-QUARTER-2022-RESULTS.

128   **would spend $6.8 trillion:** "IDC FutureScape: Worldwide Digital Transformation 2021 Predictions," IDC, October 2020, https://www.idc.com/getdoc.jsp?containerId=US46880818.

128   **disconnect is deepest:** "The Experience Advantage: Transforming Customer and Employee Experience for the Future of Work," Salesforce and Edelman DXI, 2022, https://www.salesforce.com/form/pdf/the-experience-advantage.

128   **develop digital mindsets:** Tsedal Neeley and Paul Leonardi, "Developing a Digital Mindset," *Harvard Business Review*, May–June 2022, https://hbr.org/2022/05/developing-a-digital-mindset.

128   **32 percent of employees:** "The Experience Advantage."

128   **most poorly rated dimensions:** "The Experience Advantage."

129   **Figure 7.1:** "The Experience Advantage."

130   **critical role of technology:** "Uncovering ROI: The Hidden Link Between Technology Change and Employee Experience," Eagle Hill, https://www.eaglehillconsulting.com/insights/new-technology-change-employee-engagement.

130   **companies that provide:** "The Experience Advantage."

130   **Strong tech helps high-performing teams:** "The Experience Advantage."

132   **facts about IT leaders:** "2022 Connectivity Benchmark Report."

133   **When the COVID-19 pandemic hit:** "The Changing Role of the IT Leader," Forrester Consulting on behalf of Elastic, April 2021, https://www.elastic.co/pdf/forrester-the-changing-role-of-the-it-leader.

133 **IT spending is projected:** "Gartner Forecasts Worldwide IT
Spending to Reach $4.4 Trillion in 2022," Gartner, press release,
April 6, 2022, https://www.gartner.com/en/newsroom/press
-releases/2022-04-06-gartner-forecasts-worldwide-it-spending-to
-reach-4-point-four-trillion-in-2022.

134 **technology as key to customer engagement:** Andrea
Guerzoni, Nadine Mirchandani, and Barry Perkins, "The CEO
Imperative: Will Bold Strategies Fuel Market-Leading Growth?,"
EY, January 10, 2022, https://www.ey.com/en_gl/ceo/will-bold
-strategies-fuel-market-leading-growth.

134 **"Poor leadership and lack of vision":** "The Experience
Advantage."

134 **more than nine hundred unique applications:** "2022
Connectivity Benchmark Report."

136 **Highly automated organizations:** "2021 Global Customer
Experience Benchmarking Report," NTT, https://services.global
.ntt/en-us/insights/crossing-the-cx-divide.

136 **will not just value efficiency:** Tom Puthiyamadam and José
Reyes, "Experience Is Everything. Get It Right," PwC, 2018,
https://www.pwc.com/us/en/services/consulting/library/consumer
-intelligence-series/future-of-customer-experience.html.

136 **only 33 percent of employees agree:** "The Experience
Advantage."

137 **Figure 7.5:** "IT and Business Alignment Barometer," MuleSoft,
https://www.mulesoft.com/lp/reports/it-business-alignment
-barometer.

138 **57 percent now collaborate more closely:** "The Changing Role
of the IT Leader."

138 **two-thirds (64 percent) of CIOs:** "The Changing Role of the IT
Leader."

Chapter 8. Culture: An Era of Experience

142 **A genuine culture:** Marc Benioff, *Trailblazer: The Power of
Business as the Greatest Platform for Change* (New York:
Currency/Random House, 2019).

142 **"Culture eats strategy":** David Campbell, David Edgar, and
George Stonehouse, *Business Strategy: An Introduction*, 3rd ed.
(London: Palgrave Macmillan, 2011), 263.

142 **misattributed to Peter Drucker:** "Did Peter Drucker Say
That?," Drucker Institute, https://www.drucker.institute/did-peter
-drucker-say-that.

143 **You'll learn why culture is:** "The Experience Advantage:
Transforming Customer and Employee Experience for the Future

of Work," Salesforce and Edelman DXI, 2022, https://www
.salesforce.com/form/pdf/the-experience-advantage.

144   **43 percent of EX executives cite:** "The Experience Advantage."

144   **To change a business's culture:** Larry Bossidy and Ram
Charan, *Execution: The Discipline of Getting Things Done* (New
York: Crown/Archetype, 2002), 85.

145   **In 1993, after passing:** Louis V. Gerstner Jr., *Who Says
Elephants Can't Dance?* (New York: HarperBusiness, 2002), 182.

145   **Nabisco CEO Lou Gerstner Jr:** *Encyclopaedia Britannica
Online*, s.v., "Lou Gerstner," https://www.britannica.com
/biography/Lou-Gerstner.

145   **stock price had dropped:** "Lou Gerstner's Turnaround Tales at
IBM," Knowledge at Wharton, December 18, 2002, https://
knowledge.wharton.upenn.edu/article/lou-gerstners-turnaround
-tales-at-ibm/.

146   **"You can quickly figure out":** Gerstner, *Who Says Elephants
Can't Dance?*, 182.

146   **"culture isn't just one aspect":** Gerstner, *Who Says Elephants
Can't Dance?*, 182.

146   **"This codification, this rigor mortis":** Gerstner, *Who Says
Elephants Can't Dance?*, 185.

147   **the guiding principles:** "IBM Management Principles &
Practices," IBM.com, https://www.ibm.com/ibm/history/documents
/pdf/management.pdf.

147   **"everyone's pay was based":** Gerstner, *Who Says Elephants
Can't Dance?*, 211.

147   **"If you want to out-execute":** Gerstner, *Who Says Elephants
Can't Dance?*, 234.

149   **"It is the policy":** "Building an Equal Opportunity Workforce,"
IBM.com, https://www.ibm.com/ibm/history/ibm100/us/en/icons
/equalworkforce.

149   **eight diversity task forces:** David A. Thomas, "Diversity as
Strategy," *Harvard Business Review*, September 2004, https://hbr
.org/2004/09/diversity-as-strategy.

149   **"We made diversity":** Thomas, "Diversity as Strategy."

149   **"Hopefully cutting-edge equipment":** "Thomas Watson, Jr.
Speaks About IBM's Commitment to Service," IBM.com, https://
www.ibm.com/ibm/history/multimedia/ibmservice_trans.html.

150   **"Management doesn't change culture":** Gerstner, *Who Says
Elephants Can't Dance?*, 187.

150   **end of Gerstner's reign:** "Case Study: IBM's Turnaround Under
Lou Gerstner," MBA Knowledge Base, https://www.mbaknol.com

/management-case-studies/case-study-ibms-turnaround-under
-lou-gerstner/.

150   **were the topics of 53 percent:** "Organizational Culture: From
Always Connected to Omni-Connected," Accenture, 2022, https://
www.accenture.com/us-en/insights/strategy/organizational
-culture.

150   **"1-in-5 global employees":** "The Experience Advantage."

151   **"companies that focused on culture":** "Digital Transformation,"
BCG, https://www.bcg.com/capabilities/digital-technology-data
/digital-transformation/how-to-drive-digital-culture.

151   **"one in two CEOs":** "Organizational Culture: From Always
Connected to Omni-Connected."

151   **Figure 8.1:** "The Experience Advantage."

152   **78 percent of employees:** "2021 Trust Barometer Special
Report: The Belief-Driven Employee," Edelman, https://www
.edelman.com/trust/2021-trust-barometer/belief-driven-employee.

152   **trusted and empowered:** "2021 Trust Barometer."

152   **top CX supporters:** "The Experience Advantage."

153   **Psychological empowerment is positively:** Scott E. Seibert,
Gang Wang, and Stephen H. Courtright, "Antecedents and
Consequences of Psychological and Team Empowerment in
Organizations: A Meta-Analytic Review," *Journal of Applied
Psychology* 96, no. 5 (2011): 981–1003, https://doi.org/10.1037
/a0022676.

153   **an inclusive workplace culture:** "Hybrid Work: Making It Fit
with Your Diversity, Equity, and Inclusion Strategy," *McKinsey
Quarterly*, April 20, 2022, https://www.mckinsey.com/business
-functions/people-and-organizational-performance/our-insights
/hybrid-work-making-it-fit-with-your-diversity-equity-and
-inclusion-strategy.

154   **Lack of C-suite accountability:** "The Experience Advantage."

154   **their company excels:** "The Experience Advantage."

154   **A culture is defined:** Adam Grant (@AdamMGrant), "To
understand the values in a culture, we often examine which
behaviors get punished. But we also need to consider which
behaviors *don't* get punished—what people get away with. . . ."
Twitter, April 20, 2021, 8:01 a.m., https://twitter.com
/AdamMGrant/status/1384477310875799554.

157   **alignment is the greatest hurdle:** "Harvard Business Review:
The Power of Employee Alignment," Betterworks, updated June
22, 2021, https://www.betterworks.com/magazine/harvard
-business-review-power-employee-alignment/.

157 **toward a meaningful goal:** "Bersin by Deloitte: Effective Employee Goal Management Is Linked to Strong Business Outcomes," Cision PR Newswire, December 17, 2014, https://www.prnewswire.com/news-releases/bersin-by-deloitte-effective-employee-goal-management-is-linked-to-strong-business-outcomes-300011399.html.

158 **What you appreciate:** Lynne Twist, "What You Appreciate Appreciates," Chopra, August 7, 2014, https://chopra.com/articles/what-you-appreciate-appreciates.

158 **"one of the most meaningful rewards":** "Employee Recognition: The Secret Ingredient to High Employee Engagement," Korn Ferry, 2017, https://focus.kornferry.com/employee-engagement/employee-recognition-the-secret-ingredient-to-high-employee-engagement-asean.

159 **"10 million cars":** Carlos Santos, "VW Emissions and the 3 Factors That Drive Ethical Breakdown," UVA Darden Ideas to Action, October 17, 2016, https://ideas.darden.virginia.edu/vw-emissions-and-the-3-factors-that-drive-ethical-breakdown.

159 **"rigged about 11 million":** Mengqi Sun and Jack Hagel, "Volkswagen Tries to Change Workplace Culture That Fueled Emissions Scandal," *Wall Street Journal*, updated September 30, 2020, https://www.wsj.com/articles/volkswagen-tries-to-change-workplace-culture-that-fueled-emissions-scandal-11601425486.

159 **the biggest scandal:** Charles Riley, "Volkswagen's Ex-CEO Pays Company $14 Million over His Role in the Diesel Scandal," CNN Business, June 9, 2021, https://www.cnn.com/2021/06/09/business/volkswagen-martin-winterkorn-dieselgate/index.html.

160 **VW's cutthroat management style:** Edward Taylor and Jan Schwartz, "Ferdinand Piech, Architect of Volkswagen's Global Expansion, Dies Aged 82," Reuters, August 26, 2019, https://www.reuters.com/article/us-volkswagen-piech-death/ferdinand-piech-architect-of-volkswagens-global-expansion-dies-aged-82-idUSKCN1VG26I.

160 **"There was not one":** Tom Fox, "The Watergate Hearings and the VW Internal Investigation," Compliance Week, December 14, 2015, https://www.complianceweek.com/the-watergate-hearings-and-the-vw-internal-investigation/11373.article.

160 **"There were weak spots":** Geoffrey Smith, "Why VW's 'Update' Failed to Deliver the Goods," *Fortune*, December 10, 2015, https://fortune.com/2015/12/10/why-vws-update-failed-to-deliver-the-goods.

160 **"misconduct and shortcomings":** Fox, "The Watergate Hearings and the VW Internal Investigation."

160   **"The crisis was an opportunity":** Andreas Cremer, "VW Says Only Small Group to Blame for Emissions Scandal," Reuters, December 10, 2015, https://www.reuters.com/article/us-volkswagen-emissions/vw-says-only-small-group-to-blame-for-emissions-scandal-idINKBN0TT14V20151210.

161   **"Our objective is":** Sun and Hagel, "Volkswagen Tries to Change Workplace Culture That Fueled Emissions Scandal."

161   **improve workplace culture:** Mengqi Sun, "Volkswagen Completes Compliance Monitoring After Emissions Scandal," *Wall Street Journal*, September 15, 2020, https://www.wsj.com/articles/volkswagen-completes-compliance-monitoring-after-emissions-scandal-11600191807.

161   **dedicated compliance officers:** Sun, "Volkswagen Completes Compliance Monitoring After Emissions Scandal."

161   **"established a group compliance":** Sun, "Volkswagen Completes Compliance Monitoring After Emissions Scandal."

161   **fell from third:** Sarah Vizard, "Volkswagen Vows to 'Win Back Customer Trust' as Brand Hit by Emissions Scandal," Marketing Week, September 22, 2015, https://www.marketingweek.com/volkswagens-brand-on-the-line-as-it-promises-to-win-back-customer-trust-following-emissions-scandal.

161   **"one of the most hated brands":** Rebecca Stewart, "Volkswagen Joins Shell as One of the World's 'Most Hated' Brands Following Emissions Scandal," The Drum, January 18, 2016, https://www.thedrum.com/news/2016/01/18/volkswagen-joins-shell-one-world-s-most-hated-brands-following-emissions-scandal.

162   **rigged to cheat:** Danielle Muoio, "Volkswagen Just Made a Big Move to Regain Customers' Trust After the Emissions Scandal," *Business Insider*, April 11, 2017, https://www.businessinsider.com/volkswagen-big-move-regain-trust-after-fuel-emissions-scandal-2017-4.

162   **turn their image around:** Vizard, "Volkswagen Vows to 'Win Back Customer Trust' as Brand Hit by Emissions Scandal."

162   **"We have broken":** Jennifer Faull, "Volkswagen Plots Route to Win Back Trust in First Marketing Push Since Emissions Scandal," The Drum, October 12, 2015, https://www.thedrum.com/news/2015/10/12/volkswagen-plots-route-win-back-trust-first-marketing-push-emissions-scandal.

162   **handful of a company's behaviors:** Conor Donegan, "State of the Connected Customer Report Outlines Changing Standards for Customer Engagement," Salesforce, June 12, 2019, https://www.salesforce.com/news/stories/state-of-the-connected

-customer-report-outlines-changing-standards-for-customer-
engagement.

Chapter 9. Using Metrics to Understand and Improve CX and EX

167 **Measurement is fabulous:** Seth Godin, "Measuring Without
Measuring," *Seth's Blog*, June 1, 2013, https://seths.blog/2013/06
/measuring-without-measuring/.

170 **Figure 9.1:** "PwC's 25th Annual Global CEO Survey:
Reimagining the Outcomes That Matter," PwC,
January 17, 2022, https://www.pwc.com/gx/en/ceo-agenda/
ceosurvey/2022.html.

173 **CX management market:** "Customer Experience Management
Market Size, Share & Trends Analysis Report by Analytical Tools,
by Touch Point Type, by Deployment, by End-Use, by Region, and
Segment Forecasts, 2022–2030," Grand View Research, https://
www.grandviewresearch.com/industry-analysis/customer
-experience-management-market.

174 **To calculate NPS:** Fred Reichheld, Darci Darnell, and Maureen
Burns, "Net Promoter 3.0," Bain & Company, October 18, 2021,
https://www.bain.com/insights/net-promoter-3-0/.

174 **CX drives more than:** "Creating a High-Impact Customer
Experience Strategy," Gartner, January 16, 2019, https://www
.gartner.com/en/documents/3899777.

174 **an NPS promoter:** "Are You Experienced?," Bain & Company,
April 18, 2015, https://www.bain.com/insights/are-you
-experienced-infographic.

174 **NPS above zero:** "What Is a Good Net Promoter Score (NPS)?,"
Perceptive (blog), September 6, 2022, https://www.customer
monitor.com/blog/what-is-a-good-net-promoter-score#what-is
-a-good-nps.

175 **B2B service firms reported:** Eric Gregg, "2022 NPS®
Benchmarks for B2B Service Industries," ClearlyRated, February
7, 2022, https://www.clearlyrated.com/solutions/2022-nps-
benchmarks-for-b2b-service-industries/.

175 **Figure 9.2:** Gregg, "2022 NPS® Benchmarks for B2B Service
Industries."

176 **Figure 9.3:** Grigore, "What Is a Good Net Promoter Score? (2022
NPS Benchmark)," Retently, April 18, 2022, https://www.retently
.com/blog/good-net-promoter-score/.

176 **for three months:** "Creating a High-Impact Customer
Experience Strategy."

176   **calculate your CSAT:** "What Is Customer Satisfaction Score
         (CSAT)?," Delighted, https://delighted.com/what-is-customer
         -satisfaction-score.

177   **"How easy was it":** "What's Your Customer Effort Score?,"
         Gartner, November 5, 2019, https://www.gartner.com
         /smarterwithgartner/unveiling-the-new-and-improved-customer
         -effort-score.

177   **"easy to resolve their issue":** "What's Your Customer Effort
         Score?"

178   **Customer effort is 40%:** "What's Your Customer Effort Score?"

179   **Most large organizations:** "How to Measure Customer
         Experience," Gartner, May 18, 2019, https://www.gartner.com
         /smarterwithgartner/how-to-measure-customer-experience.

179   **41 percent prefer NPS:** "The State of B2B Account Experience,"
         CustomerGauge, August 2021, 17, https://customergauge.com
         /ebook/b2b-nps-and-cx-benchmarks-report.

179   **Figure 9.4:** "The State of B2B Account Experience," 18.

180   **"Sales were declining":** Christine Porath and Douglas R.
         Conant, "The Key to Campbell Soup's Turnaround? Civility,"
         Harvard Business Review, October 5, 2017, https://hbr.org/2017/10
         /the-key-to-campbell-soups-turnaround-civility.

180   **"Campbell Soup's employee engagement scores":** Jathan
         Janove, "Doug Conant: How CEOs and HR Can Work Together
         Successfully," SHRM, February 18, 2022, https://www.shrm.org
         /resourcesandtools/hr-topics/employee-relations/pages/doug
         -conant-how-ceos-and-hr-can-work-together-successfully.aspx.

180   **"Great Workplace Award":** "The Campbell Soup Story," Conant
         Leadership, https://conantleadership.com/the-campbell-soup
         -story.

181   **"Keeping employee engagement front and center triggered":**
         Kevin Kruse, "How Employee Engagement Leads to Higher Stock
         Prices," American Express, March 27, 2012, https://www
         .americanexpress.com/en-us/business/trends-and-insights/articles
         /how-employee-engagement-leads-to-higher-stock-prices.

181   **employees are largely satisfied:** "The Impact of Cost Cutting
         on Employee Experience and Talent Outcomes," Gartner, March
         25, 2020, https://www.gartner.com/en/documents/3982502.

181   **only 19 percent of employees:** "The Employee Net Promoter
         System," Bain & Company, https://www.netpromotersystem.com
         /about/employee-nps.

182   **"explicitly tie together":** "The Employee Net Promoter System."

183 **more than half of employees:** "The Experience Advantage:
Transforming Customer and Employee Experience for the Future
of Work," Salesforce and Edelman DXI, 2022, https://www
.salesforce.com/form/pdf/the-experience-advantage.

185 **losing $1 trillion:** Shane McFeely and Ben Wigert, "This Fixable
Problem Costs U.S. Businesses $1 Trillion," Gallup, March 13,
2019, https://www.gallup.com/workplace/247391/fixable-problem
-costs-businesses-trillion.aspx.

188 **"This approach gives job seekers":** "Ratings on Glassdoor,"
Glassdoor, updated March 3, 2022, https://help.glassdoor.com
/s/article/Ratings-on-Glassdoor.

188 **cultural strength metrics:** "Close the Employee Experience
Gap," Forrester, 7, https://itbusinessinfo.com/forrester-close-the
-employee-experience-gap-research-report-2.

Appendix: Research Methodology

221 **"The Experience Equation: How Happy":** "The Experience
Equation: How Happy Employees and Customers Accelerate
Growth," Forbes Insights in association with Salesforce, 2020,
https://www.salesforce.com/form/conf/forbes-ex-cx-growth.

221 **"The Experience Advantage: Transforming":** "The
Experience Advantage: Transforming Customer and Employee
Experience for the Future of Work," Salesforce and Edelman DXI,
2022, https://www.salesforce.com/form/pdf/the-experience
-advantage.

Index

automation *(cont.)*
  and order fulfillment process,
    16–17
  at Pfizer, 119, *120*
  and redundant business
    processes, 104
  at Unilever, 35
autonomy of employees, 64

back-office technology, 27–28
Bain & Company, 173
Bain Fellowship, 61
balance of work and personal life,
  87, 156
banking industry, 10
bankruptcies, 193, 202
baristas, 72, 74
Barrett, Colleen, 44
beginner's mind, 213, 214
"The Belief-Driven Employee," 152
benchmarks, 167, 175, *176,* 181, 186
benefits for employees, 71, 85, *87,*
  187, 194–95
Benioff, Marc, 142, 152
Best Buy, xv, 83–86, *85,* 89
Best Career Growth award, 125
Best Companies to Work For
  award, 152
Best Company Culture award, 125
Best Company for Women award, 125
Best Company Perks & Benefits
  award, 125
Best Employer for Women award,
  43–44
Best for Vets award, 44
Best Places to Work list, 76, 206
Bezos, Jeff, 13
billing systems, 135
blind spots, 117
boards of directors, 207
bonuses, 170. *See also* wages and
  compensation
Boston Consulting Group (BCG),
  150–51
branding and brand loyalty
  and benefits of prioritizing
    employee experience, 42
  brand ambassadors, *72,* 75, 94
  brand awareness, 53
  brand promises, 22
  and customer effort
    requirements, 10

customer experience associated
  with, *6, 9*
  importance of employees in, 20
  and scandals/unethical
    behavior, 162
  and Zappos, 5
Branson, Richard, xvi, xix, xxii
Brazil
  and ownership of employee
    experience, *53*
  and prioritization of customer/
    employee experience, *51, 52*
  and seamless technology, 129
bureaucracy, 82, 103, 108, 114, 119,
  121, 146
business-for-environment (B4E),
  21, 88
Business Roundtable Pledge, 36
business-to-business (B2B)
  and career development for
    employees, *92*
  and CX metrics, 174, *175,* 179, *179*
  and departmental siloing, 110
  and development of Experience
    Mindset, xxi–xxii
  and employee recruitment, *90*
  and redundant business
    processes, 105
  *See also specific industries and
    companies*
business-to-consumer (B2C)
  and career development for
    employees, 92, *92*
  and customer experience
    dilemma, 13
  and CX metrics, 174, *176*
  and development of Experience
    Mindset, xxi–xxii
  and employee effort level, 28
  and employee recruitment, *90*
  and recruitment/onboarding
    process, 89–90
  *See also specific industries and
    companies*
business-to-employee (B2E), xxi–xxii
buy-in from employees, 36
buy online, pick up in store
  purchases (BOPIS), 16

call centers, 15, 118, 132, 140,
  169–70, 172. *See also*
  customer service

251

and brand loyalty, *6*
characteristics of superior service,
    7–9
at Chipotle Mexican Grill, 125
and culture of companies, 62,
    142–44, 151–52, 157
and customer effort requirements,
    9–12
data on prioritizing, 46–50, *47*
and departmental siloing, 109–11
and design thinking, 114–15
development of customer-centric
    approach, 1–3
and development of Experience
    Mindset, xx–xxii
diagram, *xxiii*
dilemma of, 12–14
and diminishing returns, 11, 17
and employee effort level, 28–29
and Experience Mindset process, *77*
and factors favoring employee
    experience, 76–78
and goals of business, xvii–xviii
and Growth IQ, xix
and IBM's company culture, 147
impact on employees, 88
importance of employees in, 20
and improvement of employee
    experience, 22–23, 25–27
and leadership-employee
    disconnect, 55
and management prioritization of
    customer experience, 29–31
and motivations of employees, 87
and performance metrics, 167–68,
    170–71, 173–79, 181–82, 186,
    188–89
and PPTC framework, 81, 83
and priorities of executives, *56,*
    56–58, *57*, 78
and prioritization of customer/
    employee experience, *52*
and redundant business processes,
    103–4
relationship with technology, 14–16
senior management prioritization
    of, 50–51, *51*, 53
at Starbucks, 71–75
and technology advances, 128
and technology integration, 139
and transformation of business
    processes, 106, 108

and updating of outdated
    technology, 131
at Zappos, 3–9
See also customer relations
CustomerGauge, 110
customer loyalty, 10–11, 16, 42. *See*
    also branding and brand
    loyalty
customer relations
anonymous company case study,
    202–3, 206
and culture of companies, *163*
customer-centric approaches, 2, 68
customer-facing employees, 30,
    48, *85*, 110, 128–30, *129*, 155
customer relationship
    management systems, 69–70,
    132, 135, 140, 156, 205
expectations of customers, 74
and journey mapping, 117
metrics for, 10, 85, 172–74,
    176–77, 179
and redundant business
    processes, 105
surveys, 73
See also customer service
customer service
anonymous company case study,
    194, 207
customer service lines, 3–5, *4,* 8
and departmental siloing, 109–10
and IBM's company culture, 149
and management prioritization of
    customer experience, 29, 30
Southwest Airlines' focus on, 43
and technology integration, 135
See also customer relations
customer success groups (CSGs),
    164–65
CX technology, 15

data systems
data integration, 140
impact on revenues, *105*
and process hygiene, 109–10,
    113–14, 120
See also information
    technology (IT)
decision-making authority, 80,
    110, 119
Deep Thinking (Kasparov), 94
Deming, W. Edward, 101–2

253

INDEX

Deming Institute, 112
democratization of companies,
    63, 122–23
design thinking, 114–18
detractors, 174, 183
Diamond Model, 80
Diess, Herbert, 161
digital technology, 28
    democratizing effect of, 122–23
    and digital sales, 127
    and employee disengagement, 33
    and PPTC framework, 123–24
    and process hygiene, 106–9,
        119–20
    relationship with employee
        experience, 16–17
    technology advances at Chipotle,
        126–28
discretionary effort of employees, 34
disgruntled employees, 33
diversity in employment, 63,
    152–54, *154*
"Don't F*^k Up the Culture"
    (Chesky), 61–62
downstream effects, 11
Dragons' Den (television program), 97
drive-through sales, 73
Drucker, Peter, xvii, 142

earnings, 127. *See also* profitability;
    revenues
e-commerce industry, *176*
economic justice, 163
Edelman, 20, 42, 152
education, 71, 125, *126. See also*
    training
efficiency, 7, 25, 27, 136–37
effort levels, 9–12
Emerging Leader and Mentoring
    programs, 125, *126*
emissions standards, 159–62, *160*
Empathy Business, The, 96
employee development, 80–83, *81,
    82,* 204. *See also* career
    development and
    advancement
employee dissatisfaction, 31–34,
    38, 74
employee effort, 27–29
employee experience (EX)
    and adoption of Experience
        Mindset, 67, 71
    at Airbnb, 61–66, *66*

alignment with CX, xx, 16–17,
    27–28, 41–46, 58–59, 64–65,
    78–79, 95–96, 214
anonymous company case study,
    218–19, 222, 224
and automation initiatives,
    136–37, *137*
benefits of prioritizing, 37–39
and business processes, 103
and challenges facing
    management, xxi
characteristics of superior, 25–27
at Chipotle Mexican Grill,
    124–27, *126*
comparisons of companies, 52–54
connection with revenue and
    profit, 48–50, *49*
and culture of companies, 62,
    142–44, 151–52, 154–55,
    155, 157
and customer effort
    requirements, 10
and customer-focused technology,
    16–17
CX prioritized over, 29–31
data on prioritizing, 46–50, *47, 49*
and departmental siloing, 109–11
and design thinking, 114–15
and development of Experience
    Mindset, xxii
diagram, *xxiii*
and employee disengagement,
    31–34
and employee effort, 27–28
and employee expectations, 28–29
employee experience (EX) teams,
    xvi–xvii, xviii–xx, 124–25, 164
and employee feedback, 99
executive disconnection from,
    54–55, *55*
and Experience Mindset process, 77
factors favoring prioritization of,
    76–78
impact of technology on, *130,* 131
key questions, 59–60
and management priorities, *50,*
    50–51, *51*
and market leadership, 54–55
and motivations of employees,
    87, 88
and performance metrics, 167–71,
    180–88
at Pfizer, 119–20, *120*

INDEX

257

259

261

Read more from TIFFANI BOVA